OFF THE BEATEN PATH® SERIES

SEVENTH EDITION

NEVADA

OFF THE BEATEN PATH

HEIDI KNAPP RINELLA

Globe
Pequot

Essex, Connecticut

The information in this guidebook is subject to change. We recommend calling ahead before traveling.

Globe
Pequot

An imprint of The Globe Pequot Publishing Group, Inc.
64 South Main Street
Essex, CT 06426
www.globepequot.com

Distributed by NATIONAL BOOK NETWORK

British Library Cataloguing in Publication Information available

Library of Congress Cataloging-in-Publication Data available

ISSN 1537-3304
ISBN 9781493087211 (paperback)
ISBN 9781493087228 (ebook)

∞™ The paper used in this publication meets the minimum requirements of American National Standard for Information Sciences—Permanence of Paper for Printed Library Materials, ANSI/NISO Z39.48-1992.

Contents

About the Author

Heidi Knapp Rinella was a journalist for forty-five years in Ohio, Florida, and Nevada, where she was the restaurant critic and food writer for the *Las Vegas Review-Journal* for more than 20 years before retiring as a staff writer in 2022. She moved to Nevada with her husband and two daughters in the late 1990s and continues to be intrigued by the rich lode of fascinating—and yes, sometimes wacky—people and places she finds there. This edition of *Nevada Off the Beaten Path* is her 10th book.

Acknowledgments

I'm grateful to my husband, Frank, who's always ready to depart on a new adventure and has an unwavering good nature, generous capacity for cooperation and support, and deep well of tolerance, and to my daughters, Aubrey and the late Aynsley, whose quest for learning has been never-ending. Also I thank my late parents, Jean and Eugene Knapp, who gave me a lifetime of fun, educational travel opportunities and fostered the adventurous spirit that has led me to always try to explore life down any trail I may find myself on.

And a special thanks to Nevada and its people, who have always been warm, welcoming, and especially interesting, whether I'm on or off the beaten path.

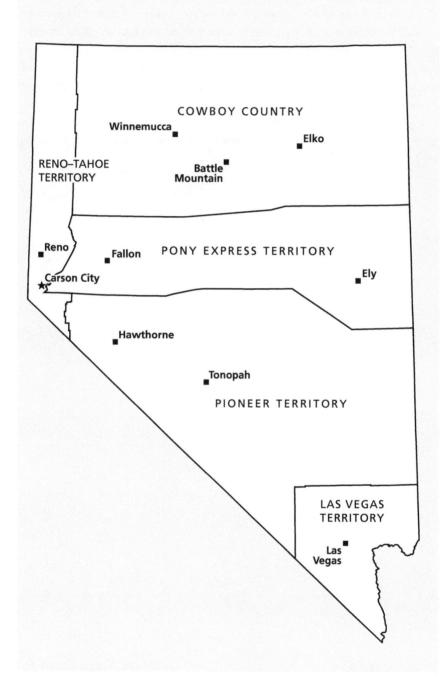

Introduction

When I first moved to the Las Vegas area in the late 1990s, it seemed that the rest of the state was but a mere backdrop to the great city of glitter and glitz.

And no wonder: The nearly 3 million people who call Las Vegas home represent more than 90 percent of the population of the entire state. Add to that the nearly 39 million people who visit Las Vegas each year and the thousands more who move there every month, and you'll understand why an ever-brighter spotlight continues to shine on the neon metropolis.

But I soon discovered that there are a lot of fascinating things to see and experience in Nevada when one leaves Las Vegas and ventures off the beaten path. My first experience with wild and wonderful rural Nevada was Virginia City, which I encountered while on a business trip. Virginia City is reached via a winding road that climbs steeply up the side of a mountain—a stark testimony to the endurance and determination of those who reached the site with mule-drawn carts over rutted tracks instead of turbo-charged vehicles over smoothly paved (if winding) highways. The town's frequent references to the Comstock Lode that built—and broke—many fortunes mirrors the effects rich caches of minerals had on various other parts of the state. And its plank sidewalks and wooden buildings recapture the spirit of Nevada's role in the history of the American West.

Despite the fact that the preponderance of the population is in Las Vegas, geographically, that metropolitan area represents but a small part of the state. Nevada is the seventh-largest state by area, with 110,543 square miles, and because just over 80 percent of its land is owned by the federal government, much of it is open range. In fact, wide-open spaces characterize the vast majority of rural Nevada, where the scenery varies from the 13,000-foot mountain peaks in the Sierra Nevada near Reno to the stark stretches of the Mojave Desert in the southern part of the state near Las Vegas.

The state's name is derived from the Spanish for "snowcapped," a reference to Nevada's mountain ranges—more than in any other state. Nevada has 51 mountains higher than 9,000 feet.

It also has sparkling-blue Lake Tahoe (in partnership with California), the third-deepest lake in North America and the highest alpine lake of its size in the country; the man-made wonder of Lake Mead, which bloomed from the desert thanks to another man-made wonder, the Hoover Dam; plus national and state parks that afford numerous recreational opportunities including hiking, fishing, boating, and wildlife-watching.

Add to that the ghost towns that dot the state, historic sites, festivals, rodeos, and Native American powwows, and it's easy to see that Nevada offers countless opportunities to experience the offbeat.

A few caveats: All of that open space means that on many Nevada roads you may not encounter another vehicle—or a gas station or other sign of civilization—for miles, so be sure your vehicle is in good working order and that you have plenty of fuel. Winter travel can be hazardous in some parts of the state, with chains required in many areas when there's snow (and sometimes roads closed for the season), and wind can restrict high-profile vehicles on some highways. In a large part of the state, summer heat can be life-threatening, so be sure you have sufficient water for your vehicle and everyone in it. And remember to stay away from abandoned mines, which are notoriously dangerous.

All of these cautions aside, Nevada has good roads, great tourism offices, and lots of friendly people. So relax and have fun as you experience its wonders.

Enjoy your time off the beaten path!

Facts at a Glance

NEVADA COMMISSION ON TOURISM

401 North Carson St., Carson City, travelnevada.com or (775) 687-4322.

Chambers of commerce, staffed by locals, are great resources for planning your trip. They can recommend lodging, dining, and sightseeing and provide directions. Folks in the rural backcountry sometimes close up shop in the summer, and those in the northern part of the state may be shuttered during the winter. Call or write to the local chambers and tourism agencies listed at the end of each chapter.

AIRPORTS

Reno/Tahoe International Airport, renoairport.com or (775) 328-6400, and Harry Reid International Airport, Las Vegas, harryreidairport.com or (702) 261-5211, are served by dozens of airlines, including major carriers Southwest, United, Alaska Airlines, American, Delta, Allegiant, Frontier, Air Canada, Hawaiian Airlines, JetBlue, Spirit, and Virgin Atlantic.

The Elko Regional Airport, flyelkonevada.com or (775) 777-7190, is served by Delta.

MOTOR HOME RENTAL COMPANIES

Bates International Motor Home Rental Systems Inc., 3430 E. Flamingo Rd., suite 224, Las Vegas 89109; (702) 737-9050.

Cruise America, 551 N. Gibson Rd., Henderson 89011; cruiseamerica.com or (702) 565-2224.

El Monte RV, 3800 Boulder Hwy., Las Vegas 89121; elmontelv.com or (702) 269-8000.

ATV RENTAL COMPANIES

Las Vegas ATV Tours & Watercraft Rentals, 661 W. Lake Mead Pkwy., Henderson 89015; lvatv.com or (702) 406-0943.

Ultimate Desert Adventures, 250 S. Moapa Valley Blvd., Overton 89040; vegasthrills.com or (702) 952-1633.

RAIL SERVICE

Amtrak, amtrak.com or (800) USA-RAIL.

CLIMATE

Temperatures range from a low of 30 degrees Fahrenheit in Ely in January to a high of 120 degrees Fahrenheit in Laughlin in July.

MAJOR PUBLICATIONS

Las Vegas Review-Journal, daily (state's largest)
Reno Gazette-Journal, daily
Nevada Magazine

NEVADA STATE PARKS

Expect to pay an entrance fee, which goes toward improvements and staff salaries. Summer ranger programs enhance the camping experience. At the Cathedral Gorge State Park, activities include hiking through volcanic formations—some of them cave-like; others resembling cathedral spires—as well as picnicking, camping, and nature study. Campers pay $15 to $30, which includes the entrance fee that's normally $5 ($10 for out-of-state vehicles). Fees at private campgrounds are often higher. Visit parks.nv.gov or call (775) 684-2770.

FUN FACTS

Nevada was part of the area ceded by Mexico to the United States in 1848. The discovery of the Comstock Lode in 1859 caused such an influx of settlers that Nevada soon had a big enough population to become the 36th state. Outside of Reno and Las Vegas, Nevada, is a vast, open country of wide ranges and towering, snow-clad mountains. It is still a land where the Old West survives, with historic main streets looking much the same today as they did in the days of Wyatt Earp and Mark Twain.

- **State capital:** Carson City
- **Largest city:** Las Vegas (2024 population 667,282, or 2,952,756 in the metropolitan area)
- **State bird:** mountain bluebird
- **State animal:** desert bighorn sheep
- **State trees:** single-leaf piñon, bristlecone pine
- **State grass:** Indian ricegrass
- **State flower:** sagebrush
- **State reptile:** desert tortoise
- **State fish:** Lahontan cutthroat trout
- **State metal:** silver
- **State fossil:** ichthyosaur
- **State rock:** sandstone
- **State precious gemstone:** Virgin Valley black fire opal
- **State colors:** silver and blue
- **State song:** "Home Means Nevada," by Bertha Eaton Raffetto of Reno; adopted in 1933

MORE FUN FACTS

- Before statehood, Nevada was part of Zion, as the Latter-day Saints (or Mormons) called their desert homeland. Based in Salt Lake City, the Mormons established the State of Deseret, a provisional government that included most of what is now Nevada and Utah and parts of seven other states.
- Nevada ranks on almost every list of top American tax havens because its taxes are among the lowest in the nation. Nevada lures businesses with these advantages: no personal income tax, no corporate income tax, no unitary tax, no inventory tax (although it does have a gross-receipts tax).
- Nevada lists as major industries tourism and logistics.

- Marriage is another major business. Nevada has few legal restrictions and doesn't require blood tests, waiting periods, or consent for those 18 and older.
- While the Bureau of Land Management does occasionally sell parcels, 80 percent of Nevada is owned by the federal government. For information about specific areas, contact the Bureau of Land Management, 1340 Financial Blvd., Reno 89502; blm.gov or (775) 861-6500.

UNIQUE WEDDINGS

Some themes played out at Nevada wedding chapels include Santa's workshop, graveyard, Dracula's tomb, 1950s and 1960s, gangster, disco, rockabilly, pirate, Egyptian, gothic, *The Hangover*, *Beetlejuice*, and zombie. Viva Las Vegas Wedding Chapel, 1205 Las Vegas Blvd. South, specializes in themed weddings: vivalasvegasweddings.com or (702) 384-0771. Out of Nevada's 15 county clerk offices, these offices issue the most marriage licenses:

- Carson City County, 885 E. Musser St., Carson City 89701-4475, (775) 887-2087 or (775) 887-2085;
- Clark County Marriage License Bureau, 201 E. Clark Ave., Las Vegas 89101, (702) 671-0600;
- Washoe County Clerk's Office, 1001 E. 9 St., Reno 89512, (775) 328-2003;
- Douglas County Administration Building, 175 Hwy. 50, Stateline 89449, (775) 586-7290 or 1616 E. St., Minden 89423, (775) 782-9017.

HELPFUL WEBSITES

- travelnevada.com. Nevada Commission on Tourism provides general information, activities, events, and travel articles.
- visitlasvegas.com. Las Vegas Convention and Visitors Authority offers a calendar of events plus information on where to stay and eat and what to do.
- visitrenotahoe.com. Reno-Sparks Convention and Visitors Authority site has information on lodging and attractions, plus trip-planning tips.
- visitcarsoncity.com. Learn about the state capital and find itineraries on this site from Visit Carson City.
- visitvirginiacitynv.com. Virginia City Tourism Commission lists attractions, lodging, directions, and events.
- tonopahnevada.com. Learn about recent developments and attractions in the Queen of the Silver Camps.

- visitfallonnevada.com. A closer look at things to do in a small town that calls itself "the Oasis of Nevada."
- recreation.gov. The federal government's centralized travel planning and recreation platform is a reservation hub and has information on camping at national and state parks in Nevada.

DETAILED MAPS

The website travelnevada.com has maps and all sorts of tips, plus information on 10 road trips in the state, including the Burner Byway (think Burning Man), Death Valley Rally, and Loneliest Road in America. Free physical highway maps and downloadable maps on cities, counties, and historical tours are available at the site of the Nevada Department of Transportation, dot.nv.gov. The DOT store offers numerous other maps, including a 150-page atlas.

MOVIES FILMED IN NEVADA

The Las Vegas Story (1952), with Vincent Price and Jane Russell, filmed partially in Las Vegas.

The Misfits (1961), Clark Gable's last movie, filmed in Dayton and Virginia City.

Viva Las Vegas (1964), with Elvis Presley and Ann-Margret.

The Shootist (1976), John Wayne's last movie, filmed in Carson City.

Top Gun (1986), with many flight scenes filmed over Fallon.

Rain Man (1988) includes scenes filmed at Caesars Palace.

Austin Powers: International Man of Mystery (1997), filmed almost entirely in Las Vegas.

Fools Rush In (1997), with Matthew Perry and Salma Hayek, has a pivotal scene filmed on Hoover Dam.

Casino (1995), a fictionalized accounting of the mob era in Las Vegas.

Miss Congeniality (2000) captures the crazy, nonstop action of Las Vegas.

Ocean's 11 (2001) is a casino heist film set in a thinly veiled Bellagio.

The Hangover (2009) proves that not everything that happens in Vegas stays in Vegas.

POWWOWS AROUND THE STATE

At powwows you learn about the Native American inhabitants of the state. The Paiutes, Shoshone, and Washoe once thrived in Nevada's unique environment. Before attending a powwow, view the richly detailed dioramas of tribal life at Carson City's Nevada State Museum, or learn about Native history and culture at the Lost City Museum in Overton.

Powwows consist of fancy and traditional dances, referring both to dress and dance style. Each tribe adds its own variation to the dance based on its heritage and tribal lifestyle.

- **Stewart Father's Day Powwow,** Jun, Carson City; (775) 687-7410.
- **Moving Forward Together Social Powwow,** Jun, Fallon; (775) 423-7433.
- **Schurz Pine Nut Festival Powwow,** Sept, Schurz; (775) 773-2306.
- **Snow Mountain Powwow,** Oct, Snow Mountain Paiute Reservation, Las Vegas; (702) 386-3926.
- **Nevada Day Powwow,** late Oct, Carson City; (775) 450-9655.
- **Pahrump Social Powwow,** Nov, Pahrump; (775) 209-3444.

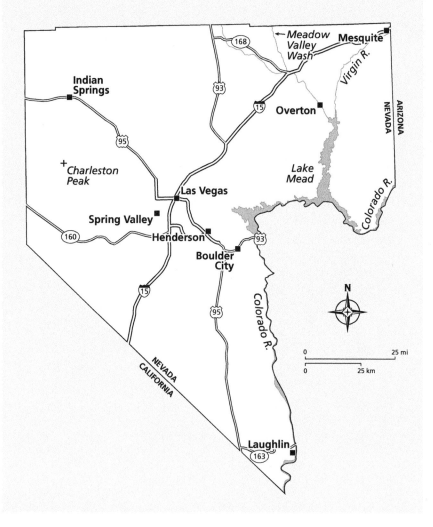

Las Vegas Territory

Clark County

There's no better place to start a book about Nevada than Las Vegas—the most exciting city in the world and the source of numerous sightseeing, sports, entertainment, and dining options. It's visited by some 39 million people each year and is home to nearly 3 million more.

"Ummm . . . ," you're likely saying right about now. "But Las Vegas isn't exactly off the beaten path, now is it?"

Point well taken, but that's where this book comes in: Las Vegas, like the rest of Nevada, is home to plenty of quirky—and fascinating—places unseen by the average tourist. And once visitors do discover Las Vegas's offbeat charms, they often find that it's the ideal gateway for exploring the rest of wild and wonderful Nevada.

Las Vegas actually has been drawing visitors for centuries. You might say the first tourist was Rafael Rivera, who came along in the early 1700s—and without a beer in one hand and a bucket of quarters in the other. That long-standing tradition would begin later.

But back to Rafael. During the early part of the 18th century, Spanish explorers looked on the journey through this part of the West as the *jornada de muerte*, or journey of death, for the high summer temperatures and dry desert conditions during almost any time of the year.

Rafael Rivera, a young scout, is considered the first European to gaze upon the valley. And when he gazed, he saw wild grasses and trees—and therefore a supply of water, from the natural springs in the valley. It wasn't news to the Native Paiutes (or the Anasazis who came before them), who had dwelled in the region for centuries, but it was to the Europeans. This newly discovered oasis would become a new stop for the adventurers and cut their journey by several days. Inspired by the green vegetation in the midst of the desert, they named it *las vegas*, Spanish for "the meadows."

The Spanish explorers and missionaries who quickly followed them established the Spanish Trail by about 1829. (Parts of it can still be seen today in outlying areas, but most notably, parts of it eventually became the wagon road between Salt Lake City and Southern California, used by settlers making their way west, which today is roughly mirrored by I-15.)

It took a while for the news to get out, however. Conventional wisdom has it that not until explorer John Frémont wrote of Las Vegas in 1844 did word spread beyond the circle of Spanish explorers and missionaries. Frémont wrote:

> We ate the barrel cactus and moistened our mouths with the acid of the sour dock. Hourly expecting to find water, we continued to press on to midnight, when after a hard and uninterrupted march of 16 hours, our wild mules began running ahead; and in a mile or two we came to a bold running stream.

The "bold running stream" is now known as the Muddy River, which runs through the northeastern part of the valley, most visible near the present-day

AUTHOR'S TOP PICKS

Las Vegas Strip, Las Vegas

Sphere, Las Vegas

Resorts World, Las Vegas

Springs Preserve, Las Vegas

The Mob Museum, Las Vegas

The Neon Museum, Las Vegas

Ethel M Chocolate Factory and Botanical Cactus Garden, Las Vegas

Red Rock Canyon National Conservation Area, outside Las Vegas

Hoover Dam, Boulder City

Valley of Fire State Park, Moapa Valley

communities of Logandale and Overton. It's generally not as "bold" or as "running" anymore, but it sustained several communities for decades.

Once Frémont's writings about the valley were published, word spread quickly.

In 1855, Brigham Young dispatched a group of Mormon colonists to establish a fortified mission in the Las Vegas area as a link between California and Utah. The settlement

trivia

Mormon settlers arrived at Las Vegas in 1855, sent by Brigham Young to establish a way station on the Mormon Road from Utah to a settlement in San Bernardino, California.

was abandoned in 1858. The adobe remnant of the original mission, known as *Old Mormon Fort,* is the oldest building in Nevada and listed on the National Register of Historic Places. The fort is at 500 E. Washington Ave. and is open from 8 a.m. to 4:30 p.m. Tues through Sat (with last admission at 4 p.m.). Admission is $3 for adults, free for children 12 and younger. For information, visit parks. nv.gov or call (702) 486-3511.

Located nearby, at 900 Las Vegas Blvd. North, is the *Las Vegas Natural History Museum.* Kids of all ages will be thrilled with the feeling of entering Tut's tomb in "The Treasures of Egypt." There also are huge, animated dinosaurs, international wildlife displays, live sharks, and stingrays in the Marine Life Gallery, a geology gallery, and displays of Nevada wildlife that can be seen, heard, touched—even smelled. The many hands-on exhibits keep kids interested for hours. Museum admission is $14 for most adults, $12 for seniors, members of the military, and youths ages 12 to 18, and $3 for children ages 3 to 11; children younger than 3 are admitted free. There are discounts for Nevada residents, and memberships are available. Hours are 9 a.m. to 4 p.m. daily. For information, visit lvnhm.org or call (702) 384-3466.

Lied Discovery Children's Museum in the Symphony Park area piques the interest of children with 3 floors of hands-on exhibits that allow them to visit a life-size pirate ship, a medieval castle, or a metropolitan and environmentally friendly mini-city; perform in a family theater; or explore the "language" of art, the core principles of energy science, or the movement and power of water (complete with kid-sized hooded raincoats). Hours are from 10 a.m. to 5 p.m. Tues through Sat and 12 to 5 p.m. Sun). Admission is $16 ($13.50 for Nevada residents) or $3 for those with EBT, SNAP, or WIC cards. Lied Discovery Children's Museum is at 360 Promenade Place. For information, visit discoverykids lv.org or call (702) 382-3445.

The Old Mormon Fort may be the oldest building in Nevada, but habitation wouldn't have been possible without the springs that gave the city its name—the wellspring, if you will. Kids and adults can learn more about Las

Vegas's origin story at *Springs Preserve,* which has 180 acres of hiking trails and botanical gardens. Plus there's the Origen Museum, which serves as an introduction to the preserve and has such delights as a 5,000-gallon flash-flood exhibit; Nevada State Museum, covering everything from ichthyosaurs to atomic tests; Boomtown 1905, a life-size model of the core of the early city; a butterfly habitat during fall and spring; and a playground, splash pad, train rides, live animal exhibits, plenty of wildlife, and more. At 333 S. Valley View Blvd., it's open from 9 a.m. to 4 p.m. Thurs through Mon; visit springspreserve.org or call (702) 822-7700.

In America's glittering city in the desert, casinos and resorts grow more lavish and imaginative each year. The *Las Vegas Strip* is the only place in the world where, in a single day, you can stroll past the Eiffel Tower, a giant Egyptian pyramid, a medieval castle, the streets of Manhattan, and a Roman temple, or shop your way through a Venetian square complete with indoor and outdoor canals. The Fontainebleau, the city's newest hotel-casino, reflects its Miami roots and is the state's tallest habitable building, with 67 floors. Resorts World has soaring digital displays on the building's exterior, 3 hotels, 6 pools, a massive casino, a sprawling food market, and a "street" of shops and restaurants. Bellagio welcomes you with a choreographed ballet of water, music, and lights on a 9-acre lake out front. Wynn Las Vegas and Encore are a celebration of elegance.

trivia

The *Rat Pack* was comprised of the five biggest names in show business in the 1960s: Frank Sinatra, Sammy Davis Jr., Dean Martin, Joey Bishop, and Peter Lawford. They performed together at a number of properties, including the Sands, while in Vegas to film the original *Ocean's Eleven.*

The legendary Caesars Palace evokes ancient Roman excess, and Mandalay Bay is a tropical paradise. Check out the big names on the marquees—Adele, Lady Gaga, Katie Perry, Taylor Swift, Carrie Underwood, U2, Bruno Mars, Christina Aguilera, David Copperfield, and Usher. Heck, you can even see Elvis all over town. Production shows range from the traditional—personified by Donny Osmond and Carrot Top—to the avant-garde—Blue Man Group, the mind-freaking magic of Criss Angel, impressive impressions by Terry Fator, and the nightly naughtiness of Absinthe and Fantasy, plus the numerous companies of Cirque du Soleil (Bellagio, Treasure Island, New York–New York, MGM Grand, and Mandalay Bay).

Cirque du Soleil's **O** is performed at Bellagio resort. Through Cirque du Soleil's cunning mix of diving, synchronized swimming, aerial acrobatics, character actors, and musicians, *O* rises to the apogee of live entertainment. The

Making the Cirque Circuit in Las Vegas

In Las Vegas these days, life's a circus—or at least a Cirque. Since **Cirque du Soleil's Mystere** became the showpiece of Treasure Island (3300 Las Vegas Blvd. South) in 1993, numerous other Cirque productions have been established on the Las Vegas Strip, each slightly different from the others. Currently, there are four other shows: *O*, in which the star is a 150-by-100-foot pool at Bellagio (3600 Las Vegas Blvd. South); *KÀ*, which is brought to life on a moving stage that is at times vertical, at MGM Grand (3799 Las Vegas Blvd. South); *Michael Jackson ONE* at Mandalay Bay (3950 Las Vegas Blvd. South); and *Mad Apple*, an adults-only celebration of "The City that Never Sleeps," at New York–New York (3790 Las Vegas Blvd. South). For tickets and information, visit cirquedusoleil.com, call (877) 773-6470, or visit the websites of the individual resorts.

stage is the first of many surprises. Performing in, on, and above a 1.5-million-gallon pool, the cast appears otherworldly: stunningly masked, costumed, and painted. To the creators of Cirque du Soleil, imagination is without limits as long as reality is well masked. A team of 15 divers changes sets underwater. Props are continuously raised, lowered, and docked. Bubbles from a perforated hose along the bottom of the pool mask this flurry of underwater activity. Performances begin at 7:30 and 9:30 p.m., Wed through Sun. For information, visit cirquedusoleil.com or call (877) 773-6470.

Las Vegas is always looking ahead. At press time, the ***Mirage***—where a nightly erupting volcano kicked off a few decades of offbeat (and sometimes off-kilter) public attractions at Strip hotels—is in the process of becoming the ***Hard Rock Hotel***, with the faux-geologic spectacle scheduled to give way to a 36-story, nearly 600-foot guitar-shaped hotel tower in 2027. (Go to hardrockhotels.com for more.) The landmark Tropicana closed in 2024 to make way for a baseball stadium for the A's.

When the ***Four Seasons*** opened in 1999, it was the first deluxe non-gaming hotel on the Strip and also the first hotel within a hotel, with 424 guest rooms atop Mandalay Bay's main tower. It was joined in the former category 10 years later by ***Vdara*** and ***Mandarin Oriental***, both part of the ***CityCenter*** complex on the middle Strip; the Mandarin Oriental became the ***Waldorf Astoria*** in 2018. And the hotel-within-a-hotel trend would continue, with the ***W Las Vegas*** at Mandalay Bay, ***Venezia*** at The Venetian, ***NoMad*** at Park MGM, and ***Nobu Hotel*** at Caesars Palace. And when ***Resorts World*** opened in 2021, it was with three hotels in the complex—***Crockfords, Conrad,*** and ***Hilton***.

Lots of other trends have died as new ones have come to life. The lions, tigers, and dolphins—not to mention the nightly battle between two full-sized pirate ships—are gone from the Strip, replaced by clubs, restaurants, and top-drawer specialty shops. About the only fauna you're likely to spot these days is a Fluffy or two, as more local hotels are accepting pets. For something resembling wildlife, you'll want to hit the **Flamingo Wildlife Habitat,** a 4-acre space that's home to exotic birds, turtles, and fish, set among waterfalls and ponds. It's open from 7 a.m. to 8 p.m. daily; visit caesars.com/flamingo-las. vegas.

But while Las Vegas, in its frequent rebirths, is fond of imploding its history, it has somewhat recently begun to appreciate it. **The Mob Museum** opened in 2012 in a neoclassical building that, since 1933, has housed various federal facilities including the post office and courthouse and, in 1950, was the site of the Kefauver hearings into organized crime. The 4 floors of exhibits, many of them interactive, depict various aspects of organized crime, including the birth of the mob, a century of made men and the efforts to defeat them, famous mob hits, a crime lab, firearms-training simulation, how casino skimming operated, and 300 bricks from the infamous St. Valentine's Day massacre wall. The basement holds exhibits on the Prohibition era and, appropriately enough, a speakeasy and distillery. Admission to the museum at 300 Stewart Ave., which is open from 9 a.m. to 9 p.m. daily, ranges from $34.95 to $54.95. Visit themobmuseum.org (which has a cool nickname generator) or call (702) 229-2734.

The glitz and glimmer that made Las Vegas famous originally came from miles and miles of neon, much of which has been replaced by LED lighting in static and elaborate video displays. But more than 250 classic neon signs

The Mafia

Benjamin "Bugsy" Siegel, Meyer Lansky, Frank "Lefty" Rosenthal, and Anthony "the Ant" Spilotro were some members of the Mafia who transformed a sandy desert into a multimillion-dollar business called Las Vegas. Explore the Mafia connection in these five books:

Beyond the Mafia: Italian Americans and the Development of Las Vegas, by Alan Richard Balboni.

The Black Book and the Mob: The Untold Story of the Control of Nevada's Casinos, by Ronald A. Farrell and Carole Case.

Bugsy, by James Toback.

The Enforcer: Spilotro—The Chicago Mob's Man over Las Vegas, by William F. Roemer.

War of the Godfathers: The Bloody Confrontation Between the Chicago and New York Families for Control of Las Vegas, by William F. Roemer.

dating to the 1930s, many of which are art in and of themselves, have been preserved in the unrestored state at the **The Neon Museum,** where they've come to rest in the Neon Boneyard. Among the famous signs on display are those from the Stardust, the El Cortez in the Bugsy Siegel era, and the City Center Motel, designed by Betty Willis, creator of the famous WELCOME TO FABULOUS LAS VEGAS sign. The museum's *Brilliant* exhibit reanimates 40 vintage signs in a 360-degree audiovisual experience, and the visitor center is in the restored lobby of the former La Concha hotel, with its sweeping mid-century lines. Daytime or evening admission, with or without guided tours, starts at $20 for adults, $10 for children 7 to 17, with discounts for seniors and military. The museum is at 770 Las Vegas Blvd. North; visit neonmuseum.org or call (702) 387-6366. *Note:* Fifteen restored signs, including those from the Silver Slipper, Horseshoe, and Pair-A-Dice—are available for free public viewing 24/7 along Las Vegas Boulevard in the downtown area.

For history of a more ancient era, consider **Discovering King Tut's Tomb** at—appropriately enough—Luxor, 3900 Las Vegas Blvd. South. The exhibits take visitors back to Howard Carter's discovery in 1922. Visitors start by lighting a torch, breaking the seal, and entering to see the king's nested coffins, death masks, and more. Tickets are $33 for adults, $23 for children 4 to 12.

TOP ANNUAL EVENTS

Rock 'n' Roll Las Vegas marathon and half-marathon
The Strip, Las Vegas, Feb
runrocknroll.com

Henderson St. Patrick's Day Parade and Festival
Water Street, Henderson, Mar
cityofhenderson.com

Pennzoil 400
Las Vegas Motor Speedway, Las Vegas, Mar
lvms.com

Viva Las Vegas Rockabilly Weekend
The Orleans, Apr
vivalasvegas.net

Electric Daisy Carnival
Las Vegas Motor Speedway, Las Vegas, May
lasvegas.electricdaisycarnival.com

Life Is Beautiful Festival
Downtown Las Vegas, Sept
lifeisbeautiful.com

Las Vegas Greek Fest
St. John the Baptist Greek Orthodox Church, Las Vegas, Sept
lasvegasgreekfest.com

Art in the Park
Boulder City, Oct
bchcares.org

Wrangler National Finals Rodeo
Thomas & Mack Center, Las Vegas, Dec
nfrexperience.com

Las Vegas Great Santa Run
Downtown Las Vegas, Dec
opportunityvillage.org

Upgraded packages include options such as an audio tour narrated by Carter, a virtual reality (VR) experience, and a souvenir photo. Hours are 10 a.m. to 8 p.m. daily. For more information, visit kingtutvegas.com.

You'll come back to the future with a visit to—or even a sighting of—the **Sphere,** 255 Sands Ave. It's an 18,600–seat performance venue but so much more. When U2 or another scheduled act aren't on stage, you can indulge in the Sphere Experience, with tickets starting at $69. That gets you inside the gargantuan globe, where you'll be greeted by Aura, a humanoid robot, and see avatar captures and a 50-foot-high holographic-like image. You can also settle into a haptic chair for *Postcard from Earth*, an immersive film from Darren Aronofsky that merges science fiction and nature documentary on the world's largest high-definition screen. But speaking of high definition: The exterior of the Sphere is one 336-foot-high, 516-feet wide, 4-acre programmable LED screen. Images vary; you may see a very realistic-looking basketball during NBA Summer League, a patriotic display on the 4th of July, fireworks, or an eyeball that borders on the creepy. And best of all, the exterior views—which can be seen over much of the tourism corridor—are free. Visit thespherevegas .com, or call (725) 258-0001.

While you're encountering the futuristic, experience local travel of tomorrow via **The Loop,** an underground system from Elon Musk's Boring Company. It has 6 stations, with 1 at Resorts World, 1 at the Westgate, and 4 at the Las Vegas Convention Center. While it takes about 25 minutes for convention-goers to walk from the center's South Hall, The Loop makes the trip in 2 minutes. Recently, 18 more stations have been approved and will come online as construction proceeds. Rides in the three-passenger Teslas are free within the convention center complex for attendees, with day passes for the Resorts World and Westgate legs priced at $5.

Another way to get around town is the **Las Vegas Monorail,** which may not be so futuristic but is still a rarity as public transportation. The monorail connects 6 resorts and the Las Vegas Convention Center. It's a very efficient way of traveling along the east side of the Strip, especially for people attending shows at the Convention Center. It starts at 7 a.m. and runs as late at 3 a.m., depending on the day. Fares start at $5.50 for one day ($1 for locals), with passes for as many as 7 days available. Visit lvmonorail.com or call (702) 699-8200.

And while you're riding high above the city, take time to hitch a ride on the **High Roller,** which is hard to miss even on Las Vegas's spectacular skyline. At The LINQ, at 3535 Las Vegas Blvd. South, it stretches 550 above the Strip, making it the tallest observation wheel in North America, and is dotted with 28 spherical cabins. Options for riding it are numerous and include regular rides, for a full rotation in 30 minutes or happy hour 30-minute rides, complete with open bar and bartender, for groups up to 25. Daytime rides start at $25 for adults, $10 for kids 4 to 12, and nighttime rides at $35.50 for adults, $19 for kids. Happy (half) hour starts at $61.50 for those 21 and older. Visit caesars. com or call (800) 634-6441.

Another high-flying experience at The LINQ is the *Fly LINQ Zipline*, with riders taking off from a 12-story tower and gliding—more than 1,000 feet at 35 mph—from the Strip along The LINQ Promenade to land near the High Roller. It starts at $40.50; visit caesars.com or call (702) 777-2782.

The mega resorts of the Strip are so spacious and spread out you'll do a lot of walking if you don't take advantage of public transportation or ride-sharing, but there are a few places in Las Vegas that are more compact.

The name *Area 15* is clearly a play on the legendary (or notorious? non-existent?) Area 51 north of the city, where secret experiments on aliens and spaceships are supposedly conducted, but this complex at 3215 S. Rancho Dr. doesn't rely on conspiracy theories for its existence. It's billed as an immersive experience, and it is; but its avant-garde nature shouldn't be discounted and becomes obvious when you encounter the sculpture displays out front that appear to have escaped from Burning Man.

Inside you'll find Meow Wolf's Omega Mart, which has several aspects including a "supermart" with only-in-your-imagination merchandise. Virtual reality (VR) attractions abound at Area 15, as well as some linked to actual reality, such as Dueling Axes. The complex also has bars and restaurants. It's free if you just want to walk through, and passes start at $49 for 6 attractions per day and go to $250 for 3 days of unlimited attractions, most of which are open to all ages. Visit area15.com.

An attraction that offers kids a chance to cut loose and be kids is the *Downtown Container Park* at 707 Fremont St. Part of the Downtown Project conceived by the late visionary Tony Hsieh, it's a complex of shipping containers that have been remodeled and repurposed to house shops and restaurants. At the entrance is a fire-breathing praying mantis that debuted at Burning Man, and at the center of the complex is a sprawling play area, anchored by a multi-story treehouse, with innovative equipment for climbing and spinning. Kids are permitted until 9 p.m.; after that, the complex is for those 21 and older. Visit downtowncontainerpark.com.

Most of the downtown casinos—which by and large are smaller than those on the Strip—are sheltered by the towering electronic canopy of the *Fremont Street Experience,* which extends from Main Street to 4th Ave. South. The largest LED canopy screen in the world is 1,375 by 90 feet and has 16.4 million pixels, with sound and light shows featuring musical acts such as Katy Perry, Shakira, and Las Vegas's own Imagine Dragons. Shows, which begin on the hour nightly from 6 p.m. (or after dark, depending on the time of year) to 2 a.m., are free.

While you're there, you can ride another zipline attraction, **Slotzilla.** Choose the traditional zipline in a sitting position, 77 feet up for 350 feet, or opt for the zoomline to soar like a superhero 114 feet in the air for 1,750 feet. Rates start at $49 for the zipline and $69 for the zoomline. Visit vegasexperience.com.

While most of the downtown casino-resorts are proudly vintage—the **Golden Gate,** at 1 Fremont St., is the oldest in Las Vegas, dating to 1906—there's a new kid on the block(s) in the form of **Circa Resort & Casino,** 8 Fremont St., which opened in 2020 as the first-from-the-ground-up casino built in 40 years. The 35-story resort has 26 room types and is packed with high-tech features, with the exception of the historic neon Sassy Sally that graces the lobby and a parking garage dubbed the Garage Mahal. The rooftop Stadium Swim has 6 pools and a 143-foot video screen for really seeing the game.

Circa is also home to some of Las Vegas's best restaurants, including **Barry's Downtown Prime,** from legendary Las Vegas chef Barry Dakake, and exudes lots of old-school glamour. Visit circalasvegas.com or call (702) 247-2258.

While Barry's is a newish restaurant that honors the past, there are some restaurants in the downtown area that actually date back to the Rat Pack era. The brick-lined **Hugo's Cellar** at the Four Queens, 202 Fremont St., has such old-school touches as a tableside cart for custom-made salads, a rose for every lady, and a menu of dishes such as rack of lamb, beef Wellington, a signature hot-rock appetizer, and tableside bananas foster or cherries jubilee. Visit fourqueens.com or call (702) 385-4011.

And the recently expanded **Golden Steer,** 308 W. Sahara Ave., which opened in 1958, was an actual hangout for the Rat Park, who would pop in after performing at the Sahara across the street. Ask nicely and they'll point out Frank Sinatra's booth. The Golden Steer has an extensive steak menu, lots of updated throwback dishes, and tableside caesar salads, bananas foster, and cherries jubilee. Visit goldensteer.com or call (702) 384-4470.

An area in central Las Vegas that's come into its own over the past decade or so—roughly following the path set by downtown as a whole—is the off-the-beaten-path **Arts District,** roughly 18 square blocks in the vicinity of Charleston Boulevard and Main Street that not long ago was home to some businesses that had seen better days and some that never would. The most public face of the Arts District is presented during the First Friday events held monthly, weather permitting. This bazaar-on-the-street is a colorful pastiche of art exhibits and demonstrations, food, music, and more. Since parking can be an issue, a free shuttle service is offered from the City of Las Vegas parking garage at 500 S. Main St.

The Arts Factory at 17 E. Charleston Blvd., long a studio space for artists, was the de facto birthplace of the district and still its center, currently showcasing more than 30 artists and art galleries (theartsfactorylv.com), while other makers and creators have opened spaces branching out from the heart and public art is becoming more plentiful. Stroll through the area and you're likely to find *Priscilla Fowler Fine Art* at 1300 S. Main St. (priscillafowler.com), *Conrad West Art Gallery* at 15 W. Colorado Ave. (conradwestgallery.com), and *Recycled Propaganda* at 1114 S. Main St. (recycledpropoganda.com).

The more daring among us might want to stop by *Zak Bagans' The Haunted Museum,* where the master of the Discovery Channel's *Ghost Adventures* displays his collection of the supernaturally spooky such as the Dybbuk box, said to be the world's most haunted object, and the original staircase from the Indiana "demon house." At 600 E. Charleston Blvd., it's open from 10 a.m. to 8 p.m., Wed through Mon, and admission starts at $54 for most adults older than 14; $48 for locals, seniors, and members of the military. Flashlight ghost tours—if you dare—are $204. Visit thehauntedmuseum.com or call (702) 444-0744.

Now that we've covered death, know that bars and restaurants have given new life to the Arts District, beginning in 2013 with the intimate *Velveteen Rabbit,* founded by a pair of sisters at 1218 S. Main St., which serves a creative and eclectic mix of cocktails, wine, and spirits (velveteenrabbitlv.com). *Garagiste,* 197 E. California Ave., prides itself on seeking out and featuring excellent obscure wines (garagiestlv.com).

Main Street Provisions at 1214 S. Main St., from veteran Las Vegas restaurateur Kim Owen, serves "modern American comfort food" such as short rib dumplings, duck breast with farro, and the daily chef-inspired Main Street affogato (mainstprovisions.com). Wolfgang Puck's organization has skin in this game, too, with *1228 Main* at . . . well . . . 1228 S. Main St., which specializes in baked goods, such as crème brûlée croissants and lemon cruffins, but also has built a following for brunch dishes such as classic quiche lorraine and Tunisian shakshuka (1228mainlv.com).

Among the most prominent faces in the area these days are Kristen Corral, who has become an activist of sorts in the district and has the *Tacotarian* plant-based Mexican restaurant at 1130 Casino Center Blvd., and chef-restaurateur James Trees.

Trees, a James Beard Award nominee, opened *Esther's Kitchen* on California Avenue in 2018, naming it for the aunt who helped him get through culinary school. It wasn't long until Esther's truly became the toughest ticket in town, beloved for its house-made retinue of updated and innovative Italian-style dishes and phenomenal house-baked bread.

In 2023 he opened a new Esther's Kitchen, just around the corner at 1131 S. Main St. (with plans for a new concept in the original space and more on the way). Even if you're not in the neighborhood, it's worth a jaunt for that unforgettable bread and dishes such as mafalda amatriciana with guanciale, egg tagliatelle with clams and smoked butter, and saffron and carrot risotto. Oh, and don't miss the massive charcuterie board. Lunch is served weekdays; dinner is served daily. Visit estherslv.com or call (702) 570-7864.

Lodging in the Arts District hasn't kept up with the art galleries, restaurants, bars, and coffee shops, so you'll probably want to stay downtown. Good bets are the aforementioned Circa or Golden Gate or the **Golden Nugget,** 129 Fremont St., which has an elaborate pool area complete with shark tank. Visit goldennugget.com or call (702) 385-7111.

One thing that escapes many visitors to Las Vegas is that the city has an active and vibrant Chinatown area, and it's not far from the Strip. Extending mostly along Spring Mountain Road between Valley View and Jones Boulevard, and around the corner stretching north on Jones, the area is home to scores of Asian businesses, many of which don't bother with English-language signs. While the neighborhood has really become pan-Asian and even has prominent Western businesses such as **Sparrow + Wolf** restaurant at 4480 Spring Mountain Rd. (sparrowandwolflv.com) and **The Golden Tiki,** a Disney-esque, high-fantasy bar at 3939 Spring Mountain Rd. (thegoldentiki.com), the main emphasis remains Chinese.

The neighborhood's centerpiece has long been and remains the **Chinatown Plaza** at 4205 Spring Mountain Rd. (lvchinatownplaza.com), home to the Asian supermarket 99 Ranch Market, the Chinatown Outlet gift store, T&T Ginseng, the Lohan School of Shaolin, and restaurants including Xiao Long Dumpling, Pho Vietnam, and 888 Korean BBQ.

Las Vegas casinos draw thousands of Asian tourists each year, and while most of them cater to the visitors with culturally appropriate restaurants and other services, it's not unusual to see a bus pull up in Chinatown Plaza and unload its Asian-national passengers to do their shopping and dining. For Westerners, it's also not unusual to be seated in a Chinatown restaurant and have the server go get someone else because he or she doesn't speak English, or to be slipped a fork just in case chopsticks are unfamiliar.

The city also has a number of major cultural events including the Lunar New Year, which is huge and widely celebrated. The **Las Vegas Greek Fest** at St. John the Baptist Greek Orthodox Church, 5300 El Camino Rd., was founded in 1973 and draws more than 25,000 people each September for three days of Greek food, music, and vendors, as well as amusements for the kids. Visit lasvegasgreekfest.com.

In October, the **Snow Mountain Powwow** attracts Native Americans and other visitors from across the country for traditional dances and Native American crafts such as handmade jewelry, beadwork, and clothing, with artisans demonstrating their skills. It's on the Snow Mountain Reservation off US 95/I-11 north of Las Vegas. Visit lvpaiutetribe.com.

And the heritage of Las Vegas's Latin population is celebrated each May with an annual festival in the Sammy Davis Jr. Festival Plaza at Lorenzi Park, 3333 W. Washington Ave. **Cinco de Mayo** activities include music, food, dancing, and artisan vendors. Visit lasvegasnevada.gov.

While city residents have long been proud of the University of Nevada, Las Vegas, sports teams, the arrival of professional teams in the past few years has generated a great deal of excitement and dedicated pools of fans among locals and visitors alike, and this has added "sports" to the reasons people are drawn to Sin City.

The **Vegas Golden Knights** National Hockey League (NHL) team, which was the first to come to town in 2017 and retains an extremely loyal fan base, plays at T-Mobile Arena on the Strip near New York–New York. Visit nhl.com/goldenknights. They were followed by the **Las Vegas Raiders,** a National Football League (NFL) team that arrived in 2020 and plays at Allegiant Stadium near Tropicana Avenue and Valley View Boulevard. Visit raiders.com. The Women's National Basketball Association's **Las Vegas Aces,** who were the WNBA champions in 2022 and 2023, play at Michelob Ultra Arena at Mandalay Bay on the Strip. Visit aces.wnba.com.

At press time the **Oakland Athletics** had committed to move to Las Vegas, following in the footsteps of the Raiders. The Tropicana resort on the Strip has been demolished to make way for their new stadium; they're expected to start playing baseball there in 2028.

Las Vegas also has the **Las Vegas Lights** Football Club (FC), a professional soccer team that plays at Cashman Field (visit lasvegaslightsfc.com); the minor-league **Las Vegas Aviators,** who play at Las Vegas Ballpark at Downtown Summerlin (milb.com/las-vegas); and the professional lacrosse team **Las Vegas Desert Dogs,** who play at Michelob Ultra Arena at Mandalay Bay (lasvegasdesertdogs.com).

The **Wrangler National Finals Rodeo** in December continues to be among Las Vegas's biggest sporting events, with a total attendance of 173,500. There is more than a week of rodeo competitions at the Thomas & Mack Center on the campus of UNLV, and other associated events, such as Cowboy Christmas at the Las Vegas Convention Center. Visit nfrexperience.com.

Take a drive out to the City of Las Vegas's *Floyd Lamb Park* at 9200 Tule Springs Rd., 10 miles off US 95/I-11 north of the city. The green oasis is a great haven for bird-watching (it's doubtful you'll miss the screeches of the roaming peacocks), fishing, or just having a picnic under the groves of trees. Native Americans used this spot as a watering hole for generations. Later it became a privately owned working ranch, as well as a guest/dude ranch; the historic Tule Springs Ranch within the park provides a peek at the way things worked in the old days. The park has fishing ponds and 680 acres of land. Admission is $6 per vehicle (no cash accepted). It's open daily from 8 a.m. to 8 p.m. Apr through Sept, and 8 a.m. to 5 p.m. the rest of the year. Visit lasvegas nevada.gov or call (702) 229-8100.

trivia

The second Saturday in June of each year is **Nevada's Free Fishing Day,** the only day you can fish without a license. For more information on Nevada's Free Fishing Day or to locate the best angling sites, visit ndow.org or call (702) 486-5127 for recommendations. Lakes Mead and Mohave on the Colorado River are Nevada's largest fisheries in terms of angler use and offer year-round angling for striped bass, largemouth bass, and rainbow trout.

Continue to explore the northern part of Clark County. From Floyd Lamb Park, head south on US 95/I-11 about 2 miles to Route 215 East to I-15, then north about 34 miles to exit 75, and 12 miles to the western entrance of an archaeological and geological wonder. *Valley of Fire State Park* encompasses 40,000 acres of unusual sandstone formations, petrified trees, and ancient petroglyphs. Between 1930 and 1950, this was a popular site to film westerns. Within Nevada's oldest state park, breathtaking views abound as you travel through rugged rust-colored rock outcroppings.

One look and you'll fall in love with the Nevada desert. The Valley of Fire was formed millions of years ago from the great shifting of sand dunes. Oxidized iron gives the park its name and eerie appearance. Basins, canyons, uplifts and overthrust belts, and mountain ranges represent a geologist's dream. Several loop roads within the park lead you to intriguing sites, hiking trails, and picnicking and camping areas.

The visitor center is located in the center of the park, just off the main road. It has excellent displays on geology and the area. The visitor center presents a variety of interesting and informative programs, such as desert survival, desert wildflowers, moonlight hikes, and archaeology and geology.

You can get a copy of the park brochure with a road map and points of interest at the visitor center but try to pick one up at the entrance booth so you won't have to double back to see some sights.

Take the scenic loop road that goes off to your left to reach Atlatl Rock, the site of many petroglyphs carved high on the bluff. A long metal stairway reaches high above the desert floor to bring you face-to-face with the ancient rock carvings, including one of an atlatl, a notched stick used to add speed and distance to a thrown spear. It was a predecessor to the bow and arrow.

Stop at the Beehives, unusual sandstone formations weathered by eroding wind and water. Proceed to the Petrified Logs, washed into the area from ancient forests more than 225 million years ago. Next, it's time to take out your camera for a shot of Rainbow Vista and the towering red giants. A 0.5-mile hiking trail takes you through a sandy canyon to Mouse's Tank, a natural basin where water collects after each rainfall, and allegedly the hiding place for a Paiute fugitive nicknamed Mouse. Along the way, interpretive signs point out petroglyphs.

For shaded picnic areas with grills, choose between the one at the Seven Sisters rock formation and the one at the 1930s Civilian Conservation Corps stone cabins. Be sure to take a look inside the cabins; it's tough to imagine travelers staying there, no matter the era.

Valley of Fire has 72 campsites—some of which will accommodate RVs, with some hookups available—with shaded tables, grills, water, and restrooms. Camping fees are $20 per night, or $25 per non-Nevada vehicle. Hookups are $10 extra.

This would be a good time to point out that Valley of Fire is aptly named and, especially in summer, is not an environment that's really compatible with human life. Its proximity to Las Vegas makes it a popular spot for day trips but, occasionally, even seasoned hikers have perished in the heat. Be sure to carry plenty of water—a gallon per person is ideal—and avoid being outdoors during the hottest part of the day. Current weather conditions are available via a link on the park's website, and information on surviving the heat is available at the visitor center.

Admission to Valley of Fire State Park is $10, or $15 for non-Nevada vehicles. For more information, visit parks.nv.gov/parks/valley-of-fire or call (702) 397-2088.

If you're driving a four-wheel drive, high-clearance vehicle, have a sense of adventure and 2 or 3 hours to spare, and want to really get off the beaten path, take the 28-mile ***Bitter Springs Backcountry Byway,*** which winds through remote basins and canyons. The alert and adventuresome may spot coyotes, kit foxes, wild horses, burros, roadrunners, and desert tortoises. Picturesque geologic formations include buttes, natural arches, and windows. There are ample opportunities for backpacking, hiking, and camping. A bonus is the remnants of a historic borax mining operation.

The trail is accessible from the Valley of Fire Highway, about 3 miles from I-15. For more information on the byway, visit ohv.nv.gov/trails/bitter-springs -backcountry-byway or call (702) 515-5000.

Wrap up your visit to Valley of Fire State Park by leaving by the eastern gate, on the opposite side of the park from where you entered. Before you depart, take the short, marked hiking trail from the entrance station to view Elephant Rock.

Exiting from the park's eastern entrance, turn north on SR 169 and travel 8 miles to *Overton.* On the edge of town, stop at the *Lost City Museum.* This excellent museum houses one of the nation's most complete collections of early Pueblo Native American artifacts. Learn the history of the Anasazi (the Ancient Ones) and the ruins of the Pueblo Grande de Nevada (Lost City's original name), situated along the Muddy and Virgin River Valleys until the people mysteriously disappeared 1,200 years ago. The Lost City ruins were discovered by explorer Jedediah Smith around 1826. In 1924 Nevada governor James Scrugham arranged for a New York archaeologist, M. R. Harrington, to investigate the sites.

The Anasazi had established a highly developed culture and were engaged in agriculture, mining, and trade. They cultivated corn, beans, squash, and cotton and developed permanent dwellings along the entire length of the Moapa Valley before they disappeared. Just inside the entrance to the museum is the 1935 Gallery, housed within the original adobe brick museum built by the Civilian Conservation Corps and listed on the National Register of Historic Places. It displays materials dating to the discovery of the Pueblo Grande de Nevada.

At the center of the main exhibition hall is an actual archaeological site excavated in the 1930s, which illustrates the stages of an archaeological excavation. The hall also captures the Lost City's culture with displays of baskets, pottery, jewelry, and interpretive exhibits. Outdoors is a model of a pit dwelling.

Lost City Museum

Overton has the finest Native American exhibit in Nevada. The Southern Paiute lived around the springs of the Las Vegas Valley and the tributaries of the Colorado River. Their predecessors were the Anasazi, also known as the Ancient Ones. More than 1,000 years ago, these ancients constructed large adobe colonies along the Muddy River in the Moapa Valley south of Las Vegas. Artifacts from the area, as well as an actual archaeological site and a model of an Anasazi home, are on display at the **Lost City Museum** in Overton. For unique regionally themed gifts at reasonable prices, visit the museum shop; (702) 397-2193.

The museum was originally called Boulder Dam Park Museum, constructed under the auspices of the National Park Service to display artifacts recovered from local archaeological sites. The name was changed when ownership transferred to the State of Nevada in the mid-1950s. Much of the original Lost City has lain beneath the waters of Lake Mead since the 1930s, with the construction of Hoover Dam. Overall, 21 sites with more than 600 buildings were excavated and investigated.

The museum is at 721 S. Moapa Valley Blvd. and is open from 8:30 a.m. to 4:30 p.m., Tues through Sun. Admission is $6 for adults, free for children 17 and younger. For more information, visit lostcitymuseum.org or call (702) 397-2193.

If you're feeling hungry while you're in Overton, don't miss **Cablp,** the somewhat oddly named restaurant owned by the Mindfreak Master himself, Criss Angel. Angel, a Strip headliner, became familiar with the area when his family was looking for a place for his eldest son, Johnny Crisstopher, to go dirt biking. He purchased a local restaurant that had roots to 1938, when it was the Lost City Café, and renovated it into Cablp, which stands for "Criss Angel's breakfast, lunch, and pizza," though it serves dinner as well.

Cablp serves breakfast dishes, appetizers, salads, sandwiches, burgers, pizza, and entrées such as Long Island Fish & Chips and Spaghetti Fa You! There's a bar and a coffee bar, and a window serving Italian ices made in Angel's Mindfoods plant in Las Vegas.

And, well, this wouldn't be Angel's restaurant without a bit of magic. There's a bookcase at the rear of the restaurant. Figure out the hidden trigger and it swings back to reveal the Magic Room displaying some of Angel's memorabilia.

Cablp is at 309 S. Moapa Valley Blvd. For more information, visit eatblp.com or call (702) 397-8084.

You may have noticed that the original name of the Lost City Museum was the Boulder Dam Park Museum, which hints at the proximity of both the dam (more on the name later) and Lake Mead National Recreation Area near Boulder City. To get there, retrace your path past the museum, heading south on SR 169 and SR 167 for about 56 miles (the route also becomes known as North Shore Road) to Lakeshore Road and turn left. After about 12 miles, follow US 93 BUS and SR 172 to the **Hoover Dam** Access Road.

Park in the parking garage (fee: $10), which exhibits art deco styling that ties it artistically to the 1930s-era architecture of Hoover Dam buildings. To be sure, the engineering marvel of the dam will attract your attention. The dam is not only a National Historic Landmark but also a National Historic Civil Engineering Landmark.

Hoover Dam rises to a height of 770 feet at its crest, with a top width of 45 feet spanning Black Canyon. Work crews placed 4.25 million cubic yards of concrete in its construction. Seventeen generating units create in excess of 2,000 megawatts of power. Behind the dam, Lake Mead encompasses 700 miles of shoreline and has a maximum depth of 500 feet. It is the largest man-made lake in the Western world.

trivia

In 1994 the *Hoover Dam*, which harnesses the lower Colorado River, was named one of America's seven Modern Civil Engineering Wonders.

Hoover Dam and subsequent downstream dams enable use of Colorado River water to irrigate more than 1 million acres of land in the United States and an additional 0.5 million acres in Mexico; provide domestic water needs for more than 18 million people in Las Vegas, Los Angeles, San Diego, Phoenix, Tucson, and other Southwestern towns and Native American communities in Arizona, Nevada, and California; and generate low-cost hydroelectric power to those same states.

As you view the lake, you may notice a broad white band that locals have come to call the "bathtub ring." It's caused by the declining levels of the lake over the past two decades. Recent unusually heavy rains and heavy snowpack on the Western Slope of the Rocky Mountains, which feeds the Colorado River, and conservation measures have raised the level of the lake somewhat from the record low of a few years ago, though at press time the lake's future prospects remain somewhat precarious.

It wasn't long ago that vehicular traffic traveled along the top of the dam. There was a line that delineated the border between Nevada and Arizona and clocks illustrated the difference during the months of the year when the states were in different time zones. But the events of 9/11 and the completion of the I-11 bypass and the Mike O'Callaghan-Pat Tillman Memorial Bridge changed that, and vehicular travel across the dam is no longer possible, although you still can walk it. Note the artwork at the center columns above the brass doors.

Start at the visitor center, which has photos and other exhibits that tell the story of the dam. The original cost of the dam exceeded $165 million, which has been recovered through power sales; the complex remains self-funded. To get a better understanding of this engineering marvel, take the $15 Guided Power Plant Tour, which takes you through the original construction tunnels to a viewing platform; you'll also see 8 of the commercial generators. The $30 Guided Dam Tour includes the power plant tour plus an elevator ride to the top of the dam, a walk through the inspection tunnels at the center of the dam, and a view of the river through an inspection ventilation shaft.

Two of our favorite Hoover Dam sites that you won't find in the brochures are the gravesite of the construction crew's mascot and the Dedication Plaza. Across the road from the escalator leading to the tour center, look for a shallow niche in the canyon wall and a plaque that tells the story of a puppy who was adopted by the crews and grew up to become the construction mascot. After he was accidentally run over by a truck in 1941, he was buried in a site below the current plaque.

To reach the Dedication Plaza, exit the parking garage and follow the sidewalk to the left. You'll see the stone mosaic with the exact settings for star positioning at the moment of dedication: 8:56:2.25 A.M., SEPT 30, 1935. The flagpole was positioned to point to the center of the equinox at that time. Flanking it are two 1930s statues with hands and wings raised to the sky in triumph.

In his dedicatory address, President Franklin D. Roosevelt said:

Ten years ago the place where we are gathered was an unpeopled, forbidding desert. In the bottom of a gloomy canyon, whose precipitous walls rose to a height of more than 1,000 feet, flowed a turbulent, dangerous river. The mountains on either side of the canyon were difficult of access, with neither road nor trail, and their rocks were protected by neither trees nor grass from the blazing heat of the sun. The site of Boulder City was a cactus-covered waste. The transformation wrought here is a twentieth-century marvel.

Head back on US 93 toward Boulder City and stop at the ***Lake Mead Visitor Center*** at the intersection with Lakeshore Road. Inside you can get maps and brochures on the recreation area and get your National Parks Passport stamped. You can view the *Life in the Desert* film and see a large relief map of the park. The store's gift shop has books on the park and the area, Native American crafts, and the usual postcards and maps. Hours are 9 a.m. to 4:30 p.m. daily. Visit nps.gov/lake/planyourvisit/visitorcenters.htm, which has hiking information and maps. Or call (702) 293-8990. Park admission is $25 per vehicle.

One of the easy hikes is the ***Historic Railroad Tunnel Trail***, a 7.5-mile round trip that follows the railroad bed used to transport materials for dam construction and passes through 5 tunnels. The trail is open to both hikers and bicyclists, so be on the alert for either. You'll have spectacular views of Lake Mead and Boulder Basin. Look out for raven and owl nests and be on the watch for rattlesnakes and scorpions. Park below the visitor center.

Lake Mead National Recreation Area has 900 campsites in 15 locations from lakeside to desert. They have restrooms, running water, dump stations, grills, and picnic tables—and shade—for RVs, trailers, and tents. Some are operated by private concessionaires. At the 5 NPS-managed campgrounds, camping is $20 a night. For more information or to reserve a site, go to nps.gov/lake/plan yourvisit/campgrounds.htm or recreation.gov.

Temple Bar Marina, off US 93 in Arizona about 48 miles from the dam, offers motels and cabins, watercraft rental, a café, bar, and gift shop. Visit templebarlakemead.com or call (855) 918-5253.

Callville Bay Marina offers houseboat and small boat rentals. Houseboats sleep 6 to 15 people; rates for a 50-foot Sirius houseboat, which sleeps 6, start at $476 per day. Pontoon boats, skiffs, ski boats, and tritoons also are available for rent, starting at $299 a day. Visit callvillebay.com or call (855) 918-5253 for houseboat rentals; call (702) 565-4813 for small craft.

Lake Mead Cruises embark on Hoover Dam Sightseeing Cruises and champagne brunch and dinner cruises on the 3-level *Desert Princess*, equipped with a full bar and the Paddlewheel Grill serving burgers and sandwiches. The 90-minute sightseeing cruise is $42 for adults and $22 for children ages 2 to 11. Visit lakemeadcruises.com or call (866) 292-9191.

You'll see references to Hoover Dam and Boulder Dam, which can get a little confusing because it's the same dam. The name was originally to be Boulder Dam, for Boulder Canyon in which it was to be situated, but by the date of the dedication, it was changed to Hoover Dam in honor of former president Herbert Hoover, under whose tenure the dam was begun. Adding to the confusion is the fact that Boulder Canyon was deemed to be unsuitable; the dam actually was built in Black Canyon.

Thus, the reason *Hoover Dam Rafting Adventures* offers Hoover Dam raft tours in Black Canyon. You can experience the canyon's awesome sights as you float along the Colorado River on a guided motor-assisted raft. The 3-hour tours start just below the dam end at Willow Beach on the Arizona side of the river and frequently pass such wildlife as bighorn sheep, osprey, and great blue herons. The fare, which includes a box lunch, is $125 for adults and $110 for kids ages 5 to 15; adults also pay the $15 national park entrance fee unless they have passes. Round-trip transportation to selected Las Vegas hotels is $69 per person. Visit hooverdamraftingadventures.com or call (800) 455-3490.

The federal government created *Boulder City* (population just under 15,000), beginning in 1931, in conjunction with the construction of Hoover Dam. The town was needed because of the remote location of the large construction project and the need to house 4,000 dam engineers and construction workers. The government hired pioneer and noted city planner Saco Reink DeBoer from Denver, who created a lovely city with government buildings situated at the crest of a hill and a large park serving as the city's focal point. The

National Register of Historic Places lists the original townsite as the Boulder City Historic District.

The website of the **Boulder City Chamber of Commerce,** bouldercitychamber.com, lists two walking tours, one focusing on the town's murals and the other on historic sites. There's also a self-guided audio tour on the site.

Start your tour at the 1933 **Boulder Dam Hotel** at 1305 Arizona St., which was built to accommodate dignitaries and guests visiting the dam. Guests have included Bette Davis, Mr. and Mrs. Cornelius Vanderbilt, Will Rogers, Henry Fonda, Boris Karloff, and Shirley Temple.

The hotel has been renovated over the years and now offers king and queen rooms and king suites with kitchenettes, with amenities including free Wi-Fi and parking and coffee from 5 to 10 a.m. in the guest center. There's a cocktail lounge and breakfast-and-lunch restaurant on-site. Rates start at $104; visit boulderdamhotel.com or call (702) 293-3510.

It might seem a little unusual to have a museum in a hotel, but Boulder City doesn't revel in the usual. The **Boulder City/Hoover Dam Museum** is a collection of three-dimensional, interactive exhibits that tell the story of those who struck out in the desert to build the dam and the city. The story starts with the 1929 stock market crash and resulting Great Depression and the horror of the Dust Bowl that collectively led these people to leave their homes and make their way west, where the dam project offered work that was otherwise nearly impossible to find.

You'll hear the stories of men relating the dangers of building the dam, mothers talking about the difficulties of setting up households in such an unforgiving area, and life in the fledgling city created by the government. This one's fun for kids too; they can open a door to get a blast of what the desert air felt like to those working in the canyon or try their hand at emptying one of the huge buckets that transported concrete to the dam site.

The Boulder City Museum and Historical Association also maintains an archive of 11,000 photographs, a 600-book research library, and 3,500 artifacts. Museum hours are 7 a.m. to 7 p.m. daily; admission is free. Visit bchdmuseum .org or call (702) 294-1988.

The **Boulder City Art Guild** also makes its home at the hotel, with a gallery that is open daily with an artist always in attendance. The guild produces shows, holds exhibits and monthly workshops, and awards scholarships. Gallery hours are 9 a.m. to 3 p.m. Visit bouldercityartguild.com or call (702) 293-2138.

The hotel is on the aptly named Hotel Plaza, which is the center of Boulder City's historic area, so take a stroll to see what's around. Antique shops abound, such as **Sherman's House of Antiques** at 1228 Arizona St. (shermanshouse ofantiques.com) and **Bella Marketplace** at 1212 Wyoming St. (bellamarketplace bouldercity.com). Clean up at *Boulder City Soap & Candle,* 501 Nevada Way (bouldercitysoap.com). Or just relax in the 7-acre, shaded Bicentennial Park at the center of town, where you'll find a gazebo, playground, picnic tables, and grills (bcnv.org).

Bicentennial is just one of the cluster of parks in the center of town that form the site of *Boulder City Art in the Park,* which draws 100,000 people to this tiny town each October. It's a juried show over 2 days, with dozens of exhibitors displaying their paintings, sculptures, woodworking, metalwork, and fiber arts—about anything you can imagine—to benefit the Boulder City Hospital. Go to bchcares.org.

By now you've no doubt worked up an appetite, so it's a good thing there are 10 restaurants in close proximity to the hotel. Good choices include *Milo's Cellar* at 538 Nevada Way for wine and dishes to go with it such as paninis and braised boneless short ribs (milosbouldercity.com); *The Dillinger* at 1224 Arizona St. for appetizers, burgers, sandwiches, and wraps (thedillinger.com); *The Coffee Cup* at 512 Nevada Way for breakfasts such as Loco Moco or smothered burritos and lunch sandwiches and salads (worldfamouscoffeecup .com); and *Boulder Dam Brewing Company* at 453 Nevada Way for craft beer and everything that goes with it, such as beer-battered pickles or mushrooms, wings, and burgers (boulderdambrewing.com).

Then get into your car, because here's an insider tip for something a lot of Las Vegas locals don't even know about: Follow Nevada Way to the Boulder City Bypass, also known as Boulder City Parkway/Great Basin Highway/US 93 BUS, and turn right. About a mile along, turn left on Ville Drive and follow it to the city's *Hemenway Park* at the end. There, depending on the time of day, you may see up to a couple dozen bighorn sheep coming down the nearby mountainside to graze in the shade of the park. They're not pets, so don't get close, but you'll be able to get pictures from not too far away. Visit bcnv.org (check bcnv.org/1026/Ram-Cam to see if any are around). There also are picnic shelters and a playground if the sheep don't delight.

While you're in the area, go back to the bypass road, turn right, and drive about 2 miles to *Tom Devlin's Monster Museum* at 1310 Boulder City Pkwy. The museum, owned by a veteran of movie makeup effects, is dedicated to the art and history of those amazing creations. You'll see props used on-screen, creature suits, and other bits of movie monster mayhem. Hours are 10 a.m. to 6 p.m. daily. It's $20 for adults and $10 for children older than 5; for $75, you can get a private tour with Devlin for your group of up to 8 people. Visit tomdevlins montermseum.com or call (702) 294-1313.

Or ride into the past at the *Nevada Railway Museum Boulder City* at 601 Yucca St. (about 0.5 mile farther along the bypass road, turn right on Yucca

Street; it's well marked). Here you'll find exhibits related to rail history, dam construction—even a 5/8 scale replica of a Wells Fargo stagecoach. More recent local rail history is represented by two locomotives that moved reactors and nuclear rocket motors around the Nevada Test Site. There are also temporary exhibits such as two Amtrak rail locomotives.

And, of course, train rides, on Sat, Sun, and some holiday Mons (plus special trains for Santa and the Easter Bunny). The fare for the 40-minute ride is $10 for adults and $5 for kids 4 to 11. Cab and caboose rides are extra. Museum hours are 9 a.m. to 3:30 p.m. daily. Visit boulderrailroadmuseum.org or call (702) 486-5952.

To reach the City of **Henderson** (population 343,791), follow Boulder City Parkway north to I-11/SR 95/SR 93 and then about 7 miles north to the Wagonwheel Drive interchange. After exiting, turn right; after you cross the freeway ramps, turn left onto Boulder Highway/SR 582. Follow the road to 1830 S. Boulder Hwy. and the **Clark County Museum.**

The museum became known to TV audiences nationwide because the former director, the prodigiously bearded and broad-brim-hatted Mark Hall-Patton, was frequently called in to consult for the *Pawn Stars* reality show on the History Channel. Hall-Patton has retired, but his beloved museum remains a fine place to visit.

One of the most striking features on the 30-acre museum site is Heritage Street, a collection of full-sized local buildings that reflect various aspects of life in Southern Nevada, such as a railroad cottage, a number of other houses, a wedding chapel, and the Boulder City train depot.

The indoor exhibits are designed to take visitors from the Ice Age to the Age of Entertainment with a look at Native Americans from the ancient pueblo-dwellers to the current Paiute, the daily lives of early Anglo pioneers, mining technology and the gaming and entertainment heritage of Las Vegas.

The museum is open from 9 a.m. to 4:30 p.m. daily except holidays. Admission is $2 for most adults and $1 for seniors and children. Visit clark countynv.gov or call (702) 455-7955.

Henderson was born during World War II with the opening of the Basic Magnesium Plant, which supplied the government with materials for munitions and airplane parts. (Today you'll see reminders of the plant in the form of Basic Road and Basic Academy of International Studies, formerly Basic High School, in the downtown area.) The plant had 14,000 employees, but most of them moved away after the government shut down the plant in 1947, reducing school enrollment by 67 percent. In fine Nevada fashion, it seemed Henderson was about to become a ghost town; the United States War Asset Administration actually offered the town for sale as surplus war property.

The Nevada Legislature stepped in in the nick of time, giving the Colorado River Commission of Nevada the right to purchase the industrial plants, and the city was saved. Today, its industrial roots are still visible—though well screened by landscaping—along Lake Mead Parkway in the form of factories including TIMET, the sole American producer of the titanium sponge used in aircraft, satellites, and missiles.

Over the past decades, though, Henderson mostly grew into a bedroom community for Las Vegas and the state's second-largest city. Most recently it became somewhat of a sports hub, with Raiders headquarters and the city-owned Lee's Family Forum, home to the American Hockey League team Henderson Silver Knights and the America First Center, a practice facility for the Silver Knights and home of the Vegas Golden Knights youth programs.

The America First Center was also an early anchor for the Water Street District, a redevelopment area near City Hall that's become a major draw for its restaurants, bars, and residential units (visit waterstreetdistrict.com). To get there from the Clark County Museum, turn left on Boulder Highway/SR 582. Drive about 2 miles and turn left onto Basic Road and then right onto Water Street in about 0.5 mile.

During a visit to Southern Nevada, President John F. Kennedy predicted that Henderson would be a "city of destiny." Truer words were never spoken.

But don't leave Henderson without making a sweet stop that draws buses full of visitors from all over. Follow Water Street to Lake Mead Parkway and turn left. A short distance down the road, turn right onto I-11/US 95/US 93 north to Sunset Road; exit and turn left. Drive about 2 miles to the intersection where Sunset Road hangs a left; you'll want to turn right, onto Sunset Way, then left onto Cactus Garden Drive.

Ethel M Chocolates is a chocolate factory and cactus garden. Take the self-guided factory tour to the gift shop, where you'll find a vast assortment of the company's products (including M&M's) and the opportunity for a tasting experience. Outside, the 3-acre Botanical Cactus Garden is home to more than

It's a Chocolate Holiday

My favorite time of year to visit ***Ethel M Chocolates*** is during the Christmas season, when the cactus garden is illuminated by thousands of colored lights, giving it a glow that seems magical even this close to Las Vegas, the neon metropolis.

In fact, for a very pleasant spin on Christmas shopping, take the factory tour, then proceed to the gift shop to purchase a prepackaged or custom box of chocolates for that special someone, or perhaps find a cactus, M&M's, or Southwest-themed item. Then wander into the garden. You'll be in the Christmas spirit all evening.

300 species of plants and is a great place for a gentle stroll. The complex is open from 10 a.m. to 6 p.m. daily, and admission is free. Visit ethelm.com or call (702) 435-2608.

Retrace your steps to I-11/US 95/US 93 and head south to the interchange just before Boulder City where US 95/I-11 breaks off to head south. In about 60 miles, turn left onto SR 163; in about 20 more miles, you'll be in **Laughlin** (population 8,371). Laughlin lies on the banks of the Colorado River and is mainly a collection of medium-sized casino-resorts that have led many to call it "the way Las Vegas used to be."

It's also in the heart of desert country, with the average summer high a toasty 108 degrees and holding Nevada's highest recorded temperature at 125 degrees in 1994. But there are plenty of ways to escape the heat with activities centered on the Colorado River.

To get an up-close-and-personal look at the river, take a sightseeing cruise on the *Grand Celebration*, a 150-passenger yacht. Narrated 90-minute cruises presented by **Laughlin River Tours** depart from the Aquarius Casino Resort, 1900 S. Casino Dr., with prices starting at $19 for adults and $12 for kids 4 to 10. Or take a 2-hour sunset dinner cruise, with fares starting at $79 for adults. Visit laughlinerivertours.com or call (725) 253-2619.

If you want to get closer to the water, **Rocky River Adventure Center,** 1900 S. Casino Dr., offers Jet Ski rentals for $119 for 1 hour, $209 for 2 hours, $329 for a half-day, or $429 for a full day. Visit rockyriverfun.com or call (702) 299-1500.

Or, if you'd rather keep your distance, take a jaunt on the **Laughlin Riverwalk,** a paved walking path that extends about a mile along the casino corridor, 7 of the 9 casino resorts on the Laughlin Strip. Go to visitlaughlin.com or call (702) 298-3221.

The **River Passage Water Taxi** is an option for traveling between the 9 casino resorts, stopping at the Riverwalk dock of each from 9 a.m. to late evening. One-way rides are $5, all-day passes $25, or you can take a round-trip ride for $10. Visit riverpassagewatertaxi.com or call (725) 529-2629.

Gearheads will soak up the atmosphere at **Don Laughlin's Classic Car Collection** in two exhibit areas at the Riverside Resort, 1650 S. Casino Dr. It's a rotating collection of more than 80 antique and collectible vehicles, such as the Laughlin Motorsports Race Truck, a 1955 Buick Century Riviera, and a motorcycle once driven by Steve McQueen. It opens at 10 a.m. daily. Admission is $5, or free with a King of Clubs Players' Card. Visit riversideresort.com or call (800) 227-3849.

All of this activity will no doubt work up an appetite, and those 9 resorts are filled with places to eat and drink. Take a trip back to the way things used to be at the French-inspired *Gourmet Room* at the Riverside, with classics such as coquilles Saint-Jacques or steak au poivre (riversideresort.com or 702-298-2535). *Saltgrass Steak House* at the Golden Nugget, 2300 S. Casino Dr., specializes in Certified Angus Beef steaks (goldennugget.com or call 702-298-7153). *Bumble-berry Flats* at the New Pioneer, 2200 S. Casino Dr., is the place to get Southern comfort foods like fried green tomatoes and barbecued shrimp and grits and a brunch buffet on weekends (laughlinpioneer.com or 702-298-2442). And the wood- and rock-lined *Bighorn Café* at the Laughlin River Lodge, 2700 S. Casino Dr., serves American dishes such as burgers, short ribs, and steaks, with a great view of the river (laughlinriverlodge.com or 702-298-2242).

Then it's back outside, to the *Colorado River Heritage Greenway Park & Trails,* 9 miles of new trails that depart from 3 trailheads near the north end of the casino strip. For more information on the trails or Laughlin itself, go to visitlaughlin.com.

If you'd like to see an authentic ghost town—and a living ghost town, at that—cross the Colorado River into Bullhead City, Arizona, and head south on US 95/I-11 about 15 miles. Turn east on Boundary Cone Road when you get to Fort Mohave, then continue on Oatman Road. *Oatman* is notable for the abandoned mining structures you'll see scattered about, but it's perhaps best known for the wild—or maybe not so wild—burros that make their way into the center of town each day, only to return to the hills at night. The burros are under the purview of the US Bureau of Land Management, which watches over them carefully and restricts the food visitors may give them, and they're so tame that one may try to climb into your car as you prepare to depart. Tiny Oatman also is the site of numerous colorful shops and a few restaurants and bars; the Oatman Hotel was the site of the 1939 honeymoon of Clark Gable and Carole Lombard and is rumored to be haunted—although by neither of that famous couple. Go to oatmangoldroad.org or call (928) 577-9139.

Then it's time to retrace your steps to Laughlin, then drive east on SR 163 to US 95/I-11 and about 19 miles north to *Searchlight* (population 208), home of the late prominent US senator Harry Reid. The historical marker alongside the road tells you that G. F. Colton discovered gold here in 1897. The town boasted 1,500 residents in the early 1900s but by 1910 the decline had set in. Total district production is estimated at more than $5 million. A quick drive around town rewards you with dilapidated miners' shacks and weathered wooden headframes worthy of photos. Local lore claims that Colton found gold while lighting his pipe with Searchlight brand matches, thus giving birth to the mining camp name.

The *Searchlight Historic Museum* in the Searchlight Community Center at 200 Michael Wendell Way tells the story of this town that once surpassed Las

Vegas in population and was a contender for the county seat. It's open from 9 a.m. to 2 p.m., Mon through Thur. Admission is free. For information, visit searchlightmuseum.org or call (702) 305-8474.

East of Searchlight, 14 miles, on SR 164, you'll find ***Cottonwood Cove Resort & Marina*** on Lake Mohave. There you'll find camping and a motel and houseboat and other watercraft rentals. A 50-foot Sirius houseboat, complete with waterslide that sleeps 6, starts at $476 per day. Single kayaks start at $85 per day, canoes at $105, and WaveRunners at $389.

The RV park has 72 spots with full hookups that start at $41. The lakeside Cottonwood Cove Motel has rooms with covered outdoor patios and outdoor grills. Rates start at $134.10. Visit cottonwoodcoveresort.com or call (702) 297-1464.

Leaving Cottonwood Cove, head west on SR 164 for 44 miles through the historic town of Nipton, California, and then turn north on I-15, back toward Las Vegas. After you pass through Primm, you'll see ***Seven Magic Mountains,*** a "large-scale desert artwork," which consists of seven towering stacks of boulders erected by Swiss artist Ugo Rondinone. The installation, produced by the Nevada Museum of Art and Art Production Fund, initially was to exist two years after it was erected in 2016, but its popularity has led to its continued existence, with periodic repainting as the desert environment fades the colors.

To reach it, drive north on I-15 to Jean, then head east on SR 161 to Las Vegas Boulevard, then north on the boulevard and you'll see it on the right, along with a parking lot. Admission is free. Visit sevenmagicmountains.com or call (702) 381-5182.

Return to I-15 and head north about 27 miles to the "Spaghetti Bowl" near downtown Las Vegas, then continue north on US 95/I-11 about 25 miles to SR 157/Kyle Canyon Road, turn west and climb your way up ***Mount Charleston*** to a completely different climate.

Mount Charleston, where temperatures routinely are at least 20 degrees lower than they are in the Las Vegas Valley, is in the Spring Mountains National Recreation Area, part of the 6.2-million-acre Humboldt-Toiyabe National Forest, which sprawls across Nevada and parts of California and is the largest national forest in the lower 48. You can learn all about this oasis in the Mojave Desert at the 90-acre ***Spring Mountain Visitor Gateway,*** which has a visitor center, two amphitheaters, trailheads, and spots with benches to just relax. In the visitor center, you can get the lay of the land and learn about hiking trails, scenic byways, biking and climbing opportunities, picnicking, camping, winter sports—well, you get the picture, or you can get a better one by visiting gomountcharleston.com. For more about what the national forest's Mount Charleston Wilderness has to offer, go to fs.usda.gov.

Mount Charleston has an elevation of 11,915 feet at its peak, but you won't be able to get that high, unless maybe you're a seasoned mountaineer. Two roughly parallel roads, SRs 157 and 156, lead up the mountain. As you continue up SR 157/Kyle Canyon Road, you'll begin to cool off immediately in the face of sheer cliffs and copious aspen and evergreen trees. While snow is extremely rare in the Las Vegas Valley, it's just part of winter up here, making this the place a lot of valley kids first encounter snow.

The road ends near the **Mount Charleston Lodge** at 5375 Kyle Canyon Rd. At an elevation of 7,800 feet, it had long been an extremely popular restaurant, bar, and place to escape since 1957. Yes, *had*. Unfortunately, the lodge burned down in 2021, and plans are to start the rebuilding in early 2025. But wait! There's more!

While the lodge building is gone temporarily, the resort has 22 modern, comfortable cabins that sleep from 2 to 6 people, and you can sit on your deck and try to spot bobcats, deer, elk, gray foxes, mountain lions and wild turkeys, and watch hummingbirds flutter about. Weekday rates start at $123. Visit mtcharlestonlodge.com or call (702) 872-5408.

Head back down Kyle Canyon Road about 4.5 miles and you'll come to **The Retreat on Charleston Peak** at 2755 Kyle Canyon Rd., which you passed on the way up. It's at 6,700 feet and has rooms and suites starting at $151.18 per night. It has concierge service, the Tavern Gaming Bar, and Barks and Brews, a pet-friendly patio. Be particularly aware of your surroundings; our lunch was once graced by the view of a wild horse right outside our window.

The Retreat's full-service Canyon Restaurant opens for breakfast at 7:30 a.m. for those eager to get into the great outdoors, and it also serves lunch and dinner, with dishes such as burgers, fish and chips, and a 40-ounce ribeye tomahawk steak. Visit retreatoncharlestonpeak.com or call (702) 872-5500.

Just across Kyle Canyon Road, almost opposite the Retreat, you'll spot another state road on this mountain, SR 158, also known as Deer Creek Road, which connects the two principal routes that go up (and down). Keep your eyes peeled for the **Desert View Overlook** on the right side of the road. Here you'll find a smallish parking lot and a well-paved, wheelchair-accessible, 0.4-mile round-trip trail that winds down to viewing platforms, benches, and educational panels that indicate distant points of interest such as the Nevada Test Site and bomb-detonation viewing sites during the Atomic Era. Visit gomtcharleston.com.

After your walk, continue on SR 158/Deer Creek Road to SR 156/Lee Canyon Road and turn left. Continue climbing and, in a few minutes, you'll reach the **Lee Canyon** skiing and snowboarding resort. With a base lodge elevation of 8,661 feet, the resort has 5 lifts and 312 trails and a pro shop with rentals.

There's also a coffee shop, restaurant, and bar—at press time, the only food and drink options on the mountain other than the Retreat. In summer, you can go mountain biking on the trails, take a scenic chairlift ride, or participate in archery, axe-throwing, or disc golf. Visit leecanyonlv.com.

Then it's back down the mountain to US 95/I-11, going south, to SR 215 West, and about 22 miles around the loop to the Charleston Boulevard exit. Turn left on Charleston, then right on South Pavilion Center Drive, through the traffic circle and right onto Summerlin Centre Drive into *Downtown Summerlin.*

Downtown Summerlin isn't an organically formed downtown area, or a downtown in the traditional sense of the term. Like the unincorporated Summerlin community in which it's located, it's a planned development, which opened in 2014 and has become the beating heart of the area.

Downtown Summerlin is a mixed-use development with some residential and some office space and lots of restaurants and stores. It's also home to City National Arena, where the Vegas Golden Knights practice and host many of their youth-hockey programs, and Las Vegas Ballpark, home of the Las Vegas Aviators Triple-A affiliate of the Oakland Athletics. And much more is in Downtown Summerlin's future; among other things, at press time, Sony Entertainment and Summerlin developer Howard Hughes Holdings announced plans for a $1.8-billion movie studio and mixed-use development in the area also supported by Hollywood actor and Las Vegas resident Mark Wahlberg. Visit summerlin.com.

Make your way back out to Charleston Boulevard, heading west. You'll wind through some of the westernmost residential areas in Las Vegas and in less than 2 miles you'll arrive at the entrance to Red Rock Canyon National Conservation Area. In this oasis a mere 20 miles from

howard hughes

Billionaire recluse *Howard Hughes* lived for four years in the since-demolished Desert Inn Hotel behind heavily draped windows. At the time of his death, Hughes owned casinos, an airline, stretches of undeveloped and commercial properties, mining claims, Hughes Aircraft, and the Howard Hughes Medical Institute. Hughes died in 1976, mad from drug abuse and maybe genetics, weighing 92 pounds. He also died without a will. Who would control or inherit his $6.2 billion fortune? Con artists by the thousands presented wills. Even the states of California and Texas claimed Hughes as a resident to get inheritance tax money. The big winners were finally an assortment of heirs (including twenty-two cousins and an actress who claimed to have been married to Hughes), the tax man, Howard Hughes Medical Institute, and Nevadans. Much of his land was eventually developed into Summerlin, named for his grandmother. And Spring Mountain Ranch State Park, once owned by Howard Hughes, is now a 520-acre shady retreat for picnics and outdoor concerts.

the Strip you'll see towering cliffs with alternating bands of red sandstone and white limestone, their color contributed by the minerals in the soil. Throw in colorful desert flowers and frequent wildlife sightings and you have the makings of a great excursion.

This is an extremely popular place with more than 4 million visitors a year because of its rare beauty and proximity to Las Vegas, so plan ahead. If you're visiting between 8 a.m. and 5 p.m. Oct 1 through May 31, and want to access the scenic drive, you'll need a timed reservation, which is available at recreation.gov. (*Note:* The scenic drive opens at 6 a.m. daily and during some of those months is open later than 5 p.m., if you forget to plan.)

After entering the gate, stop at the visitor center for maps and information on climbing, hiking, bicycling, and other activities. Outside, you'll see four interpretive exhibits, each themed to one of the four elements. The visitor center opens daily at 8 a.m. and closes at 4:30 p.m. except for Thanksgiving and Christmas Day, when it closes at noon. The entry fee for the scenic drive is $20 per vehicle; America the Beautiful passes of the National Park Service and Federal Recreational Lands Pass program are accepted.

The loop drive is a one-way, 13-mile paved road dotted by parking areas providing access to scenic overlooks, informative displays, trailheads, picnic areas, and restrooms. This is a very popular place for rock climbing, drawing athletes from all over the world, and the first couple of overlooks, Calico I and Calico II, are good places to pull over, park, and watch climbers honing their skills. If you want to participate, *Mountain Skills Rock Climbing Adventures* can give you a leg up with local guides, some of them Red Rock–climbing pioneers, who can lead the way up classic multi-pitch routes or to places that are known to few. Daily rates, which go down with each additional person in your group, start at $400. Visit climbing schoolusa.com or call (575) 776-2222.

white-knuckle rides

The world's highest thrill rides are at **The Strat Hotel, Casino & Tower,** 2000 Las Vegas Blvd. South (thestrat .com or 800-998-6937), where you'll find the Big Shot, which shoots you even higher into the sky, X-Scream, a roller-coaster-type ride that propels you 27 feet over the edge of the (866-foot-high) tower, and the SkyJump, on which you—yes—jump off the tower. Or make your way to New York–New York for a thrill, Gotham-style, on the Big Apple Coaster, which twists and turns and loop-de-loops as it races over the faux New York skyline (new yorknewyork.mgmresorts.com or 866-815-4365).

Or, if you have proper footwear, are dressed for the weather, and carrying plenty of water, strike out on one of the many marked trails, some of which start at trailheads near parking areas. As you walk, keep a wary eye out for rattlesnakes. If you're lucky, you may spot a desert tortoise, or lizards, bighorn sheep, mule deer, or roaming burros. A 2.4-mile, 2-hour, easy-to-moderate round-trip hike into Pine Creek Canyon, for which the trailhead is right off the scenic drive past the Red Rock Wash overlook, leads to the ruins of a historic homestead surrounded by large ponderosa pines and diverse plant communities at the base of the canyon walls. The 2.2-mile, 2-hour (and strenuous) Ice Box Canyon trail, which is accessed off the scenic drive past Lost Creek, leads to a shady box canyon with waterfalls December through April. For detailed trail maps and more information, visit blm.gov/programs/national-conservation -lands/nevada/red-rock-canyon or redrockcanyonlv.org.

If you're just looking for a place to relax and enjoy the scenery, there are plenty of opportunities for that as well. It's not unusual to see a couple sharing a bottle of wine at one of the overlook areas.

The Red Rock loop road is a very popular place for bicyclists, as you'll soon see. If you didn't bring a bike, *Escape Tours* is standing by to help with half-day and full-day guided and self-guided bicycle tours of the canyon, plus mountain bike and e-bike tours. Rates, which include bike rental, helmet, water, and round-trip transportation to the Strip, start at $139.99 for self-guided tours, $149.99 for guided. Visit escapeadventures.com or call (702) 596-2953.

If you'd rather see the scenery from the back of a horse, *Silver State Tours* is ready to help you saddle up. Rates start at $70 for a morning or afternoon trail ride; options include rides paired with breakfast, lunch, dinner, or a chuckwagon show—or even a private proposal. Visit silverstatetour.com or call (702) 805-1911.

Or tour with a different kind of horsepower. *Pink Jeep Adventure Tours* offer tours of Red Rock Canyon, or you can opt for the Rocky Gap Off-Road Tour. Rates start at $114 for adults, $104 for kids 3 to 12, and private group tours are available. Visit pinkadventuretours.com or call (800) 873-3662.

Leaving Red Rock Canyon National Conservation Area, turn right on SR 159 and drive about 8.5 miles to *Spring Mountain Ranch State Park.* The focus of the 520-acre park, which lies at the base of the grand Wilson Cliffs in Red Rock Canyon, is the ranch house that dates to the late 1940s or early 1950s and was built by a radio star of the era as a retreat from his family's Los Angeles home. Subsequent owners of the ranch included Vera Krupp, whose 33.19-carat diamond later was owned by Elizabeth Taylor—and which was stolen while Krupp lived at the ranch but later recovered—and Howard Hughes, who bought it in 1967 but never actually lived there.

Today, tours of the ranch house, which serves as the park's visitor center, are offered daily. Other points of interest include a sandstone cabin that dates to the early 1800s and an 1860s blacksmith shop. The park also has hiking trails and shaded picnic areas with tables and grills. There's also an amphitheater, where summer productions by local community theater groups are very popular with Las Vegans who bring their blankets and picnics for an evening away from the heat. For more on that, visit supersummertheatre.org.

Park admission is $10 per vehicle, or $15 for non-Nevada vehicles. The park opens at 8 a.m. daily; closing hours vary by the season. Visit parks.nv.gov/parks/spring-mountain-ranch or call (702) 875-4141.

Leaving Spring Mountain Ranch State Park, turn right and continue a little less than 4 miles to the hamlet of **Blue Diamond** (population 294). This unincorporated town started out, like so many, as a mining town, but has morphed into a bedroom community for those willing to make the 45-minute commute. The draw: lots of shade trees, a small-town feel, and—especially for those who live on the north end of town—stunning views of Red Rock Canyon.

Blue Diamond doesn't have much in the way of businesses but a new addition in the past few years is **Cottonwood Station,** a restaurant in a historic building that has built a loyal following among Red Rock day-trippers, hikers, bicyclists, and climbers. Owned by a couple of local residents, it gets the morning started with artisanal coffee and pastries before moving to a menu of appetizers, pizzas, paninis, and salads. Visit cottonwoodstationeatery.com or call (702) 875-4332.

The Blue Diamond/Red Rock area is a likely place to spot wild horses and burros, especially at dusk. Remember that these are wild animals and far from tame, and those caught feeding them face hefty fines.

But such sightings tend to be memorable. One evening when I was sitting on the Cottonwood Station's deck, having pizza and a glass of wine with friends visiting from the Midwest, one spotted a couple of burros wandering through the restaurant's parking lot. And we saw a larger group of them in the town park as we drove out of Blue Diamond and back to Las Vegas, so our friends could catch their plane for home—one of their last delightful memories of their Las Vegas visit.

Places to Stay in Las Vegas Territory

BOULDER CITY

Hoover Dam Lodge
18000 US 93
hooverdamlodge.com
(800) 245-6380

HENDERSON

Railroad Pass Hotel & Casino
1500 Railroad Pass Casino Rd.
railroadpass.com
(702) 294-5000

LAS VEGAS DOWNTOWN

The D Casino & Hotel
301 Fremont St.
thed.com
(800) 274-5825

The English Hotel
921 S. Main St.
theenglishhotel.com
(725) 888-4920

Golden Gate Hotel & Casino
1 Fremont St.
goldengatecasino.com
(800) 426-1906

LAS VEGAS STRIP

Aria
3730 Las Vegas Blvd. S.
aria.mgmresorts.com
(702) 590-7111

Caesars Palace
3570 Las Vegas Blvd. S.
caesars.com
(866) 227-5938

The Cosmopolitan of Las Vegas
3708 Las Vegas Blvd. S.
cosmopolitanlasvegas.com
(702) 698-7000

Four Seasons/ Mandalay Bay
3960 Las Vegas Blvd. S.
fourseasons.com
(702) 632-5000

Hilton/Conrad/ Crockfords, Resorts World
3000 Las Vegas Blvd. S.
rwlasvegas.com
(702) 676-7000

MGM Grand Hotel/Casino
3799 Las Vegas Blvd. S.
mgmgrand.mgmresorts.com
(877) 880-0880

Nobu Hotel, Caesars Palace
3570 Las Vegas Blvd. S.
caesars.com
(800) 727-4923

NoMad, Park MGM
3772 Las Vegas Blvd. S.
nomadlasvegas.mgmresorts.com
(702) 730-7000

Park MGM
3774 Las Vegas Blvd. S.
parkmgm.mgmresorts.com
(702) 730-7777

The Strat
2000 Las Vegas Blvd. S.
thestrat.com
(800) 998-6937

The Venetian (and Palazzo)
3355 Las Vegas Blvd. S.
venetianlasvegas.com
(866) 659-9643

Waldorf Astoria
3752 Las Vegas Blvd. S.
hilton.com
(702) 590-8888

Wynn Las Vegas (and Encore)
3131 Las Vegas Blvd. S.
wynnlasvegas.com
(702) 770-7000

LAUGHLIN

Aquarius Casino Resort
1900 S. Casino Dr.
aquariuscasinoresort.com
(800) 662-5825

Don Laughlin's Riverside Resort Hotel & Casino
1650 S. Casino Dr.
riversideresort.com
(702) 298-2535

Golden Nugget Laughlin
2300 S. Casino Dr.
goldennugget.com
(702) 298-7111

MESQUITE

Casablanca Resort Casino
950 W. Mesquite Blvd.
casablancaresort.com
(877) 438-2929

Eureka Casino Resort
275 Mesa Blvd.
eurekamesquite.com
(702) 346-4600

Virgin River Hotel, Casino & Bingo
100 Pioneer Blvd.
virginriver.com
(877) 438-2929

PRIMM

Buffalo Bill's
31900 Las Vegas Blvd.
South
primmvalleyresorts.com
(702) 386-7867

SUMMERLIN

Suncoast
9090 Alta Dr.
suncoast.boydgaming.com
(702) 636-7111

Places to Eat in Las Vegas Territory

BOULDER CITY

Cornish Pasty Company
1300 Arizona St.
cornishpastyco.com
(702) 268-7864

Fox Smokehouse BBQ
930 Nevada Way
foxsmokehousebbq.com
(702) 489-2211

HENDERSON

Gaetano's Ristorante
10271 S. Eastern Ave.
gaetanoslasvegas.com
(702) 361-1661

Todd's Unique Dining
4350 E. Sunset Rd.
toddsunique.com
(702) 259-8633

LAS VEGAS DOWNTOWN

Andiamo Steakhouse, The D Casino & Hotel
(steak and Italian)
301 Fremont St.
thed.com
(800) 274-5825

The Pepper Club, The English Hotel
(Asian Fusion)
921 S. Main St.
thepepperclub.com
(725) 228-2393

Triple George Grill
201 N. 3rd St.
triplegeorgegrill.com
(702) 384-2761

LAS VEGAS STRIP

Bardot Brasserie,
(French), Aria,
3730 Las Vegas Blvd. S.
aria.mgmresorts.com
(702) 590-8610

Bazaar Meat by José Andrés, The Sahara
2535 Las Vegas Blvd. S.
saharalasvegas.com
(702) 761-7610

The Bedford, Paris Las Vegas (Martha Stewart)
3655 Las Vegas Blvd. S.
caesars.com
(702) 946-4361

Dominique Ansel, Caesars Palace
3570 Las Vegas Blvd. S.
caesars.com
(702) 731-7865

Eataly, Park MGM (Italian)
3770 Las Vegas Blvd. S.
eataly.com
(702) 730-7777

Giada, The Cromwell
(Italian)
3595 Las Vegas Blvd. S.
caesars.com
(855) 442-3271

Hell's Kitchen, Caesars Palace (American)
3570 Las Vegas Blvd. S.
gordonramsayrestaurants
.com
(702) 731-7373

Nellie's Southern Kitchen, MGM Grand
3799 Las Vegas Blvd. S.
mgmgrand.mgmresorts
.com
(702) 640-0156

The Peppermill (American)
2985 Las Vegas Blvd. S.
peppermilllasvegas.com
(702) 735-4177

Restaurant Guy Savoy, Caesars Palace (French)
3570 Las Vegas Blvd. S.
caesars.com
(702) 731-7286

Spago, Bellago
(California Italian)
3600 Las Vegas Blvd. S.
bellagio.mgmresorts.com
(702) 693-8181

Yardbird, The Venetian
(Southern)
3355 Las Vegas Blvd. S.
runchickenrun.com
(702) 297-6541

LAUGHLIN

The Brew Brothers, Tropicana Laughlin
(American)
2121 S. Casino Dr.
caesars.com
(702) 298-4200

Casa Serrano, Don
Laughlin's Riverside
Resort (Mexican)
1650 S. Casino Dr.
riversideresort.com
(800) 227-3849

MESQUITE

D Thai Bistro
1085 W. Pioneer Blvd.
dthaibistromesquitenv.com
(702) 613-0442

Katherine's, Casablanca
(American)
950 W. Mesquite Blvd.
casablancaresort.com
(702) 346-6846

SUMMERLIN

Honey Salt (American)
1031 S. Rampart Blvd.
honeysalt.com
(702) 445-6100

La Strega (Italian)
3555 S. Town Center Dr.
lastregalv.com
(702) 722-2099

FOR MORE INFORMATION

Boulder City Chamber of Commerce
100 Nevada Way
bouldercitychamber.com
(702) 293-2034

City of North Las Vegas
2250 Las Vegas Blvd. N.
cityofnorthlasvegas.com
(702) 633-1000

Henderson Chamber of Commerce
400 N. Green Valley Pkwy.
hendersonchamber.com
(702) 565-8951

**Las Vegas Convention
& Visitors Authority**
3150 Paradise Road
lvcva.com
(702) 892-0711

Mesquite Nevada
460 N. Sandhill Blvd.
visitmesquite.com

Moapa Valley Chamber of Commerce
PO Box 361, Overton
moapavalleychamber.com
(702) 398-7160

Oatman Chamber of Commerce
PO Box 423
oatmanchamberofcommerce.com
(928) 577-9139

Vegas Chamber
575 Symphony Park Ave.
vegaschamber.com
(702) 641-5822

Visit Laughlin
LVCVA, 3150 Paradise Rd.
visitlaughlin.com
(877) 847-4858

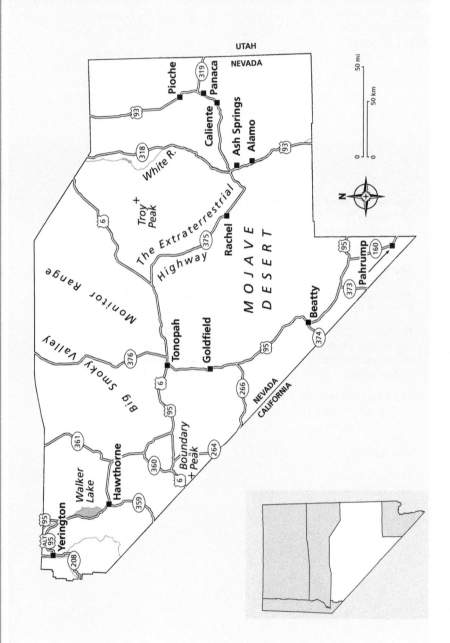

Pioneer Territory

Lincoln County

From Las Vegas, travel to Lincoln County on I-15 North to US 93 North. Shortly after the turnoff you'll see, on the right, the massive solar array that helps power MGM Resorts' Las Vegas properties and, on the left, the **Pahranagat National Wildlife Refuge** and Lower and Upper Pahranagat Lakes. The 5,382-acre refuge is a great place to spot waterfowl and songbirds migrating along the Pacific Flyway, as well as willow flycatchers and birds of prey. You also may see cottontails, jackrabbits, deer (watch for highway signs warning of "major" deer crossings), and the occasional elusive mountain lion or coyote—and speaking of which, keep your eyes peeled for roadrunners, though without anvils or explosives. The refuge offers hiking, camping, fishing, and hunting. Visit fws.gov/refuge/pahranagat or call the visitor center at (775) 725-3417 ext. 100.

Continue through the hamlets of Alamo and Ash Springs to *Crystal Springs*, which enjoyed a brief moment in the sun when the discovery of silver in the Pahranagat Valley made the community the provisional county seat in 1865. It was determined, however, that too few legal voters lived there. Formal establishment of Lincoln County took place in 1866, and the county seat moved to Hiko in early 1867, sounding the death knell for Crystal Springs.

Joshua trees, yucca flowers, and distant mountain ranges provide the imagery as you head east on US 93 to the turnoff for the ghost town of *Delamar,* which is 15 miles off the highway along a gravel and a rock road not recommended for passenger vehicles. In the late 1890s, Delamar outproduced every other Nevada gold mine. All materials arrived via mule teams from a railhead 150 miles away at Milford, Utah, and most of the $15 million in gold bullion departed in the same manner. The main mine shaft descended 1,300 feet, and underground tunnels snaked for a combined length of 36 miles. The town's boom lasted from 1894 to 1909, with a brief revival in the 1930s. At one time, up to 3,000 residents walked its streets, and the town boasted a hospital, a newspaper, a school, a theater, churches, saloons, and a stockbroker.

In addition to being famous for its peak gold production, Delamar gained notoriety as "the Widow Maker." The dry milling processes used prior to the introduction of wet methods created a fine silica dust, causing the premature death of many miners, mill workers, and town residents. Legend has it that at one time there were 500 widows in town. While other Nevada mines fought against flooding, Delamar had the opposite problem. Drilling for water proved unsuccessful, and water had to be transported by pipeline to the town and mill site from Meadow Valley Wash, 12 miles away. Three pumping stations were required to lift the water 2,000 feet in elevation.

Current mining activities in the area occasionally limit access to the Delamar site, which is located on private property. What remains today are some

AUTHOR'S TOP PICKS

Death Valley National Park/Scotty's Castle
near Beatty

Central Nevada Museum
Tonopah

Tonopah Historic Mining Park
Tonopah

Extraterrestrial Highway
Rachel

Little A'Le'Inn
Rachel

Rhyolite Ghost Town
near Beatty

Goldwell Open-Air Museum
near Beatty

Mizpah Hotel
Tonopah

Belvada Hotel
Tonopah

Clown Motel
Tonopah

partially standing rock buildings, mill ruins, and a cemetery. Visit the ghost towns section on travelnevada.com.

Shortly before entering the railroad town of *Caliente* (population 1,031), you'll pass near Oak Springs Summit at 6,237 feet in elevation. Caliente is the largest town in Lincoln County, and as you enter, you'll spot the town's highlight, the *Caliente Railroad Depot,* at 100 Depot Ave. The depot, which was built in 1923 to replace one that had burned two years previously, is one of two Mission-style buildings in Lincoln County. It once housed a restaurant, 50-some hotel rooms, and an Amtrak station. Adapted as a community center, it normally also houses the offices of the city of Caliente, which have temporarily been moved farther up Depot Avenue. At press time the depot was shrouded in scaffolding and closed for renovation. The adjacent *Caliente Box Car Museum* exhibits artifacts and documents from the town's railroad past. Visit lincolncountynevada.com or call (775) 726-3131.

The railroad did not come easily to Caliente. A bitter battle and legal fight between E. H. Harriman's Union Pacific Railroad and Senator William Clark's San Pedro, Los Angeles & Salt Lake Railroad, waged over rights-of-way in the late 1890s, was settled in 1901 by a shotgun-wielding William Culverwell, who owned the canyon that was wide enough for only one set of tracks. Union Pacific prevailed, and the railroad line was completed in 1905.

Also testimony to its railroad heritage is the row of company houses on Spring Street (US 93) north of the railroad tracks. The first 18 houses were constructed in 1905. At one time, the town's population topped 5,000. On Culverwell Street is the stone Methodist Church, built in 1905. It began its life as the Caliente School and exhibits the Classic Box style of architecture popular in the early 20th century.

Caliente, which originated in 1901, took its name from the area's hot springs. You can partake of them today at the *Caliente Hot Springs Motel and Spa,* 2 Youth Center Dr. The 18 rooms include 6 with piped hot spring water; the property also has a bathhouse with 4 tiled private soak rooms with step-down tubs. Visit calientehotspringsmotelandspa.com or call (775) 726-3777.

Stop for a bite to eat at the "world famous" *Knotty Pine Restaurant and Lounge* at 690 Front St., which serves breakfast, lunch, and dinner, including such homey fare as chicken noodle or hamburger soup, a taco salad, and fried chicken and more substantial choices like shrimp scampi and prime rib—the latter priced at less than $25. A friendly place, it also offers slot machines and special events including a weekly pool tournament, which may be canceled if Amy is off. Hours are 6 a.m. to 8 p.m. Sun through Wed, 6 a.m. to 2 p.m. Thurs, and 6 a.m. to 9 p.m. Fri and Sat. Call (775) 726-3767.

The **Side Track Restaurant** at 190 Clover St. serves salads, sandwiches, smoothies, wraps, burgers, and pizza at lunch and dinner. Call (775) 726-3164.

Go south of Caliente on SR 317 to the entrance to **Kershaw-Ryan State Park,** at the northern end of Rainbow Canyon. Wild grapevines climb up the sheer rock cliffs, and Gambel oaks, cottonwoods, and elms provide shade. The Samuel Kershaw family homesteaded the canyon in the 1870s and planted apple, plum, apricot, peach, and cherry trees, many of which survive today. The Kershaws sold the property in the early 1900s to James Ryan, who donated the Kershaw Gardens as a public park in 1934. The Civilian Conservation Corps built restrooms, picnic tables, campsites, a caretaker's cabin, and a wading pond, and it opened as one of Nevada's first four state parks in 1935. Flash floods in the 1980s destroyed most of the structures, though the wading pond survives. The park now offers camping, picnicking, and hiking. Visit parks.nv .gov/parks/kershaw-ryan or call (775) 726-3564.

Kershaw-Ryan is in **Rainbow Canyon,** which has tinted cliffs and unique geologic formations and such historic sites as the Old Conaway Ranch, the Tenille and Dula Ranches, Stine Power Station, Ballou Ranch, and the Elgin and Bradshaw End of the Rainbow Ranch (details at lincolncountynevada.com). Park on the right shoulder of SR 317 near the US 93 junction and walk up the wash and a narrow tunnel to Etna Cave. About 400 feet past the tunnel, keep your eyes open for red-orange prehistoric pictographs on the tan cliff face. The cave, halfway up the wall on the opposite cliffs, was excavated in the 1930s, netting hundreds of artifacts representing 5,000 years of prehistoric occupation.

To reach **Beaver Dam State Park** (about 38 miles from Caliente), drive north on US 93 for 6 miles to the park sign, then 19 miles on a gravel road, and 13 miles on a dirt road. Piñons and juniper trees abound and stream fishing and bird-watching are popular activities. Primitive camping sites are especially a draw for hunters during turkey and deer seasons. Visit parks.nv.gov/parks/ beaver-dam or call (725) 728-8101.

Wind north on US 93 and head east on SR 319 to the community of **Panaca** (population 1,039), which was settled in 1864. During the 1870s, coke ovens here produced charcoal for the smelters at Bullionville, now a ghost town site. Panaca ranks as Nevada's second-oldest town, second only to Genoa. Its name comes from a Southern Paiute word meaning "metal" or "wealth." The Panaca Spring, with a steady flow of water, makes the desert oasis of Meadow Valley possible.

Panaca has changed little over the past 160 years. A short tour will give you a flavor of what life is like in this agricultural town on the edge of robust mining activity. The **Panaca Heritage Center/N. T. Wadsworth & Sons General Store** currently occupies the adobe building at 4th and Main streets that opened as the Panaca Mercantile Store in 1868. It originally was a cooperative institution with more than 100 stockholders; goods were hauled in from Salt Lake City aboard wagons drawn by six-mule teams.

The Wadsworth roots also survive in the form of the N. J. Wadsworth home at 5th and Main streets. Composed of brick and natural stone, it features Victorian and Italianate styling and is the most prominent house in town.

One mile west of Panaca, return to US 93. Turn north and proceed another mile to the entrance to *Cathedral Gorge State Park* on the left. Prepare yourself to view one of Nevada's real off-the-beaten-path treasures. Impressive outcroppings form picturesque spires that give the park its name and can keep you enthralled for hours. A visitor center provides information on how the unusual formations evolved. As you drive through the park, notice the now-abandoned 1930 Civilian Conservation Corps water tower.

Millions of years of erosion sculpted the churchlike formations and caverns. At various places you can walk between the crevices and slot canyons and venture through the labyrinth. While inside, peer up at the sky and see the jagged fingers reaching for the heavens. For a view from a different vantage, exit the main park entrance and head north about 1 mile to the *Miller Point Overlook.* The wife of a Bullionville mill superintendent in the 1890s, Mrs. W. S. Godbe, found the formations awe inspiring and recommended calling the area Cathedral Gulch, which later was changed to Cathedral Gorge. It has been a state park since 1935.

The Panaca Formation is the remnant of a Pliocene-era lake bed. As the climate changed over the eons, the lake gradually dried up and erosion started its work on the sediments, creating the cathedral-like forms.

Picnic areas, showers, and campsites are available. The fee is $10, or $5 for Nevada vehicles; camping is $20 per vehicle per night ($15 for Nevada vehicles), with utility hookups $10 extra. Bike riders are admitted for $2 each. For more information, visit parks.nv.gov/parks/cathedral-gorge or call (775) 728-8101.

Head 9 miles north on US 93 to *Pioche* (population 1,111) and see one of the Old West's most rip-roaring towns ever. By 1875 more than 10,000 people had flocked to Pioche and the area silver mines, and violence came with them. Guns were the only law, and Pioche made Bodie, Dodge City, Tombstone, and other well-known Western towns pale by comparison (Pioche was the scene of dozens of murders each year in the

trivia

When *Pioche* was a frontier boomtown, mining companies employed professional gunmen, reportedly bringing in 20 a day to protect their interests. It's not surprising the word "gunfighter" entered the American usage with these words: "I'm Cemetery Sam, and I'm a gunfighter from Pioche."

1870s, while there were just a few in Tombstone.) Legend has it that gunfire sent 72 men to Boot Hill, the local cemetery, before anyone died of natural causes, and that in 1871 and 1872, 60 percent of Nevada's killings took place in Pioche. The *Territorial Enterprise* in Virginia City reported in July 1873, "Pioche is overrun with as desperate a class of scoundrels as probably ever afflicted any mining town on this coast and the law is virtually a dead letter." Anyway, you get the picture. Enjoy your stay in Pioche, but mind your manners.

Surveyed in 1869, Pioche maintains its authentic flavor with an abundance of historic buildings. The most notable, of course, is the famed ***Million Dollar Courthouse.*** The original budget for the 1871 courthouse and jail combination came in at $26,000. Design changes, construction cost overruns, and corruption pushed the tab for the Classical Revival structure to $800,000 in 1872 dollars. Closure of the principal silver mines caused Pioche to delay payments on the courthouse, and refinancing with bonds pushed the total to $1 million by the time the final payment was made in 1938. At that point, lead and zinc mining were pouring cash into government coffers; the new courthouse was under construction and the 1872 building was reportedly crumbling.

Lincoln County's Five State Parks

Beaver Dam State Park is Nevada's most remote park with piñon and juniper forest, deep canyons, streams, and waterfalls and is a designated Watchable Wildlife Area. It's 6 miles north of Caliente on US 93, then 28 miles east on a graded gravel road.

Cathedral Gorge State Park. Trails abound in this long, narrow valley where erosion has carved dramatic patterns in the clay walls and sights include cave-like formations and cathedral-like spires. The Miller Point Trail overlooks the canyon. Located 2 miles north of Panaca, west of US 93.

Echo Canyon State Park has a 65-acre reservoir for boating, swimming, and fishing, and showcases eastern Nevada's abundant wildlife, native plants, and unique rock formations. Located 12 miles east of Pioche via SRs 322 and 323.

Kershaw-Ryan State Park is situated at the end of a canyon with 700-foot-high walls and is an oasis for wildlife that come to drink from the spring-fed pond that's also a children's wading pool. Wild grapevines climb the sheer cliffs. Located 3 miles south of Caliente via US 93 and SR Route 317. Visit parks.nv.gov.

Spring Valley State Park has the 59-acre Eagle Valley Reservoir that offers fishing for rainbow, tiger, and German brown trout, plus boating and fishing. Hiking and historic ranch-house tours also are available. Located 20 miles east of Pioche on SR Route 322.

The Million Dollar Courthouse was restored in the 1970s and added to the National Register of Historic Places in 1978, and it now houses a fine museum. Don't miss the opportunity to step into "The Tank," the jail with two-foot-thick rock walls, located at the rear of the courthouse on the second floor. The building is at 69 Lacour St.; visit piochenevada.com or call (775) 962-5207.

The *Lincoln County Historical Museum*, 63 Main St., occupies the building constructed by A. S. Thompson around 1900. It has a fine display on area mining, local artifacts, and Native Americans and plenty of historic Pioche photographs. Admission is free. Hours are 10 a.m. to 3 p.m. daily. Visit piochenevada .com or travelnevada.com or call (775) 962-5207.

Start your *self-guided Pioche walking tour* at the Lincoln County Museum, where docents can provide context and information on various local attractions, most of which are within walking distance. They include the circa-1873 Thompson Opera House, the Historic Gem Theater, the 1909 Mission-style Pioche School, and the false-fronted Masonic St. John Lodge, in continuous operation since 1873. Detailed information on all of them is available at

TOP ANNUAL EVENTS

Caliente Memorial Day Weekend Homecoming Celebration
Caliente, May
lincolncountynevada.com

Jim Butler Days & Nevada State Mining Championships
Tonopah, May
jimbutlerdays.com
(775) 482-9466 or (775) 482-4533

Pahrump Wild West Extravaganza
Pahrump, May
visitpahrump.com
(775) 209-6200

Tonopah Star Parties: Dark Sky & Moon Nights
Tonopah, May through Oct
tonopahnevada.com

Walker Lake Days
Hawthorne, Jun
visitminearalcounty.com
(775) 945-5854

Tonopah Rock & Bottle Show
Tonopah, Jul
tonopahnevada.com
(775) 277-0804

Summer Classic Cornhole in the Park
Pioche, Jul
piochenevada.com

Goldfield Days
Goldfield, Aug
goldfieldnevada.org
(702) 904-3347 or (541) 218-8236

Beatty Days
Beatty, Oct
beattynevada.org
(775) 553-2424

Pahrump Social Powwow
Pahrump, Nov
pahrumppowwow.com
(775) 209-3444

piochenevada.com, where you can also download a free 36-page pamphlet with driving and walking tours of Lincoln County.

No trip to Pioche would be complete without a drive up to the infamous **Boot Hill Cemetery** at the end of Comstock Street. The cemetery's sectioned-off Murderers' Row holds 100 graves. While some are unmarked, others—many with wooden markers—carry such colorful epitaphs as MORGAN COURTNEY: FEARED BY SOME, RESPECTED BY FEW, DETESTED BY OTHERS. SHOT IN THE BACK FIVE TIMES FROM AMBUSH. And JOHN B. LYNCH: SHOT DURING DISPUTE OVER A DOG. The cemetery's still in use, so be respectful.

Overhead the **Pioche Aerial Tramway** skims over part of the cemetery; it operated primarily by gravity, with buckets full of ore from the mines providing the momentum for the empty buckets to return for another load. Heading south out of town on US 93 provides other opportunities to stop and walk around abandoned mining structures such as headframes. Here it is important to remember that mine sites are dangerous places.

For a safer view of an ore train and mine entrance, stop at the park in Pioche as Main Street turns south onto US 93. Besides, it's a wonderful place for a picnic. With picnic tables and a gazebo, what more could you ask for?

The **Historic Silver Café,** which has been serving for more than 100 years, is at 723 Main St. Breakfast, lunch, and dinner are served from 7 a.m. to 8 p.m. daily. Food prices are moderate, and the decor will keep you busy until your food arrives. Call (775) 962-5124.

Echo Canyon State Park lies less than 30 minutes from Pioche. Take SR 322 (Mount Wilson National Backcountry Byway) east for 4 miles, then turn right (south) onto SR 323 and travel 8 miles southeast. Enjoy the scenery on the way while you contemplate catching some of the 65-acre reservoir's rainbow trout or crappie for dinner. A boat ramp is available. Day-use fees are $5 per vehicle ($10 for non-Nevada vehicles), while $15 ($20 for non-Nevada vehicles) will get you an overnight campsite, with hookups $10 extra. Hikers can explore the nearby canyons and hills. The park is open year-round. For more information, visit parks.nv.gov/parks/echo-canyon or call (775) 962-5103.

Spring Valley State Park also is open year-round and offers hunting opportunities. To reach it, stay on SR 322 after leaving Pioche and travel approximately 20 miles to the park entrance. At the 65-acre Eagle Valley Reservoir, you can fish for rainbow and German brown trout. The park also offers hiking (walks around the reservoir offer great views of the valley), and visitors can see historic ranches. Fees are $5 per vehicle ($10 for non-Nevada vehicles) and $15 ($20 for non-Nevada vehicles) for a campsite. Visit parks.nv.gov/parks/spring-valley or call (775) 962-5102.

Talk about off the beaten path: To get to **Rachel** (population about 48), you'll need to backtrack west on US 93 to Crystal Springs and continue on Route 375. Rachel is the lone community on this stretch of 375, and all of 50 cars pass through it on a given day. Despite this remote location, Rachel receives quite a bit of publicity and more than its share of visitors from faraway places—especially those who are interested in otherworldly creatures.

Despite (or because of) its location north of the Nevada Test Site and east of Nellis Air Force Base, Rachel has played host to a number of UFO sightings. In fact, not to take matters such as these lightly, the Nevada Department of Transportation in April 1996 officially dedicated Route 375 the **Extraterrestrial Highway,** which made Rachel famous around the world—at least in some circles. The highway sign depicts several flying saucers, and speed-limit signs warn you to reduce your approach to WARP 7. Reportedly, there are also 1,500 geocaches on the north side of this stretch of road.

One since-departed local hang-around known as Ambassador Merlyn Merlin II (who at one point was a registered lobbyist who campaigned for the road's designation) once said that Rachel would become a destination point for intergalactic tourists: "Now that it is official, they will be here in three years." Other celebrities reportedly sighted at the dedication ceremony included Darth Vader and Elvis. The dedication took place exactly 34 years after the most notable UFO sighting in Nevada history, making it kind of an anniversary event. That sighting consisted of a fireball visible across Nevada and in several neighboring states.

Aliens Have Landed?

The **Roswell Incident** of 1947 continues to provide wonderful entertainment for believers and skeptics alike, as any *X-Files* fan knows. The July 8 edition of the *Daily Record* in Roswell, New Mexico, reported that a "flying disc" had crashed on a nearby ranch and that soldiers from the 509th Bomb Group, stationed at Roswell Army Air Force Base, had recovered the remains.

In 1994 an Air Force investigation confirmed that the debris at the crash site wasn't an alien spaceship: It was debris from Project Mogul, a secret experimental listening device that used balloon-borne detectors to monitor Soviet nuclear tests. The Pentagon issued a 231-page report explaining what really happened at Roswell. The report argues that the humanoid corpses Roswell residents claimed to have seen were probably humanoid crash-test dummies that were used in high-altitude impact tests, dropped from airplanes to test parachutes. These dummies were bald, had no eyebrows, no hair, no ears, bluish skin, and were between 5 feet 3 inches and 5 feet 6 inches tall.

Tips for Area 51 Sleuths

Area 51, Dreamland, Groom Lake, the Ranch, the Box—all these names refer to the top-secret research installation located 100 miles north of Las Vegas that has prompted speculation about captured alien spacecraft and hidden bodies of extraterrestrial beings. The facility and surrounding areas are also associated with UFO and conspiracy stories.

You cannot intrude into *Area 51* because you can't cross the 13 miles of open desert between public land and the Groom Lake base. The guards along the military border are used to tourists, but don't annoy them. Drive past the restricted area signs and you'll be captured and fined about $500. You can only see the Area 51 base from Tikaboo Peak, a 90-minute drive from Vegas followed by an hour-long drive on dirt roads and an hour's hike up a mountain. You will need binoculars or a telescope to see anything of the base; hangars are 26 miles away.

David Darlington detailed the history, legends, and characters involved with Area 51 in his book *Area 51: The Dreamland Chronicles.*

While in town, stop at the *Little A'le'Inn* (pronounced "alien"). The restaurant, motel, RV park, gift shop, and UFO seminar headquarters features racks of UFO T-shirts, caps, and books. You can't miss it—look for the building with a picture of an alien and an EARTHLINGS WELCOME sign on it. Owner Connie West or one of her helpers will serve you a World-Famous Alien Burger (complete with Alien Sauce, of course) or some other out-of-this-world fare. Or order a Beam Me Up Scotty beverage, which reportedly helps the staunchest skeptic see UFOs. For more information, call (775) 729-2515.

trivia

In 1989 *Bob Lazar* claimed on a Las Vegas television station that he had worked with alien spacecraft at Papoose Lake, south of Area 51.

To fully partake of the ET Highway experience, visit travelnevada.com, the website of the Nevada Commission on Tourism, or call (800) 638-2328. And before you pull back onto the highway, be especially careful in case one of those 50 cars passing through is whizzing by in excess of WARP 7 speed.

Nye County

To get to *Tonopah,* the next stop on the Pioneer Territory tour, proceed west along SR 375 for 109 miles. Tonopah (population 1,777) is the seat of Nye County, which has a very unusual shape (sort of like a fat "T") and encompasses more than 18,000 square miles. This size and shape mean that the county seat and Pahrump, Nye County's largest city, are 167 miles apart, for a road trip of about 2.5 hours. Along the way to Tonopah, you'll pass Warm Springs Summit, at 6,293 feet in elevation, and Tonopah Summit, at 6,270 feet. Tonopah, which became famously known as the "Queen of the Silver Camps," is at 6,030 feet.

Jim Butler kicked off Tonopah's boom with his May 1900 discovery of silver in "them thar hills." According to local lore, Butler picked up a stone to throw after his recalcitrant burro and discovered the rock to contain fine-grained quartz. An assay reflected 395 ounces of silver, plus 15.5 ounces of gold to the ton, sparking Nevada's first 20th-century mining rush and great mining camp, with a population of 10,000 people.

Tonopah's peak production years occurred during 1910 and 1914, with an annual yield averaging $8.5 million. Unlike other boomtowns, the majority of which disappeared almost overnight, Tonopah prospered for many years. After World War I, its mines continued to produce until the Great Depression interrupted production. Today, some small-scale mining continues.

The **Central Nevada Museum,** 1900 Logan Field Rd., has a yard full of intriguing displays, such as antique mining equipment, a blacksmith's shop, a miner's cabin, a 1934 Mack fire truck, horse-drawn freight wagons, and a 1927 Universal Power Shovel. An old mining ledger serves as the sign-in sheet. Inside, displays and collections will teach you about central Nevada Native Americans, Nevada boomtowns, area railroads, and the region's Asian population, and there's also a growing research library. The museum is open from 8 a.m. to 4 p.m. Tues through Fri and admission is free. Visit centralnevada museum.com, or call (775) 482-9676.

The **Tonopah Historic Mining Park,** which is routinely voted best museum in rural Nevada by readers of *Nevada Magazine,* allows visitors to see original mining claims, headframes, and hoist houses with original equipment, a five-story mill, ore crusher, mineral display, an underground tunnel, a mineral collection, and more. It covers more than 100 acres and portions of four of the original mining companies. Admission to the visitor center and movie is free. The self-guided walking tour is $5 for most adults; $3 for seniors, children 8 to 17, and Nevada residents; and free for veterans and active-duty members of the military. Guided Polaris tours are $12 per person, down to $7 per 5 people, or free for disabled visitors. Hours are 8 a.m. to 4 p.m. daily. Visit tonopahmining park.com or call (775) 482-9274.

By far one of the most colorful buildings left from the boom times, the **Mizpah Hotel,** a five-story structure built in 1907, has been fully restored, with rooms and suites, including the Wagon Suite, in which the bed is a hand-carved wagon and decorations date to 1908. Modern amenities include free Wi-Fi and trivia

Boxer *Jack Dempsey* once worked as a bouncer and bartender at the Mizpah Hotel.

smart TVs with streaming, but a sense of history is everywhere.

The dining room, named after Jack Dempsey, refers to the young man who worked in the historic Mizpah before his rise to fame and glory. Dempsey also worked in the Tonopah mines and participated in the drilling and prizefighting contests popular in those days. He left the West to win the heavyweight championships in 1919 and eventually earned more money than any previous boxer in history.

After losing to Gene Tunney in 1926 and in a contested match the following year (attended by more than 145,000 people, with a gross of $2.6 million in gate receipts), Dempsey returned to Tonopah in the late 1920s, breezing into the Ace Club on Main Street to see the proprietor, an old friend. Upon leaving, Dempsey turned and punched the proprietor's son, sending the young boy reeling but not to the ground. "Now you can say you took a punch from Jack Dempsey and didn't go down," said Dempsey.

Dempsey may be long gone, but some of the others associated with the Mizpah Hotel's early days remain. Guests have reported strange goings-on, such as encountering a ghost dressed in a red gown or finding their own red shoes moved or missing. One of the former members of the housekeeping staff, a levelheaded woman as far as we could tell, periodically caught glimpses of people in old-fashioned clothes and heard doors mysteriously opening and closing. According to legend, a local sex worker was stabbed to death at the Mizpah Hotel by a jealous lover years ago and refuses to leave.

Then there's the ghost of Senator Key Pittman, who allegedly died in the hotel of natural causes on election night, before the final votes were tallied. According to the story, his political cronies put the senator on ice until after he was declared the winner, in order to save the victory for the party. After his election they announced that he died during the victory celebration. Historians have denounced the whole tale as a myth, but it's a myth that persists.

Today, the Mizpah Hotel revels in the reported ghostly goings-on, with ghost and paranormal tours offered most evenings by prior arrangement. The hotel has been named the "no. 1 haunted hotel in America" by *USA Today's* 10 Best Readers' Choice Awards. It's at 100 N. Main St.; visit themizpahhotel.com or call (775) 482-3030.

The couple who owned and restored the Mizpah subsequently restored the 1906 bank across the street to create the ***Belvada Hotel***, modern lodgings with numerous nods to history. Like the Mizpah, its historical artifacts and skillful reproductions mean it's worth a quick tour even if you're not staying. Or grab a cup of java in the Belvada Coffee Shop off the lobby or a quick bite over at the Mizpah's Pittman Café. The Belvada is at 101 S. Main St.; visit belvadahotel. com or call (775) 277-3950.

And no trip to Tonopah would be complete without at least a gander at the **World Famous Clown Hotel** at 521 N. Main St. It calls itself "America's scariest motel," although that might apply mainly to people who are afraid of clowns, since there are more than 5,000 of them on the property. Then again, it no doubt doesn't hurt that the 1901 Tonopah cemetery is right next door. Visit theclownmotelusa.com or call (775) 624-9098.

If you're in Tonopah near the end of May, you might be able to catch Jim Butler Days, with state mining championships, a craft fair, live music, and more. Visit jimbutlerdays.com or call (775) 482-9466.

Tonopah is also among the best stargazing sites in the country, thanks to a shortage of light pollution. For more information, visit tonopahnevada.com.

A side trip from Tonopah takes you to another fascinating Nevada ghost town. Travel 5 miles east on US 6, turn left on SR 376 for 13 miles, and then take the right fork for 27 additional miles to reach **Belmont.** The town was the county seat from 1867 until 1905, when upstart Tonopah took over those honors; prior to that, Ione served as the county seat. Declining ore quality and finds in other areas around 1868 depleted Belmont's population, but rich discoveries in 1883 brought another round of prosperity until 1887, when most mines were shut down. The post office departed in 1911. The mines lay dormant until the Monitor-Belmont Company built a flotation mill in 1914 to treat old mine dumps. Several years later, all mining activity ceased.

Nevada's Volcanic Past

Two million years ago, volcanic activity began in the desert region between Tonopah and Ely. Molten lava surfaced along a fault line in the earth's crust, forming a 100-square-mile landscape of fantastic cinder cones, lava flows, and craters. *Lunar Crater,* the area's most outstanding phenomenon, is almost 4,000 feet across, 430 feet deep, and more than 400 acres in size. Because of its appearance—a bowl-shaped depression almost devoid of vegetation—it looks more like a meteor impact than a collapsed cinder cone. The Shoshone Native American tribe avoided the place, leaving it to the powerful spirits that resided there. First mapped by Lt. George M. Wheeler's surveying party in 1869, it was named to the National Natural Landmark Register in 1973. The Lunar Crater volcanic field is 79 miles east of Tonopah on US 6 on the right-hand side of the road. A loop road provides views of the crater. No services are available at this remote site, so fill your tank and check your spare tire in Tonopah. The road into the area is graded but quite narrow. Visit blm.gov/visit/lunar -crater or call (775) 482-7800.

All but a few of Belmont's 2,000 residents have long since departed, but in their haste, they left behind some well-preserved, picturesque historic ruins. Workers built the Belmont Courthouse on Cedar Street in 1876 for $22,000, using bricks manufactured in nearby kilns and locally quarried stone for the foundation. The entire town of Belmont, including the courthouse, was added to the National Register of Historic Places in 1972, and the landmark today is preserved thanks to the efforts of the nonprofit Friends of the Belmont Courthouse.

The town cemetery is on the west end of town with a few weathered, hand-carved wooden markers remaining. Today there is no electricity, gas or food in Belmont, although you might encounter an open antique/gift shop or be able to stop by Dirty Dick's Belmont Saloon, which tends to open on weekends and regularly hosts shuffleboard tournaments and potlucks. Its bar originally came from the deserted Cosmopolitan Saloon, down the street.

In the true tradition of mining camps, the Belmont Catholic Church, built in 1874, uprooted itself in 1908 after being vacant for seven years and moved to **Manhattan,** becoming the Manhattan Catholic Church. The Manhattan Mining District first came into being in 1867. A discovery of gold in 1905 reactivated the boom, with 4,000 people flooding into the region. The San Francisco earthquake of 1906 and the financial panic of 1907 dried up investment money and curtailed mining activities. In 1909 another boom started, with 13 mining and 16 placer operations producing ore. Dredging operations started in 1939 and continued for eight years.

Besides the church, you'll spot ruins of the Nye and Ormsby County Bank, which still hold the old safe; there also are old wooden headframes and dilapidated buildings around the town. At press time, the Manhattan Bar & Motel had closed and was awaiting new ownership. To reach Manhattan, take the gravel road west out of Belmont for 13 miles. Along the way you'll pass the large stack from the Belmont-Monitor Mill.

Retrace your steps toward Tonopah, then take US 95/I-11 North to SRs 316/361 North to Gabbs, then Route 844 East to **Berlin-Ichthyosaur State Park.** The 1,500-acre park encompasses the old mining town of **Berlin,** which is maintained in a state of arrested decay.

Nevada state senator T. J. Bell first discovered silver here in 1895. At its peak, Berlin supported a post office, a store, a stage line, and 250 people. The mine and 30-stamp mill shut down in 1909; however, between 1911 and 1914 a 50-ton cyanide plant worked the Berlin tailings. Demand for steel during World War II resulted in salvage of the mill equipment.

The impressive shell of the mills remains, as do a number of town buildings, such as the blacksmith shop, the mine foreman's house, a bachelor's quarters, a store warehouse, an assay office, a stagecoach stop, and a machine shop. An extensive trail marker system provides the history and historic features of Berlin and the mining camp of Union. A trail extends between the park's campground and the town site, and a walking-tour map is linked from the park's website.

The park is also the site of the largest known concentration of ichthyosaurs, a massive ancient marine reptile that dwelled in the ocean that covered Nevada millions of years ago. The fossils were first discovered in 1928, with large-scale excavation beginning in 1954. The bones were covered by thousands of pounds of mud and petrified over millions of years.

A large structure covers the archaeological dig area. Tours are given daily from Memorial Day to Labor Day; the rest of the year, they're by advance reservation only, or you may be able to peek through the windows on either end of the Fossil House or study the large cast of the ichthyosaur located to the right of the main entrance to the shelter.

Berlin-Ichthyosaur State Park also offers hiking trails, camping, and picnicking. Get details at parks.nv.gov/parks/berlin-ichthyosaur or call (775) 964-2440.

Seven miles north of Berlin you come upon *Ione,* which grew out of an 1863 silver discovery. An 1865 population of 600 people dwindled rapidly as the silver veins proved less productive than originally thought, and Ione lost its status as the county seat to Belmont in 1867. Periodic revivals and busts occurred up to 1880, until the post office closed in 1882. In 1907 Ione revived with the discovery of mercury and regained a bit of respectability with the reopening of its post office in 1912, only to lose it again in 1914. Then in the 1920s, quicksilver mining brought yet another period of prosperity before a final slowdown.

Among the remaining structures in Ione, which claims a population of 41, you'll see the Ione Ore House Saloon, which closed in 2005.

Mineral County

Retrace your tracks to Gabbs and then head southwest 32 miles on SR 361 to US 95/I-11, where you'll turn right and head due west to Hawthorne (population 2,739), the gateway to Walker Lake and ample recreational opportunities. *Boundary Peak,* at an elevation of 13,140 feet the highest in Nevada, lies on the distant horizon as you travel south on SR 361.

Hawthorne's roots are tied to the Carson & Colorado Railroad, because railroad president H. M. Yerington chose the spot as the division and distribution point for the railroad. The first train arrived on April 14, 1881. Two years later, Hawthorne became the Esmeralda County seat but later lost it to Goldfield after the Southern Pacific Railroad purchased the Carson & Colorado and realigned the tracks, bypassing Hawthorne. Area mining booms returned prosperity to Hawthorne, and in 1911 Mineral County was carved out of Esmeralda County, with Hawthorne regaining county seat honors. Appropriately named Mineral County has provided the nation with borax, copper, gold, iron, limestone, mercury, silver, and uranium over the years.

A catastrophic 1926 munitions explosion in New Jersey convinced the government to move its munitions operations to Hawthorne, a move that has provided a relatively stable economic base for the town. The population increased to 680 people after establishment of the Hawthorne Naval Ammunition Plant (now the Hawthorne Army Depot) in 1927. It reached a peak population of 14,000 during World War II. As you drive past the outskirts of Hawthorne, observe the row after row of government munitions facilities, concrete bunkers, and ammunition magazines.

To learn more about Mineral County and Hawthorne history, visit the **Mineral County Museum** at 400 10th Street in Hawthorne. Special collections include fire, mining, and railroad equipment; rocks and minerals; horse-drawn vehicles; and vintage clothing. Be sure to view the early 1880s mission bells and period pharmacy. The museum is open from 11 a.m. to 4 p.m. Mon through Sat. Visit mineralcountymuseum.com or call (775) 945-5142.

Mineral County is also home to the nation's first formally recognized wild burro range, consisting of 68,000 acres. Look out for them as you journey across the county.

walker lake

Walker Lake is the remnant of ancient Lake Lahontan, which covered much of central and northern Nevada during the last ice age. As the climate dried, Lake Lahontan receded, and many closed valleys became isolated dry lake beds. Walker River drains the east side of the Sierra Nevada and was inhabited 11,000 or more years ago by a hunter-gatherer society. The Paiutes traveled in small groups relying on pine nuts, game, and Walker Lake trout. Each September the Pine Nut Festival takes place in Schurz, 135 miles southeast of Reno.

For a day of relaxation, stop at **Walker Lake Recreation Area,** 11 miles northwest of Hawthorne on US 95/I-11. Jedediah Smith passed through here in 1827, followed by Peter Skene Ogden in 1829 and John C. Frémont in 1845 with his guide, Joseph Walker, for whom the lake is named. You can imagine the surprise when explorers first sighted this grand, 30,000-acre ancient lake with its clear blue waters in the middle of the desert, with Mount Grant towering 11,245 feet above. Watch for bighorn sheep on the sharp cliffs around the Sportsman's Beach Recreation Site, which has 31 individual campsites (but no potable water), 2 undeveloped camping areas, and a boat ramp. Tamarack Beach and Twenty Mile Beach offer dispersed camping.

Although the lake is no longer suitable for fishing because of declining water levels, wildlife abounds, including common loons, snow geese, white pelicans, grebe, and harlequin ducks. Other activities include swimming, water-skiing, canoeing, hiking, jetskiing, and sailboarding. If you're visiting in June, you can take part in the annual Walker Lake Days, with kayak races, the Liars Boat Race, and volleyball, cornhole, and arm-wrestling tournaments. Walker Lake is under the auspices of the federal Bureau of Land Management. For more information, visit blm.gov/visit/walker-lake-recreation-area or call (775) 885-6000. Or go to visitmineralcounty.com or call (775) 945-5854.

The area is also home to the Walker River Reservation, between Walker Lake and Yerington. The 530-square-mile reservation is home to the federally recognized Walker River Paiute Tribe of Northern Paiutes. Schurz is the only town on the reservation and is the site of the annual Walker River Paiute Tribe Pine Nut Festival in September. Festivities include a powwow, pageant. talent show, fun run, cornhole competition, vendors and horseshoe, strength, arm-wrestling and tug-of-war tournaments; camping is available. Visit wrpt.org, email pinenutfestival@wrpt.org or call (775) 773-2306 ext. 2300.

Lyon County

From Schurz, take the left fork that's Alternate US 95/I-11 and travel 24 miles to **Yerington** (population 3,119), in the lush Mason Valley. The agricultural town started out with the unflattering name of Pizen Switch, taken from the poor quality of liquor served in a small willow-thatched-hut saloon. Reportedly, as fresh liquor supplies ran low, the proprietor added a few plugs of chewing tobacco and water to the mix. Local cowboys and ranchers considered the switched mixture poison, and the Pizen Switch moniker stuck.

The town changed its name to Greenfield in 1879 and to Yerington in 1894. Some accounts contend that the name was changed to influence Henry M. Yerington to extend his Carson & Colorado Railroad into the valley near the town. The strategy did not work; however, Yerington has kept its new name to this day.

John Frémont's expedition made its way through Mason Valley in January 1844. In the snow-clogged terrain on the western edge of the Sweetwater Mountains, he abandoned the expedition's French-made howitzer, which had made the journey all the way from St. Louis, Missouri, to Oregon and into Nevada. Over the years, some claim to have found the missing howitzer, while others contend it is still out there, awaiting discovery.

The *Lyon County Museum,* at 215 S. Main St. in Yerington, displays several historical buildings including 3 one-room schoolhouses, a blacksmith shop, period gas station, and old country store with a working crank telephone. The main building, which was a Seventh-day Adventist Church dating to 1911, contains exhibits of clothing, housewares, clocks, pictures, mining artifacts, and a barbershop, and an annex has dolls, toys, firearms, gambling equipment, and Native American arts and crafts. The gift shop offers books, maps, and pine-needle baskets made by local artists. The museum is open for tours from 1 to 4 p.m. Thurs through Sat; tours also are available by appointment. Visit lyoncounty museum.com or call (775) 463-6576.

The historic *Jeanne Dini Center,* which is operated by the Yerington Theatre for the Arts, is in the old Yerington Grammar School No. 9 and represents a cherished piece of history and a look to the future. The building, which is in the National Register of Historic Places, has a first floor of rusticated blocks and the elaborate face of the building has two pedimented gables and a smaller gable over the entrance. An enlargement in 1935 preserved its Italian Renaissance Revival style. The building's grammar school days ended in 1980, and a fundraising program turned it into the cultural center, which has an intimate theater, meeting and classroom space, and two exhibition galleries. It hosts a lineup of performances, gallery exhibitions, and special events.

The most recent edition to the complex is the 6D Speakeasy, which opens at 6 p.m. on Fridays and offers craft beers available nowhere else in the area, as well as food and art. Admission is $15; memberships are available. For more information on the center, visit yeringtonarts.org or call (775) 483-1783; or visit the Yerington Chamber of Commerce at yeringtonchamber.org or call (775) 463-2245.

Esmeralda County

Return to US 95/I-11 and head south into Esmeralda County to the county seat of *Goldfield,* another boom/bust mining town, but one that's still active (population 212). Goldfield contains many remaining historic buildings, giving one a feel for the town's fleeting prosperity. Harry Stimler and William Marsh staked their gold claims here in December 1902, but the real influx of people did not begin until late 1903. The Tonopah & Goldfield Railroad reached the town in September 1905. By 1907 Goldfield sported a population of around 20,000, larger than that of either Reno or Las Vegas. From 1904 to 1918 the Goldfield Mining District was Nevada's most important gold-producing region, with $85 million mined during that time. The Goldfield Consolidated Mining Company constructed a huge, 100-stamp mill northeast of town.

The mining town boasted an opulence not normally found on the frontier. The once-luxurious four-story *Goldfield Hotel,* built in 1908 at a cost of $450,000, still stands, patiently awaiting a revival in the town's fortunes. It closed in 1936, then reopened in 1942 only to shut down again in 1945 after housing soldiers during World War II.

Further attempts to renovate the hotel have failed, leaving only the ghosts that famously haunt it, including Elizabeth, the mistress of wealthy banker George Wingfield. The story is that after she became pregnant, the married Wingfield kept her chained to a radiator in the hotel's room 109; later, both she and the baby disappeared. Ghost hunters claim to have seen her apparition or heard her crying, and others claim to smell Wingfield's cigar smoke. Other hotel ghosts are said to include two suicide victims. The hotel is occasionally opened for prearranged ghost tours; text Heather Ingalls at (775) 277-0484.

Boxing promoter Tex Rickard heavily advertised Goldfield and arranged for the world lightweight championship bout between champion Joe Gans and challenger Oscar "Battlin" Nelson to be held here on September 3, 1906. Gans won the bout on a technicality, due to a low blow by Nelson in the 40-second round. Tex Rickard's 1906 Victorian house stands at the corner of Crook and Franklin Streets.

trivia

The *Santa Fe Saloon* at 925 N. 5th Ave. in Goldfield is one of the oldest (1905) and most famous structures in Nevada. It preserves the frontier character of the days when Jim Casey, Virgil Earp, Wyatt Earp, and Death Valley Scotty strolled the town's streets.

Visiting Nevada's Ghost Towns

Trading posts along the emigrant trail, gold and silver mining towns, and railroad towns all suffered a similar fate. In fact, so many settlements were temporary that for every living town in Nevada there is a ghost town. Even the biggest, most flamboyant towns were abandoned when the rich ore gave out. *Goldfield,* Nevada's largest city in 1909 with a population of 20,000 and daily output of $10,000, is seeing somewhat of a revival. While buildings in Goldfield are restored, *Gold Point,* 30 miles south, belongs to another category of ghost town: "arrested decay." Gold Point and *Belmont* are watched over by "guardian angels," the last remaining residents who fend off souvenir hunters and greet visitors with a friendly "you can look all you want, but don't touch anything." *Rhyolite,* near Beatty, was abandoned in 1930, but a house made of bottles and the railroad depot have been restored. *Delamar,* too, was empty by the 1930s, and many of its buildings transported on wagons to Pioche. You can explore the ruins, mainly walls and foundations, but the dirt road, 16 miles south of Caliente and 15 miles south of US 93, requires a four-wheel-drive vehicle.

Intense labor disputes in late 1907 forced Nevada governor John Sparks to call in federal troops to restore order. This action broke the back of the fledgling International Workers of the World. Double disasters of the 1913 flood and 1923 fire dealt the town crippling blows from which it never recovered. Adding insult to injury, a flash flood in 1932 and another fire in 1943 nearly finished the job.

Your walking tour should include the ***Esmeralda County Court House,*** which opened in 1908. If the front door is locked, try entering through the back door used by the sheriff's dispatcher. Be sure to look at the brand display on the ground floor of the courthouse; more than 145 brands trace back to the 1870s and are seared into pieces of leather. Upstairs in the courtroom, original Tiffany lamps grace the judge's bench.

Before leaving town, stop for a sip at ***The Mozart Tavern,*** which is right across from the Goldfield Hotel. If you visit the town in August, you can attend Goldfield Days, which is a festival with a parade, street dance, raffle, car and bike show, and a land auction, in case you'd like your own piece of the place. As you leave town, notice the collection of antique mining equipment on the left. For more information on Goldfield, visit goldfieldnevada.org or call (702) 904-3347 or (541) 218-8236.

Head back down US 95/I-11 a few miles to SR 266 and tiny ***Gold Point,*** just a few miles from the California border. There you'll find the ***Gold Point Ghost Town,*** a bed-and-breakfast that offers accommodations in 2 two-bedroom houses and 3 rustic cabins with a 2-night minimum. Rates range

Tee Time in the Desert

Even though "green" might not be the first thing that comes to mind when you think about the desert, check out these desert golf opportunities. "Golf" may not be the first thing that comes to mind when you see them, either; this is extreme golf to the extreme. (*Tip:* Local duffers bring pieces of indoor-outdoor carpeting for a clean hitting surface.)

Lucifer's Anvil Golf Course
Black Rock Desert north of Gerlach
douglaskeister.com
Site of the annual Black Rock Self-Invitational Golf Tournament. Informal layout on the desert playa with the "greens" painted on the sand.

Pioche Golf Course
793 Golf Course Rd., Pioche
(775) 962-1585.
This old mining town has a nine-hole course that was carved from the sagebrush and dirt in the flat below town. Sneakers are recommended.

from $150 to $200, which includes a museum tour, stories and history, table shuffleboard in the saloon, and pool on a 1909 Brunswick table. Camping also is available for $12 per person per day.

The Gold Point Ghost Town also sponsors events to feed body as well as spirit, including the Gold Point Chili Cook-Off and a big day-after-Thanksgiving dinner, just in case you haven't already had enough turkey.

Like all other Nevada ghost towns, Gold Point got its start as a mining camp back in the 1860s. The few current residents still play on those traditions today. For more information, visit goldpointghosttown.com or call (775) 482-4653.

Nye County

Head south on US 95/I-11 and back into Nye County to **Beatty** (population 596), gateway to Death Valley National Park. Founded in 1904, Beatty served as the rail transportation hub of the bustling historic Bullfrog Mining District. By 1907 Beatty supported three railroads, a bank, and more than 1,000 people. Ash deposits from some of the world's largest volcanic eruptions provide a colorful backdrop for the town.

The **Beatty Museum,** 417 Main St., has interactive exhibits that explore the history of the area. Visit beattymuseum.org or call (775) 553-2303.

Get a taste of local color, literally and figuratively, at **Happy Burro Chili & Beer** at 100 W. Main St. Snag a seat on the porch and you can watch the flood of tourists, foreign and domestic, as they pass by on their way to and from the national park. Call (775) 553-9099.

No visit to the area would be complete without a stop at **Death Valley Nut & Candy Co.,** said to be one of the largest candy stores in the country, and we're not about to doubt it. It's part of the **Eddie's World** complex that also offers gas, a Tesla charging center, ice cream, sandwiches, and local souvenirs. Call (775) 552-2100.

And while you're here, be sure to keep your eyes open for the wild horses and especially the numerous wild burros that dwell in the area. They're most likely to come out in the early morning or around dusk. For more information on Beatty, visit beattynv.info or call (775) 553-2050.

Rhyolite—4 miles west on SR 374; turn right at the sign—is an honest-to-goodness ghost town, with the remains of a number of historic town structures and only ghosts remaining from the past, the last living resident having departed in the 1950s. There is active mining going on in the area, so be on the alert for large mining trucks crossing the roadway.

trivia

Rhyolite was voted America's most photogenic ghost town by readers of *Nevada Magazine*.

First, stop at the **Goldwell Open Air Museum** on your left as you drive toward the town site. The visitor center and gift shop, which is open from 10 a.m. to 4 p.m. Wed through Sat (though it may close earlier on hot summer afternoons), provides information on the history of Rhyolite and area mining activities. But the "museum" itself is open 24/7, hence the name. The site, which is supported by numerous arts and tourism agencies, is comprised of 8 outdoor sculptures placed amid the vastness of the upper Mojave Desert; as you walk among the art, be prepared for chukars and rabbits to scurry out of the underbrush—and watch for rattlesnakes.

The works were created by a group of artists led by the late Belgian Albert Szukalski, whose *The Last Supper 1984* is the centerpiece. It's a haunting scene, a tableau of 13 ghost-like figures. Other pieces include *Ghost Rider 1984*, with the figure posed with a bicycle on a raised platform; and *Desert Flower 1989*, with the ghostly figure holding an artist's palette evocative of a flower.

Ghostly figures don't figure in *Tribute to Shorty Harris 1994*, a steel silhouette of a miner, accompanied by . . . well . . . a penguin; *Icara 1992*, depicting a female Icarus figure; *Sit Here! 2020–2023*, a monumental couch-like mosaic; *Lady Desert, the Venus of Nevada 1992*, the title of which is self-explanatory; and the motivational metal sculpture *Keep Going 2023*. As you can see, the work is ongoing.

There's also a bronze plaque, *Rhyolite's District of Shadows*, which tells a somewhat allegorical tale of the town by filmmaker/author and "creator of alternate realities," Eames Demetrios. It fits right in with the fanciful figures juxtaposed with the desert's starkness.

In fact, Szukalski said he decided to place his interpretation of da Vinci's fresco of *The Last Supper* here in 1984 because of the Mojave's similarity to Middle Eastern deserts. He had only intended the piece to last two years.

Special events such as a painting party to restore the desert-dulled colors of *Lady Desert, the Venus of Nevada 1992*, are occasionally scheduled, as are workshops and artists' residencies. For more information, visit goldwellmuseum .org or call (702) 870-9946.

Rhyolite boomed after the 1904 discovery of gold by two penniless prospectors, Eddie Cross and Frank "Shorty" Harris. The resulting Bullfrog Mining District derived its name from the green-stained rock holding the veins of gold. Assays of $3,000 per ton drew more than 6,000 people to Rhyolite, and the town quickly established a newspaper, a post office, several hotels, two stock exchanges, ice plants, and 45 saloons to serve its residents. Three railroads (Las

Vegas & Tonopah Railroad, Tonopah & Tidewater Railroad, and Bullfrog Gold-field Railroad) hauled in supplies and shipped out gold-bearing ore.

Five-term Nevada senator William Stewart retired from politics and opened a law office in Rhyolite in 1905. But the 1906 San Francisco earthquake, coupled with the 1907 financial panic, dried up the flow of investment money into Rhyolite. By 1910 the city streetlights went out and the water company announced it would no longer service the town's remaining 600 residents. A decade later, only a few diehards called Rhyolite home.

Ahead, on the right, **Tom Kelly's Bottle House** consists of in excess of 20,000 discarded bottles. There's also a miniature village constructed of glass chips and a fence with bottle necks strung on wire. Built in 1906, the bottle house gives mute testimony to the quantity of beverages consumed in Rhyolite during its heyday. The house was reconstructed in the 1920s for the filming of Zane Grey's *Wanderers in the Wasteland.* Bureau of Land Management caretakers are periodically on-site and happy to talk to visitors.

Informative US Department of the Interior and Friends of Rhyolite markers at the building sites, as well as brochures available at the bottle house, contain early photographs of the town and buildings from Rhyolite's heyday. They bring the town alive again as you study the ruins. Among the downtown ruins, find the H. D. and L. D. Porter Store (1906); the three-story John S. Cook & Company Bank, built for the grand sum of $90,000; the Overbury Building and Bishop Jewelry Store; and the 1906 Corrill Building. Listen closely for sounds of accordion music drifting in the wind—it is reportedly the musical talent of one of the town's last residents, Tommy Thompson.

The **Rhyolite Depot,** up the hill at the end of town, features mission-style architecture with terra-cotta trim. Privately owned, it's the only intact building in town. The Las Vegas & Tonopah Railroad Depot cost $160,000, and its railyard had a capacity of 100 freight cars.

The Friends of Rhyolite organization raises funds to restore the town's ruins. Visit rhyolite.org.

Retrace your steps to Us 95/I-11 and drive north about 36 miles to Scotty's Junction, then about 21 miles west on SR 267 to the northernmost entrance to **Death Valley National Park.** The valley that became the park, which straddles the Nevada/California border, was named by the forty-niners who were awed by the inhospitable climate, which hadn't gone unnoticed by the original Native American inhabitants, who called it Tomesha, meaning "ground fire."

The park's centerpiece structure is **Scotty's Castle,** a reminder of the glory days of the Roaring '20s. The "castle" is a two-story structure built as a vacation home by wealthy Midwestern industrialist Albert Johnson, who became interested in the area when he was approached in Chicago by a man named Walter

slip slidin' away

When storms roll across Death Valley, rains flood a wide, flat, dry lake bed. The clay, hard as ceramic tile, melts into mud. After the rain, winds roar in from the southwest and barrel along the surface of the clay, sometimes at speeds up to 100 mph—just the right conditions to skid rocks across the slick area known as the Racetrack.

In 1948, James F. McAllister, a geologist at the United States Geological Survey, published the first scientific paper about the *sliding rocks of Death Valley*. Rocks weighing less than 1 pound up to more than 700 pounds leave deep tracks on the slick lake bed. It's in a remote valley, even by Death Valley standards, at least 3.5 hours from Furnace Creek. A 4x4 with high clearance and good tires is required.

Scott to invest in his Death Valley gold mine. Despite subsequent trips to California that revealed that the mine didn't exist, Johnson came to love the area and appreciated the effect the dry climate and outdoor activity had on his health. He gradually bought up land, and he and his wife, Bessie, began building Death Valley Ranch in the 1920s.

Johnson became close friends with Scott, whose nickname was "Death Valley Scotty" and who was much more of a raconteur than a gold miner. As the Johnsons' Spanish Mediterranean home began to take shape, Scott told everyone he was building it with the proceeds of that mythical gold mine, and Johnson went along with the joke. Upon Johnson's 1948 death, he willed the property to his foundation in the hopes that the National Park Service would buy it, which it did in 1970.

Scotty's Castle was never finished because of a surveying error, but the grounds, complete with swimming pool, Spanish tile, and 56-foot clock tower, reveal the luxurious retreat the Johnsons were creating. So does the interior of the house, complete with pipe organ and Spanish Mediterranean furnishings, and park employees in period dress conducted tours there for decades. But a 2015 flood that dumped a year's worth of rain in five hours did so much damage to the buildings and infrastructure that park officials said it would be years before it could reopen to the public. A 2021 fire and another record flood in 2023, though mostly in the southern part of the park, compounded the problems. While the full public opening date is estimated for fall 2025, limited tours are sometimes available by advance reservation; go to nps.gov/deva. You'll also find a virtual tour on the website in case you can't make the real thing.

In addition to being the largest national park in the lower 48 states, Death Valley is the lowest, hottest, and driest of them all. However, the 2023 flood created some historic changes. Badwater Basin, the lowest spot in the country at 282 feet below sea level, is normally a dry salt flat; horses rejecting the little sulfurous water found there gave rise to its name. But the flood and a year's worth of record rainfall created a body there known as Lake Manly that was 6 miles long, 3 miles wide, and about 1 foot deep and actually drew kayakers for a limited time. Though the "lake" is expected to be gone by press time, it will live on in photos and rangers' memories.

Be aware that Death Valley earned its name. The world-record high air temperature of 134 degrees was recorded at Furnace Creek in 1913. It's not unusual for summer highs to reach 120 or more, and there's little relief at night. It's not unusual for stranded motorists or lost hikers to die, tragically. Carry plenty of water at all times, stay on developed roads and trails, be sure your vehicle is suited for a particular road, and let someone know where you are. And, despite the dryness around you, don't discount the danger of flash floods. Note that cell phone access is limited in much of the park.

Still, the seemingly lifeless, sun-blistered desert offers much to see. Check out the colorful cliffs at Artists Palette on the road to Badwater, see the Mesquite Flat Sand Dunes, and get a bird's-eye aspect from Dante's View. Mine ruins can be viewed at the Harmony Borax Works and Keane Wonder Mine.

The park also is home to an amazing variety of wildlife from desert tortoises to lizards, desert bighorn sheep, and coyotes. Sunrises and sunsets are particularly spectacular, and with the park named to the highest level by the International Dark Sky Association, it's no surprise that viewing of stars is unsurpassed.

Park services including camping are available at a few points among the park's 3.4 million acres, but most are concentrated at Furnace Creek, where the Oasis at Death Valley is home to the historic four-diamond Inn at Death Valley, family-friendly Ranch at Death Valley, cottages and casitas, restaurants, shopping, and a gas station, and the lowest golf course in the world at 214 feet below sea level.

A Novel Golf Hazard

On my first visit to Death Valley National Park, I had just dropped my daughters off at the riding stable that was near Furnace Creek when I spotted a rather shaggy-looking dog, who was the object of furious barking from another dog standing not far away. "Aha," the light dawned—not a dog but a coyote, one of many who make their home in the park. The coyotes also are at home on the **Furnace Creek Golf Course,** where they have been known to swipe golf balls off a fairway and then roll around like puppies on the lush grass. (There are roadrunners in Death Valley as well, but they don't usually outsmart those wily coyotes.) If you're an adventurous golfer, check out the world's lowest golf course at 214 feet below sea level. The par-70 course was rated one of "America's 50 Toughest Courses" by *Golf Digest* and is a green oasis in the desert. Oh, and if you have the temerity to play nine holes on a summer morning, they'll provide the ice water. Greens fees are $32 to $78.50. Visit oasisatdeathvalley .com or call (760) 786-3373.

The park's entrance fee is $30 per vehicle. Passes are available, and admission's free on some holidays. For more information, visit nps.gov/deva (also a good place to check road and weather conditions) or call (760) 786-3200.

Leaving the southernmost part of the park on SR 190 East will take you to Death Valley Junction, site of the **Amargosa Opera House** (which is technically in California, but just across the road from Nevada). Ballet dancer Marta Becket and her husband had a flat tire there in the 1960s, and while awaiting its repair at a gas station that was across the road, she started exploring the nearby buildings abandoned by the Pacific Coast Borax Company. An old social house that had been heavily damaged by floods nonetheless spoke to Becket, who arranged to rent the building. The couple returned to New York to pack up and start life anew in Death Valley Junction.

They restored the building and Becket's first performance there was in 1968, with an audience of 12. Another flood inspired her to decorate the walls with a ready-made audience, primarily of the Renaissance period in homage to the building's design. Some sections depict Native American performers, a bullfighting family, and Becket's cats; 16 ladies are depicted on the ceiling, playing antique musical instruments.

Becket performed there regularly until shortly before her death in 2017, but her amazing creative legacy lives on with daily tours, plus occasional performances during the winter season. The hotel remains open, offering 16 rooms that are air-conditioned but have no TVs or phones. Visit amargosaoperahouse .org or call (760) 852-4441.

Just northwest of Death Valley Junction via SR 127 North and SR 373 East you'll find **Ash Meadows National Wildlife Refuge.** The refuge has the greatest concentration of locally unique species, including the Devil's Hole pupfish. This tiny, transparent, nearly extinct fish lives only in Devil's Hole, a narrow, deep pool of spring water. The refuge's visitor center has interactive exhibits, an Ash Meadows movie, bookstore, picnic area, and access to the Crystal Springs Boardwalk.

Once a large alfalfa ranch, then a cattle ranch, and now under the auspices of the US Fish and Wildlife Service, the 24,000-acre refuge has trails and a boardwalk that are open from sunrise to sunset daily. Visit fws.gov/refuge/ ash-meadows or call (775) 372-5435.

Take SR 127 North to US 95/I-11 South to SR 160 South and be on the alert for a small sign with the word JOHNNIE on it and an arrow pointing to the left. Like most other Nevada mining ghost towns, **Johnnie** sprang up overnight after the Montgomery brothers, using directions from Indian Johnnie, discovered a large quartz ledge. By 1893 the shallow veins had run dry. In 1898, Utah investors acquired the Johnnie and Congress Mines. A title dispute at the Congress

Mine raged, and a gun battle of several hours' duration left one man dead and three wounded. Another dispute between lessees and mine owners killed two more men and ended up with the 10-stamp mill being torched and burned to the ground. Dynamiting of the mine office catapulted the safe, minus its door, 200 feet away.

Johnnie's post office opened in 1905, and by 1907 the town had 300 residents. The Johnnie Mine and 16-stamp mill operated steadily until 1914, after which production became more sporadic through the late 1930s. While prevailing wisdom holds that Butch Cassidy died in South America after he and the Sundance Kid fled the country following the Winnemucca Bank robbery, people in these parts subscribe to the story that Butch lived for years in seclusion at Johnnie, dying of injuries resulting from a mining accident there around 1940.

Continue south on SR 160 to reach *Pahrump,* the largest city in Nye County. The name Pahrump comes from the Paiutes, who harvested pine nuts and seeds and hunted wild game in the area. The Paiutes discovered an abundance of water in the valley coming from natural springs and named the area *Pah* (water) *Rump* (rock).

Native Americans cultivated corn, melons, and wild grapes, and the agricultural tradition continued in the valley's fertile fields for decades. Irrigation in the 1930s turned cotton into a very profitable crop and the main cash crop into the 1980s.

While initial development was slow—the first paved road in 1954 was followed by electricity in 1963—the town's proximity to Las Vegas led to it becoming a bedroom community of sorts, as the two sprawled toward each other. Pahrump's 2024 population is estimated at 57,660.

Wineries and distilleries pepper the area. They include Sanders Family Winery (sanderswinery.com), Stonewise Mead & Cider (stonewise.com), Artesian Cellars Winery & Restaurant (artesiancellars.com), and Desert Cane Distillery (desertcanedistillery.com).

Balloons Over Pahrump offers hot air balloon rides over the valley (lasvegasballoonrides.com), and Spring Mountain Motor Resort and Country Club (springmountainmotorsports.com) has 6 miles of track and more than 50 configurations.

Pahrump hosts a number of annual events, including the ICS & Silver State Chili Cook-Off in March, the Wild West Extravaganza in May, a 4th of July Fireworks Spectacular, a Pahrump Fall Festival in September, and the Pahrump Social Powwow in November. For information on any of these, or the other things Pahrump has to offer, go to visitpahrump.com or call (775) 523-1697, or stop by the Pahrump Information Center at 400 N. SR 160.

Places to Stay in Pioneer Territory

BEATTY

Atomic Inn
350 S. 1st St.
atomicinnbeatty.com
(775) 553-2250

Stagecoach Hotel & Casino
900 E. US 95 N.
stagecoachhotelandcasino
.com
(775) 553-2419

CALIENTE

Caliente Hot Springs Motel & Spa
US 93
calientehotspringsmotel
andspa.com
(775) 726-3777

DEATH VALLEY JUNCTION

Amargosa Opera House & Hotel
SR 127 and State Line
Road
amargosaoperahouse.org
(760) 852-4441

GOLDFIELD

Santa Fe Saloon & Motel
975 N. 5th Ave.
(775) 485-3431

GOLD POINT

Gold Point Ghost Town
US 774
goldpointghosttown.com
(775) 482-4635

HAWTHORNE

El Capitan Resort Casino
540 F St.
elcapcasino.com
(775) 945-3321

Hawthorne's Best Inn
1402 E St.
hawthornebestinn.com
(775) 945-2660

Holiday Lodge
480 J St.
(775) 945-3316

PAHRUMP

Best Western Pahrump Oasis
1101 S. SR 160
bestwestern.com
(775) 727-5100

Pahrump Nugget
681 S. SR 160
goldencasinogroup.com
(775) 751-6500

Saddle West Hotel, Casino & RV Park
1220 SR 160
saddlewest.com
(775) 727-1111

PIOCHE

Hutchings Motel
411 LaCour St.
hutchingsmotel.com
(775) 962-2853.

Overland Hotel & Saloon
662 Main St.
overlandhotelnv.com
(775) 962-5895.

RACHEL

Little A'Le'Inn
9631 Old Mill St.
littlealeinn.com
(775) 729-2515

TONOPAH

Clown Motel
521 N. Main St.
theclownmotelusa.com
(775) 624-9098

Jim Butler Inn & Suites
100 S. Main St.
jimbutlerinn.com
(775) 482-3577

YERINGTON

Yerington Inn
4 N. Main St.
yeringtoninn.com
(775) 463-5310

Places to Eat in Pioneer Territory

BEATTY

Mel's Diner (American)
600 US 95
(775) 553-9003

Smokin' J's BBQ (American)
107 W. Main St.
(775) 553-9312

CALIENTE

Knotty Pine Restaurant and Lounge (American)
690 Front St.
(775) 726-3767

HAWTHORNE

Barley's Sports Bar (American)
822 Sierra Way
(775) 945-1444

El Capitan Restaurant
(American)
540 F St.
elcapcasino.com
(775) 945-3321

Lovelock Pizza
1085 US 95
lovelockpizzahawthorne
.com
(775) 945-6173

PAHRUMP

El Jefe's Restaurant 2
(Mexican)
921 S. SR 160
(775) 751-6222

TONOPAH

Bamboo Chinese Kitchen
360 N. Main St.
(775) 482-9888

**Tonopah Brewing
Company** (American)
315 S. Main St.
tonopahbrewing.com
(775) 482-2000

YERINGTON

El Superior Restaurant
(Mexican)
517 W. Bridge St.
yeringtoninn.com
(775) 463-2593

**Sherry's Stage Stop
Restaurant** (American)
11 US 95A N.
(775) 463-3707

ALSO WORTH SEEING

The Walker River runs from the Sierra Nevada to Walker Lake. It supports threatened fish and hundreds of thousands of breeding and migrating water birds, including 1,400 common loons. In spring and fall at Walker Lake, you may see western grebe, eared grebe, redheads, ruddy ducks, and American white pelicans. Bird-watching information is available from three sources:

Great Basin Bird Observatory
gbbo.org
(775) 323-4226

Lahontan Audubon Society
nevadaaudubon.org
(775) 562-1066

Sierra Club, Toiyabe Chapter
sierraclub.org/toiyabe

FOR MORE INFORMATION

Amargosa Chamber of Commerce
821 E. Amargosa Farm Rd.
Amargosa Valley
amargosachamber.org
(775) 372-1515

Beatty Chamber of Commerce
119 Main St.
beattynevada.org
(775) 553-2424

Goldfield Chamber of Commerce
165 Crook Ave.
goldfieldnevada.org
(702) 904-3347 or (541) 218-8236

Hawthorne Convention Center
932 E. St.
visitmineralcounty.com
(775) 945-5854

Lincoln County Authority of Tourism
PO Box 202, Caliente
lincolncountyneva.org
(775) 441-1101

Pioche Chamber of Commerce
644 Main St.
piochenevada.com
(775) 962-5544

Town of Pahrump
400 SR 160
visitpahrump.com
(775) 253-1697

Town of Tonopah
140 S. Main St.
tonopahnevada.com
(775) 482-6336

Reno-Tahoe Territory

Douglas County

The Carson Valley is accessed via US 395, which branches off from US 95—one of the major north-south routes in the state—about 20 miles west of Yerington. For part of the route, you'll follow the churning Walker River as it twists and turns through the rugged gorge. Stop for a picnic or overnight stay at one of the riverside campgrounds. When you are ready to continue, turn right at Holbrook Junction onto US 395 headed northwest to Gardnerville, Minden, and Carson Valley. The pine-covered rolling hills give way to flat, lush farmland. Just as in emigrant days, Carson Valley offers a respite for weary travelers plus a place to stock up on good food. More recent are the variety of activities that draw people to the area for recreation.

Gardnerville (population 6,147) now is adjacent to the county seat of Minden, as the two pioneer towns have spread toward each other. With antique shops and craft and art galleries, its downtown area is a fine place for a quiet stroll.

Gardnerville is in the region where Basque-immigrant sheepherders tended to settle, and those roots remain today at *J. T. Basque Bar & Dining Room,* which has become a

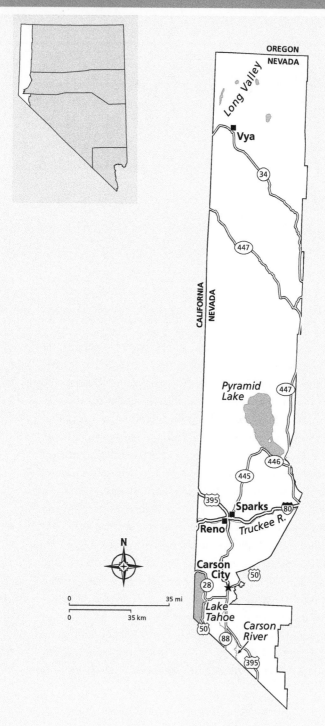

landmark over the past 60 years in a building that was moved from Virginia City in the late 1800s. Maybe start with a classic and potent Picon punch (a 19th-century cocktail about which it's said "the first is the picon, the second the punch") and be sure to come hungry; lunch and dinner include soup, salad, stew, beans, french fries, red wine, coffee, and ice cream. Entrée choices include lamb, of course, as well as the familiar sirloin steak and chicken, but also such ethnic favorites as sweetbreads or pig's feet and tripe, with prices in the mid-$30s; smaller plates, sandwiches, and sides also are available at lunch. The restaurant's right in the middle of town at 1426 US 395. Visit jtbasquenv.com or call (775) 782-2974.

A self-guided walking tour through the *Lahontan National Fish Hatchery,* on the outskirts of Gardnerville, will teach you the fish-hatching business of Lahontan cutthroat trout, an endangered native fish that's the largest cutthroat trout in the world. Scheduled visits, which must be reserved in advance, are available from 8 a.m. to 3 p.m. weekdays and cover the life cycle of the fish from the arrival of eggs at the hatchery to incubation to fry (young fish up to 1 inch long) to fingerling (young fish between 1 inch in length and 1 year of age), with 500,000 released in Nevada lakes each year. The hatchery is open all year, but the spawning season is February to May. Recreational fishing information and educational material on fish culture are available. The complex that houses the hatchery also is home to the Marble Bluff Fish Passage and Research Facility, which aids in the spawning migration of endangered fish, and the Lahontan Fish and Wildlife Conservation Office. For more information, visit fws.gov/fish-hatchery/lahontan or call (775) 265-2425.

Minden (population 3,140), which has a charming historical downtown, was born when German immigrant Heinrich Friedrich Dangberg established his ranch in 1895, before Nevada was even a state. The family deeded the streets and park to the town upon its founding in 1906, but there are no streets named for them; however, look for the "D" on the face of the Carson Valley Farmers Bank building.

The *Dangberg Home Ranch Historic Park* is a county-owned park at 1450 SR 88 in Minden. It's open from sunrise to sunset daily, and the historic buildings, with interpretive signs, can be toured from April to October. There is a kite-flying weekend in May, and various cultural events such as a Chautauqua are scheduled in spring and summer. Visit dangberg.org or call (775) 783-9417.

If you want to see the area from a loftier vantage point, check into *Soaring NV* at the Minden-Tahoe Airport. Glider pilots from all over come to Minden to take advantage of soaring conditions that include climb rates of more than 1,500 feet per minute in both thermal and wave lift as you glide over the Sierra Nevada Mountains, Yosemite National Park, and the White and Inyo ranges. If you're an aficionado you can bring your own glider, or you can rent one. Glider rides range from $219 to $530, with deep discounts if you bring a friend. A flight-training program and tow service also are available. Visit soaringnv.com or call (775) 782-9595.

Country Excursion in Minden gets you out among the wild horses, historic barns, and cemeteries in the area. Call (928) 635-6759. *Heritage Tours* can suit your customized itinerary for large or small groups or individuals. It's in Gardnerville; call (775) 315-0697.

If you're looking for a unique spot to rest your head in Minden, consider the *Carson Valley Inn,* which has an indoor pool shaped roughly like the state of Nevada. Visit carsonvalleyinn.com or call (800) 321-6983.

The *Carson Valley Museum and Cultural Center* is in the 1915 former Douglas County High School, designed by locally prominent architect Frederic DeLongchamps and included on the National Register of Historic Places. Among its collections are early newspaper and telephone displays, medical tools from when doctors still made house calls, Basque and Native American exhibits, and one on the state's free-roaming mustangs. *Main Street* depicts downtown Gardnerville as it was from 1870 to 1950. Special exhibits are mounted from time to time, such as Bed Turnings by the Carson Valley Quilt Guild. The museum is open from 11 a.m. to 3 p.m. weekdays at 1477 US 395 North in Gardnerville; visit historicnv.org or call (775) 782-2555.

A few miles north of Minden on US 395, turn left on Genoa Lane and travel 2 miles into history—to where it all began. Nevada's first white settlement, *Genoa,* grew out of a post established by Mormon traders in 1851, a full 10 years before Nevada Territory existed and 13 years before President Abraham Lincoln declared Nevada the Union's 36th state. The original Mormon Station burned in 1910, but a reconstructed trading post still holds a prominent position in historic Genoa. In addition to photos and displays such as the telegraph,

AUTHOR'S TOP PICKS

Lake Tahoe's 72-mile shoreline	Nevada Historical Society, Reno
Vikingsholm, Emerald Bay	Nevada State Museum, Carson City
Virginia & Truckee Railroad, Virginia City	Silver Terrace Cemeteries, Virginia City
	Shakespeare Festival, Sand Harbor
Virginia City Historic District	Genoa Bar & Saloon
Nevada State Capital, Reno	

Home in the Hills

In the juniper-covered hills north of Reno is the *Animal Ark Wildlife Sanctuary,* which houses such native wildlife species as cougars, black bears, wolves, bobcats, kit foxes, peregrine falcons, and burrowing owls. The focus is on non-releasable wildlife, but the operators occasionally take in orphaned animals and later return them to the wild, such as the young black bear found near Topaz Lake that recuperated from a broken hip at Animal Ark. Arrive early to see nocturnal animals before they take their naps. Signage is informative, and docents are on hand to answer questions. Feel free to bring a picnic or let the kids tackle the playground. The dirt and decomposed-granite trail is about 1 mile long; wear comfortable shoes, and, in springtime, be sure they're waterproof. Golf carts are available for rental by advance reservation. The sanctuary normally is closed from Nov through Mar, although the schedule is weather-dependent, so check the website or call. Seasonal hours are 10 a.m. to 4:30 p.m. Tues through Sun. Admission is $18 for most adults, $15 for seniors, and $10 for children 3 through 12. Animal Ark is at 1265 Deerlodge Rd. in Reno; visit animalark.org or call (775) 475-9626.

a stockade, and a wagon shed, the *Mormon Station State Historic Park* includes shaded picnic areas and outdoor grills. At its north end is the Campbell Homestead, which offers a peek into life in Genoa back to the early 1900s with a blacksmith shop, apple orchard, chicken house, and demonstration vegetable garden. The park is open daily, the museum from 10 a.m. to 4 p.m. daily May through Sep, and 11 a.m. to 3 p.m. Thurs through Mon the rest of the year. Park admission is free, museum admission $1 per person. For details, visit parks .nv.gov/parks/mormon-station or call (775) 782-2590.

In the heart of town, the *Courthouse Museum in Genoa,* in the original Douglas County Courthouse, contains displays on the Pony Express, "Snowshoe" Thompson, first-day canceled envelopes, a courtroom, classroom, a jail, and an old-fashioned parlor. Pay particular attention to the snowshoes for horses. Legendary "Snowshoe" Thompson (Jon Torsteinson-Rue, later changed to John A. Thompson) earned his reputation carrying mail and supplies across the Sierra Nevada from Placerville, California, to Genoa for more than 20 years. Born in the Telemark district of Norway, he became the human link

trivia

Brigham Young recalled the Mormons in 1857, but not before probate judge Orson Hyde allegedly placed a curse on Genoa. For a time, the town declined, but the discovery of silver in the Comstock Lode revived Genoa as an important commercial center for the bustling mining district. Genoa did lose its pioneer newspaper, the *Territorial Enterprise*, to Virginia City, where it became famous throughout the nation.

between the eastern and western slopes of the Sierra Nevada. He died in 1876 and rests in the Genoa Cemetery north of town, with a white-marble marker engraved with crossed skis and GONE BUT NOT FORGOTTEN.

The 1865 Douglas County Courthouse was in operation until 1916, when the county seat moved to Minden. The building was sold at auction for $150 and served as an elementary school for 40 years. The museum is open from 11 a.m. to 3 p.m. daily, Apr through Oct. Visit historicnv.org or call (775) 782-4325.

For a printable tour of Genoa, with a description of each historic site, go to visitcarsonvalley.org. The tour, marked out by the hour, is a pleasant way to spend a day.

Step across Nixon Street and down Main Street to the south to bend your elbow at the oldest bar in Nevada at 2282 Main. *The Genoa Bar and Saloon* traces its lineage to 1853 and is filled with historical artifacts (genoabarand saloon.com or 775-782-3870). Follow Main Street to number 2291 and the intimate *Daniel's* restaurant, with just eight tables and a dedication to fine country French food, serving dishes such as fillet of venison with apples and cranberries and grilled duck breast with foie gras (danielsgenoa.com or 774-392-1822).

TOP ANNUAL EVENTS

Eagles & Agriculture
Carson Valley, Feb
visitcarsonvalley.org
(775) 782-8144

Genoa Western Heritage Days
Genoa, Apr
visitcarsonvalley.org
(775) 782-8696

Mark Twain Days Festival
Carson City, May
visitcarsoncity.com
(775) 687-7410

Reno River Festival
Reno, Jun
renoriverfestival.com
(775) 851-4444

Carson Valley Days
Gardnerville, Jun
visitcarsonvalley.org
(775) 782-8145

Artown
Reno, Jul
artown.org
(775) 322-1538

Virginia City Camel & Ostrich Races
Virginia City, Sept
visitvirginiacitynv.com
(775) 847-7500

Genoa Candy Dance
Genoa, Sept
visitcarsonvalley,org
(775) 782-8145

Great Reno Balloon Race
Reno, Sept
renoballoon.com
(775) 391-8562

Nevada Days Celebration
Carson City, Oct
nevadaday.com
(775) 882-2600

When it's time to settle in for the evening, you have a couple of options. *The White House Inn,* 195 Genoa Ln., is a 100-year-old boutique hotel that's a place to relax and unwind a short walk from town. Its dog friendly Cottage has a fenced patio with pergola, queen bed, bath, and full kitchen, while the King Room has a full bath with tub and heated floor (if you don't mind the slanted ceiling over the bed). Rates from $145 to $400, or rent the whole property, which sleeps 13. Visit whitehouseinngenoanv.com or call (775) 870-7203.

Or go to *Holiday Inn Club Vacations David Walley's Resort,* which has grown from the hot-springs spot David and Harriet Walley built in 1862. The Walleys invested $100,000 to lavishly furnish it with 11 baths, exquisite gardens, and a grand ballroom. It operated as a hotel until 1935, when it burned down. Over the years, Walley's hosted such dignitaries as President Grant, Mark Twain, and Clark Gable.

The resort was rebuilt in the late 1980s and has been renovated periodically since then. Soothe your body in the seasonal heated pool or one of five geothermically heated mineral hot-springs tubs that range from 98 to 104 degrees (with one designated for families with kids younger than 18) while you soothe your mind by gazing at the Sierra Nevada under a starlit sky. There are aqua aerobics classes on Monday and Wednesday mornings and a fitness center with showers, steam rooms, and saunas. Or you can get in a game of volleyball or toss a disc, go on a guided nature walk or rent a bicycle. There also are two game rooms with ping pong and billiards, and scheduled activities including scavenger hunts and outdoor movies. Borrow a grill and utensils, pick up some charcoal in the on-site store, and grill your own lunch or dinner, or dine in the 1862 Restaurant & Saloon, serving all three meals including dinner entrées such as slow-braised ribs and pan-seared salmon. Rates start at $106. The resort is at 2001 Foothill Rd., 1.5 miles from Genoa; take Main Street out of town to the south. For more information, visit holidayinnclub.com/explore-resorts/david-walleys-resort or call (775) 782-8155.

If you can time your visit to coincide with the *Candy Dance* in late September, you won't be disappointed. The gala event originated in 1919 as a way to raise funds for Genoa streetlights, with townspeople making candy

trivia

Dr. Eliza Cook (1856–1947), Nevada's first woman doctor, practiced in Carson Valley. She wrote a letter stating 11 reasons why she supported women's suffrage. Reason 4: "Because being a woman, I can see things from a woman's viewpoint. Hence, no man, however willing he might be to suppress his own view on my behalf, could represent me fully at the ballot box or anywhere else."

Nevada women began voting in 1915, before the national referendum in 1920.

and hosting a dinner-dance. Today it's a 2-day festival that draws 30,000 people with more than 300 craft and food vendors, live music, and other entertainment and the Saturday-night dinner-dance. Thousands of pounds of sweets are gobbled up at Genoa Town Hall each year, with more from the various vendors. Visit genoanevada.org or call (775) 782-8696.

Take a Cruise

Lake Tahoe Bleu Wave
$125
Tahoe Keys Marina, South Lake Tahoe, CA
tahoebleuwave.com
(775) 588-9283
This 70-foot yacht that can accommodate 47 passengers offers Emerald Bay sightseeing, happy hour, and sunset cruises and charters.

MS Dixie II paddle wheeler and Tahoe Paradise yacht
Zephyr Cove Resort, Zephyr Cove, NV
$99 to $140 ($55 to $75 for kids
zephyrcove.com
(800) 238-2463
Lake Tahoe's largest cruising vessel with a capacity of 500 passengers, the MS Dixie II is available for daytime or dinner cruises and private charters all year. The two-story Tahoe Paradise offers Sipping at Sunday cruises and can accommodate groups from 25 to 90.

Sierra Cloud
Tahoe Vista Recreation Area,
Tahoe Vista, CA
$125 ($75 for kids)
awsincline.com
(775) 831-4386
This 55-foot catamaran that can carry 49 passengers offers daily 2-hour cruises, private charters, and a special July 4th Sunset & Fireworks Cruise.

Spirit of Tahoe and Safari Rose
$75 to $120
Ski Run Marina, South Lake Tahoe, CA
tahoecruises.com
(775) 588-1881
The 80-foot, 90-passenger Spirit of Tahoe runs Emerald Bay sightseeing and sunset champagne cruises daily. The 67-foot Safari Rose is available for charter.

The Tahoe Gal
$68 to $180
952 N. Lake Boulevard, Tahoe City, CA
tahoegal.com
(530) 583-0141
This 120-passenger, 64-foot sidewheel boat offers lunch, happy hour, brunch, and sunset dinner cruises on various parts of the lake. Specialty cruises and private charters available.

Carson City

Take Genoa Lane back to US 395 North to Nevada's capital, **Carson City.** The **State Capitol,** at the corner of Carson and Musser Streets, is the appropriate place to begin and is open for tours on Saturdays and by prior arrangement. Of course, oil portraits of Nevada governors over the ages grace the capitol walls. The capitol was completed on May 1, 1871, with free building stone from the state prison quarry. The annex dates to 1906, and the extension of two wings took place in 1914. In Battle Born Hall on the second floor, which opened in 2018, the *Trailblazing Nevada* exhibit highlights pioneers in Nevada and across the country before and after statehood. The five exhibit areas cover prehistory, the mining boom, statehood, Carson City through the 20th century, and a look ahead to Nevada of the 21st century and beyond. Admission is free from 8 a.m. to 5 p.m. weekdays. Go to visitcarsoncity.com or call (775) 687-4810.

Stop by another historic Carson City building, the **Nevada State Museum,** for an informative tour. The building at 600 N. Carson St. is the old Carson City Mint, which was built in 1870 and minted coins from 1870 to 1893—50 issues of silver with the "CC" mint mark. The museum's permanent exhibits include one

Physical Pleasures: Hot Springs and Spas

Carson Hot Springs Resort
1500 Old Hot Springs Rd., Carson City
carsonhotsprings.com
(775) 885-8844
This private hot springs spa offers 9 private indoor pools, an outdoor pool and patio, and an adjoining restaurant and brewery.

Holiday Inn Club Vacations
David Walley's Resort
2001 Foothill Rd., Genoa
holidayinnclub.com/explore-resorts/
david-walleys-resort
(775) 782-8155
This outdoor hot springs was originally built more than a century ago. The resort has 5 outdoor pools at varying temperature.

Spa Toscana, Peppermill Reno
2707 S. Virginia St.
peppermillreno.com
(775) 689-7190
The 24 treatment rooms provide for massage, body treatments, and skin care with hot and cold plunge pools and eucalyptus steam and cedarwood saunas.

Stillwater Spa, Hyatt Regency
Lake Tahoe
111 Country Club Dr., Incline Village
hyatt.com
(775) 886-6745
Specialty treatments include the stone massage and Tahoe Adventurer massage. Facilities include oversized tower showers, relaxation areas next to a fireplace, and fitness center with Peloton bikes.

on the history of the mint that includes Coin Press No. 1 and a complete set of Carson City Morgan Dollars. Another, "Nevada: A People and Place Through Time," is a timeline of the state's history that includes an underground mine exhibit and artifacts such as the USS *Nevada* battleship silver service made of 5,000 ounces of silver from the Tonopah mines, lined with gold from Goldfield. *Nevada's Changing Earth* displays the state's rock and minerals and *Under One Sky*, an exhibit in the words of Native Americans and from their perspective, includes the reconstruction of a Great Basin cave.

There also are temporary exhibits, such as *Fueling the Boom: Chinese Woodcutters in the Great Basin 1870–1920*, and *Our Nevada Story: Objects Found in Time*, a deep dive into state symbols and minerals that also includes a historic quilt and Native American art and artifacts.

The museum is $10 for adults, free for kids 17 and younger. Visit carsonnv museum.org (which also has some online-only exhibits) or call (775) 687-4810.

Up the block at 813 N. Carson St., kids can delight in the **Children's Museum of Northern Nevada,** located in the old civic auditorium, which fuels kids' budding imaginations with play-based learning experiences. Interactive exhibits and programs in the arts, sciences, humanities, and history are augmented with an open STEM lab, drop-in art studio, and weekly story time. Check the website for theme-of-the-week activity tables. The museum is open from 9:30 a.m. to 3 p.m. Tues through Sat, and admission is $3 for adults, $10 for children 3 to 13 and $5 for 2-year-olds. Visit cmnn.org or call (775) 884-2226.

Climb aboard a steam train at the **Nevada State Railroad Museum** and ride a bit of history. Steam train rides leave the front entrance of the museum property at 2180 S. Carson St. and make a 40-minute loop around the grounds, May through November. If you're lucky, you can ride in the cab for an extra fee. There's a Santa Train on December weekends, and the museum also offers rides in vintage Edwards and McKean motor cars.

reno-tahoe
territory trivia

What item of clothing was invented by a Reno tailor?

Who is Reno named after?

Who is Carson City named after?

(Answers on page 85)

Museum displays include the 1875 Inyo–Virginia & Truckee Railroad locomotive No. 22—which is one of the oldest operating steam locomotives in North America and was featured in movies of the 1930s. There's also an 1875 locomotive of the Carson & Tahoe Lumber & Fluming Company and two nonoperating 1873–1874 V&T locomotives, one of which was used to plow snow. The collection includes other locomotives, restored passenger coaches and freight cars, and an interpretive center that looks at railroad communications, changes wrought by the transcontinental railroad, and a collection of scale models of V&T locomotives. The museum is open from 9 a.m. to 4:30 p.m. Thurs through Mon; check the website for the train and motorcar schedules. Admission is $8 for adults and free for children 17 and younger. Steam train rides are $10 for those 12 and older and $5 for kids 4 to 11. Motorcar rides are $6 to $8 for those 12 and older and $3 to $4 for kids 4 to 11. Visit carsonrailroadmuseum.org or call (775) 687-6953.

If you're looking for a longer ride, the *V&T Railway Commission* runs one-way or 6.5-hour round trips with a 3.5-hour stopover in Virginia City in a restored 1914 Pullman coach pulled by a 1916 Baldwin locomotive. The trips leave from the Carson City Eastgate Depot at 4650 Eastgate Siding Rd., reached by taking US 50 East past the Eagle Valley Golf Course, then turning right onto Flint Drive and following the signs. Round trips are $55 for adults or $40 for children 2 to 15; one-way trips take 1.5 hours and are $40 per person. There also are Polar Express trains, as well as Toast of the Canyon evening trips between Carson City and the Carson River Canyon. For current schedules, check vtrailway.com or call (775) 686-9037.

Stop for a drink at *The Fox Brewery & Pub* (foxpubs.com; 775-883-1369). It's in the restored *St. Charles Hotel,* built in 1862 and the oldest remaining commercial building in Carson City. The hotel at 310 S. Carson St. was *the* place to stay back then and—in a sign of the times—now is an Airbnb.

Carson City is home to a number of pre-statehood structures, including Victorian houses, museums, and churches dating to the mid-1800s. Nearly 50 historic sites are included in the 2.5-mile *Kit Carson Trail,* a self-guided multimedia tour you can access for free at visitcarsoncity.com. You can follow the interactive audio guide, download the map, watch a museum docent take a stroll through history, or indulge in a guided ghost tour.

Carson City restaurants provide a wide variety of dining experiences. For a taste of Basque cooking, have lunch at the *Villa Basque Café and Deli,* 730 Basque Way, which is locally famous for its chorizo. Visit villabasquecafe

trivia

The **Carson Street Beautification Project** resulted in historic lamp-posts, iron railings, and trees lining Carson Street from 5th to Caroline Streets.

Reno-Tahoe trivia answers:

Jacob W. Davis invented a way to strengthen work pants using rivets and went into business with Levi Strauss in 1871.

Reno was named for Civil War general Jesse Reno.

Carson City was named for frontiersman and scout Christopher "Kit" Carson.

.com or call (775) 884-4451. **Cucina Lupo,** 308 N. Curry St., is an Italian restaurant focusing on foods from local producers. Specialties include gnocchi mushrooms with garlic, cream, herbs and truffle mascarpone, and cioppino with grilled bread. Visit cucinalupo.com or call (775) 461-0441.

For a classic experience, try **Duke's Steak House** in the Casino Fandango at 3800 S. Carson St. It specializes in numerous cuts of beef including three sizes of choice or prime filet mignon, choice or prime ribeyes and New York strips, and steak Diane. Seafood selections include the locally popular Petrale sole, crab, and sea bass, or try the duck leg confit, braised short ribs, or a coffee-barbecue-crusted elk tenderloin. Dinner is served from 4 to 9 p.m. Wed through Sun; visit casinofandango.com or call (775) 886-1664.

Carson City's premier annual celebration, **Carson Valley Days** in June, is 4 days of events that include a parade, live music, midway games, rides, horseshoe tournaments, craft vendors, and more. Go to visitcarsonvalley.org or call (775) 782-8145.

Storey County

The rush to the Comstock Lode started as a trickle in 1859 and turned into a flood of prospectors in 1860. Despite the vastness of the **Comstock Lode** mineral deposit, separating the wealth from the earth was not easy. Milling methods prevalent in other parts of the world did not work on the Comstock. Two of the most productive early Comstock mines, the Ophir and the Gould & Curry, spent more than $1.4 million combined on mills that were later abandoned. By 1863 construction costs mounted to $5 million per mill.

Frequent cave-ins required elaborate timbering systems designed specifically for the Comstock. It is estimated that more lumber was underground in Comstock mine shafts and tunnels than was in all the buildings in Nevada at the time. Both timber and scarce water were transported from the Lake Tahoe area to Virginia City via flumes. V-flumes sent logs flying down to the valley floor. Mule teams hauled them to the mines until the Virginia & Truckee Railroad took over that chore. Gravity flumes carried water 25 miles from Marlette Lake to Virginia City at a cost exceeding $2 million.

Despite all the expense to mine the Comstock, it was worthwhile. An estimated $1 billion in silver and gold helped build San Francisco and structures in other cities. Virginia City riches built the elaborate Sutro Baths, Fairmont Hotel, and Flood Home (later the Pacific Union Club) in San Francisco; Lucky Baldwin's Tallac House at Lake Tahoe; and Harbor Hill on Long Island. The price of Comstock mining-company stock fluctuated wildly. For example, in 1860 Ophir

The White Lode of the Comstock

I was standing in the Silver Terrace Cemeteries one morning in May, taking notes for a Memorial Day story on the old headstones that dot the seven contiguous graveyards—and shivering in a surprisingly cold wind. Suddenly I noticed white flecks on the sleeve of my navy-blue blazer—specks of insulating foam, such as those I'd noticed flying about during a construction project in downtown Las Vegas.

That's odd, I thought, looking around me at lots of quiet landscape and the vintage buildings and ancient mountains beyond. I don't see any construction projects.

And then it hit me: *Snow! Snow in May.*

My plane was leaving from Reno that afternoon, so after a quick stop for a piece of house-made, warming cobbler, I was back in my rental car for the trip down the mountain and headed to the airport. Snow was falling in Reno as well, and the pilot who was bringing in our plane had to circle again because he couldn't see the runway.

Ah, May in the Sierra Nevada.

stock sold for $60 per share and in 1863 rose to $2,500 per share, only to drop to $800 per share. Fortunes were made and lost overnight.

Elaborate saloons, ornate gambling establishments, and brothels, all looking to separate the miners from their fortunes, replaced the tent cities of the Comstock by the middle of the 1860s. Comstock Lode miners, working in 170-degree-Fahrenheit heat below the surface, earned the highest wages paid anywhere in the world—$4 per day—and more than twice the prevailing wage earned by other miners. The area prospered for more than 20 years before the boom ended. At its peak, Virginia City boasted more than 30,000 residents. Today the Virginia City Historic District includes 400 structures spaced over 14,750 acres and is a National Historic Landmark.

To get to the Comstock region from Carson City, take US 395 a few miles north to US 50 East, then SR 341 North. You will pass through Silver City, which boasted 8 mills with 95 stamps by 1871 and served as the boarding area for animals used in hauling ore-laden wagons between the Comstock Lode and mills on the Carson River.

Stop in Gold Hill for the ***Gold Hill Hotel,*** Nevada's oldest, dating back more than 150 years to 1859. Browse through the book selection in the office area—it carries tons of material on Virginia City, the Comstock Lode, and other Nevada places of interest. The patio affords a good view of the surrounding hills, and the great room's fireplace area beckons you to sit and chat. The stone hotel carries on the tradition of fine dining from the gold and silver rush days in its Crown Point Restaurant. Choose from ribeye and lobster ravioli; Crown

Point chicken with mozzarella, Parmesan, and herbs; or vegetarian arroz verde with spiced mushrooms. Prices are moderate to expensive. Breakfast, brunch, and lunch also are served, or you can stop for a drink in the historic saloon.

The hotel sponsors a historic lecture series of such events as a Chautauqua performance by living historian DebiLynn Smith as Nellie Mighels Davis, who left her birthplace in Maine to come to Carson City to be with her newspaper-editor husband. Ghost tours also are presented periodically. Rooms and suites run $75 to $180. For more information, visit goldhillhotel.net or call (775) 847-0111.

Continue on to **Virginia City** to stroll the broad board sidewalks and see the historic mansions, an old cemetery, and mines. The town's silver days may be history, but they've been captured in a wealth of museums. Start at the **Historic Fourth Ward School Museum** at 537 S. C St. The stately four-story 1876 Second Empire school (the only one still standing in the United States) produced graduating classes for 60 years before closing in 1936. Erected at a cost of $100,000, the school encompassed 16 classrooms capable of handling more than 1,000 students. The fourth floor held the gymnasium. Today the school educates the public on the history of the Comstock Lode and holds events such as a summer camp at which kids can learn to make a short film. Museum hours vary with the season, with a winter hiatus, so check the website at fourthwardschool.org. If you can't get there when it's open, the website has a virtual tour. Or call (775) 847-0975.

Continue on C Street and take a right on Flowers to 291 S. D St. for a tour of the oldest home on the Comstock. **The Mackay Mansion** was built in 1859 for George Hearst, father of newspaper mogul William Randolph Hearst. Hearst sold it in 1871 to John Mackay, who shortly after hit the Bonanza Strike, one of the largest silver strikes in history. Currently family owned, the mansion is one of the few original structures in town that survived the catastrophic 1875 fire. It has the original furniture, wallpaper, carpet, and chandeliers, and 1878 Tiffany sterling silverware, which provide a taste of the opulent life led by the "Silver Kings." The original mine office, vault, ore samples, and company records also remain.

The lush lawn and gardens with gazebo make it a popular wedding spot. Summer hours are 10 a.m. to 5 p.m. weekdays and 10 a.m. to 6 p.m. weekends; winter hours are noon to 5 p.m. on weekends. Tours are $8 for adults and $5 for kids 5 through 12; after-hours tours are $10 per person. Themed tea parties occasionally are presented, as are paranormal investigations. Visit therealmackay mansion.com or call (775) 847-0156.

The town rebuilt quickly after the fire, but production dropped rapidly after 1876. By 1880 the population had dwindled to 11,000, and at the turn of the century it plunged to 3,000, a far cry from the booming town of the 1860s when Samuel Clemens (Mark Twain) worked at the *Territorial Enterprise* and prowled its streets for stories.

Twain once wrote, "Virginia City was no place for a Presbyterian, and I did not remain one very long."

The *Virginia & Truckee Railroad Company,* "the Queen of the Short Lines," delivers the sights and sounds of historic locomotives in the heart of the Comstock while it transports you between Virginia City and Gold Hill. The lore of the Virginia & Truckee Railroad makes it the most famous of the short-line railroads. Dignitaries from all over the world rode its rails, and more than 45 trains a day arrived at and departed from Virginia City during the boom. The conductor gives you a narration of the many historic sites along the route as you travel through tunnel No. 4 and many Comstock mine sites on the 35-minute round trip.

There also are some themed trips, including Halloween and Christmas. To reach the depot, take D Street to Washington and then turn right onto F Street. Diesel locomotives run on weekdays, steam on weekends. The fare is $16 for diesel or $19 for steam for adults, $8 for children 5 to 12, with all-day passes for $35. For schedules, go to virginiatruckee.com or call (775) 847-0380.

Go up Washington Street and take the stairs up to C Street. Moving down the block, you come upon numerous museums. *Liberty Engine Company No. 1 Comstock Firemen's Museum/Nevada State Firemen's Museum* resides in a circa-1876 building between Union and Taylor. This still is an operating volunteer firefighting unit, and the volunteer firemen maintain the museum of 19th-century firefighting equipment and related artifacts. Hours are 10 a.m. to 4 p.m. daily, May through Oct. Call (775) 847-0717 for more information.

Inside the Ponderosa Saloon (formerly the Bank of California) at the corner of C Street and Taylor, arrange for the *Ponderosa Mine Tour,* a 35-minute guided underground tour. Along the way you'll see complete underground workings such as crosscuts, drifts, stopes, shafts, raises, and winzes, plus 300 pieces of antique mining equipment. Tours are offered all year; call (775) 847-7210.

The *Chollar Mine,* which dates to 1859, was one of the most successful on the Comstock, producing $17 million in gold and silver over 80 years. The 30-minute tour provides a look at original square-set timbering, silver ore, rock drills, and old mining equipment. It's open from 11 a.m. to 4:15 p.m. daily, and admission is $25. It's near the Fourth Ward School via Occidental Grade and F

trivia

Territorial Enterprise features the real newspaper office of author and reporter Mark Twain, along with his desk and the newspaper's printing facility.

jackpot!

Street. Visit chollarminetour.com or call (775) 847-0155.

The ***Courthouse Slammer & County Museum*** (or as the wags would have it, the Alcatraz of Virginia City) is in the Storey County Courthouse—built in 1875 and still functioning—at 26 S. B St. The two-tiered cellblock houses various exhibits in and around the former jail cells on the town's gunslingers, saloons, ladies of the evening, the Comstock Lode, Mark Twain and the *Territorial Enterprise*, and the Silver Terrace Cemetery. Hours are 8 a.m. to 5 p.m. weekdays; visit virginiacitynv .com or call (775) 847-0968.

The infamous ***Suicide Table,*** a faro table that reportedly got its name after three of its owners committed suicide because of gambling losses, is at the Delta Saloon at 18 C St.; call (775) 847-0789. The Silver Queen, 28 N. C St., has the tallest bar in town, built in 1876, and the **Silver Queen,** a portrait of a woman in a dress inlaid with 3,261 silver dollars (the depth of the Combination Mine Shaft) and 28 $20 gold pieces; call (775) 847-0440.

Don't miss ***The Way It Was Museum,*** at the corner of C Street and Sutton, for the world's most complete collection of Comstock artifacts as well as historic photographs, lithographs, and period maps. The entrance fee is $4; for more information, call (775) 847-0766.

Silver Terrace Cemeteries is a good place to stop. Take a right on Carson Street and then a left on Cemetery Road to reach the parking lot. The cemeteries got their start in the 1860s, when fraternal, religious, and civic organizations established their own burial grounds on this steep, windswept hillside. You'll see ornate ironwork and Masonic symbols, and elaborate monuments next to caved-in crypts and weathered wooden grave markers. Search out the monument to Captain Edward Faris Storey (1828–1860), after whom Storey County was named. *Hint:* It's on top of a hill. The headstones illustrate the draw Virginia City and the Comstock Lode had on people who had traveled from places as far away as England, France, and Scotland to seek their fortunes.

Charlotte Antonia Kruttschnitt, the wife of the Storey County assessor, was buried here in 1867 after she died in a stagecoach rollover. According to legend, her funeral was "well attended with sixty carriages and many more on horseback." Modern burials are still conducted at Silver Terrace Cemeteries. Please be respectful as you tour the grounds. For more information, go to visitvirginiacitynv.com or call (775) 847-7500.

On B Street, next to the courthouse, you'll find the most significant vintage theater in the West. **Piper's Opera House,** built in the 1880s, hosted famous singers and sustained culture in the Comstock as it entertained President Grant, Buffalo Bill, Al Jolson and Mark Twain. Tours, which are on select days April through October, are $5 (tickets are available at the opera house or the Virginia City Visitors Center). During that season, you may be able to hear a performance by the Renegade Orchestra or attend a monthly bingo night. For a schedule, visit pipersoperahouse.com or call (775) 847-0433.

"Luscious Lucius" Beebe rejuvenated the **Territorial Enterprise** in the 1950s, restoring the Enterprise Building to its former grandeur and boosting circulation to more than 5,000 across the nation. He was widely regarded as the best-dressed overdressed man in America. When spotted carrying a bucket of champagne early one morning in Virginia City, Beebe responded to the inquiry of whether he was drinking champagne for breakfast, "Doesn't everyone?"

Bob Richards, editor of Beebe's *Territorial Enterprise*, started an enduring Virginia City tradition as a jest. In a tongue-in-cheek article, Richards wrote a fictitious account of Virginia City's camel races in 1957. Camels were introduced to the Comstock Lode in 1861 as pack animals, but the rocky terrain proved too difficult for them. Richards continued the spoof, reporting that the races had to be canceled for a variety of reasons in 1958 and 1959 but declaring that the races would be held the next year. The *Phoenix Gazette* and the *San Francisco Chronicle* challenged the *Territorial Enterprise* to sponsor a real race. In 1960 *The Misfits*, directed by John Huston and starring Clark Gable and Marilyn Monroe, was being filmed in the Virginia City area during the scheduled camel races. John Huston joined the fun and entered the race on a camel borrowed from the San Francisco Zoo. Huston crossed the finish line first, and the rest is history.

trivia

Samuel Clemens arrived in Virginia City after trying his hand at mining for three weeks in 1862. He began writing under the pen name of Mark Twain for the town newspaper, the *Territorial Enterprise*.

Today, the event has evolved into the **International Virginia City Camel & Ostrich Races,** with three "heats" over the weekend at the Virginia City Fairgrounds in early September. The event also has a carnival midway and vendors. Other Virginia City events include the Rocky Mountain Oyster Fry in March, Chili on the Comstock in May, and World Championship Outhouse Races in October. Find more information at visitvirginiacitynv.com or call (775) 847-7500.

Choose from among several historic B&Bs for refined, relaxing accommodations. Longtime Nevada residents Mark and Dona Stafford operate the ***Virginia City Bed & Breakfast*** in the heart of the mining district in an 1876 building at 226 N. B St. The 3 rooms with private baths include afternoon dessert and refreshments as well as breakfast, which you can enjoy on the porch with a 100-mile view. Rates start at $160. Visit virginiacitybedandbreakfast.com or call (775) 846-0154.

The ***Cobb Mansion Bed & Breakfast*** at 18 S. A St. has 6 rooms and suites with private baths in an 1876 Victorian Italianate mansion 2 blocks from downtown. Rooms start at $167; visit cobbmansion.com or call (775) 847-9006.

As you depart Virginia City, ponder the foresight of Mr. Forman, manager of the Eclipse Mill and Mining Company. Wise in the boom-and-bust fortunes of mining towns, Forman erected his house using wooden pegs instead of nails and spikes. When the mines played out and his mill closed, he dismantled his house, loaded the pieces onto the Virginia & Truckee Railroad, and shipped it to Los Angeles for reassembly.

Washoe County

You will discover seclusion at the ***Deer Run Ranch Bed & Breakfast.*** Proprietors Muffy and David Vhay have created a peaceful retreat from life's everyday pressures. Sit back in the evening and watch the deer come out to play or watch the blue heron swoop down to the pond at dusk. Across Washoe Lake, the Sierra Nevada provides spectacular views. Listen for coyotes or mountain lions as they prowl around in the dark. It's hard to believe, but a drought in the 1980s completely dried up the sprawling Washoe Lake now before your eyes.

The B&B is located on an operating 200-acre alfalfa ranch. In 1937 Muffy's parents purchased the land, then called the Quarter Circle JP, for $2,400—the amount of back taxes owed on the property. Muffy attended the one-room schoolhouse in Franktown, directly across the lake. During Prohibition, moonshiners used the natural springs on the ranch to brew their potions. Before repeal of Prohibition in 1933, government agents blew up the stills. You can consider this while you sip your welcoming glass of wine. In your room you will find a basket full of tasty snacks.

Contractor Dave built the ranch with a passive solar system, providing warmth in the winter and coolness in the summer. Winter visitors can curl up next to the fireplace with a good book or venture outdoors to ice-skate on the frozen pond. For an added treat, ask Muffy to show you her pottery studio and some of her work.

The private guest wing has 2 comfortable bedrooms and a spacious common area. Perch yourself in the window seats and keep a vigilant watch on the Sierra Nevada. Wall after wall of bookshelves will delight any bibliophile. Navajo rugs and paintings give warmth and a feeling of home to your guest quarters. A television, DVD player, and refrigerator provide all the comforts of home.

A full ranch breakfast with Muffy's homemade jellies and muffins and dishes such as a squash-blossom frittata with Asiago cheese prepares you for the coming day. You will hate to leave, but further Nevada adventures await you. Nightly rates start at $119. To reach Deer Run Ranch Bed & Breakfast from Carson City, take I-580 North to exit 10 (Eastlake Boulevard) and turn right at the bottom of the ramp. Travel just under 4 miles, and you'll see the entrance to the ranch at 5440 Eastlake Blvd. Visit bbonline.com/united-states/nevada/carson-city/deerrun.html or call (775) 882-3643.

Leftover from the riches of the Comstock Lode days, the Bowers Mansion was built in 1864 by millionaires L. S. "Sandy" (one of the early Comstock wealthy) and Eilley (boardinghouse owner) Bowers. They combined their fortunes through marriage, but Sandy died only three years after the house was built. His widow tried to earn money by adding a third floor for more rooms and turning her home into a hotel and resort, but Eilley's fortune disappeared. She died destitute in San Francisco in 1903, but not before she had been reduced to telling fortunes to earn a meager living. Until the day she died, she insisted she could tell fortunes and locate new mines.

The two-story granite structure contains 16 rooms and cost $200,000 to construct and furnish. The Bowers Mansion is in Washoe County's *Bowers Mansion Regional Park.* Tours are given every hour on the hour from 11 a.m. to 4 p.m., weekends and holidays, between Memorial Day and Nevada Day at the end of October (although pleasant weather may bring an earlier spring opening). Tours also are available by appointment and check the website schedule for events such as the periodic Friday-evening programs on the porch. After the tour, take advantage of the park's swimming pool and picnic area. Fees for the Z-shaped heated pool complete with hydraulic lift are $6 for most adults and $5 for seniors and children 3 to 17. Mansion tours (cash only) are $10 for most adults and $7 for seniors and children 6 to 17. To reach Bowers Mansion Regional Park, take I-580/US 395 North to SR 330, and turn right. Visit washoecounty.gov or call (775) 849-0201.

Head north on I-580/US 395 to SR 431 (Mount Rose Highway) to Incline Village and "the Jewel of the Sierras," *Lake Tahoe.* Along the way you'll pass over Mount Rose Summit; at 8,933 feet in elevation, it's the highest year-round pass through the Sierra Nevada. Incline Village was named after a railway that

trivia

Lake Tahoe is the third-deepest lake in North America, containing more than 39 trillion gallons of water. The lake's pure, crystal-line water owes its intense blue to the thin mountain air, which allows the water to reflect the blue sky above. During sunsets it appears pink-orange or red, dur-ing storms a seething gray-black.

operated here between 1879 and 1896, hauling an estimated 200 million board feet of lumber and more than 1 million cords of wood to the Washoe Valley.

Leave behind the hustle and bustle that can occur in Lake Tahoe during peak season and retreat to *The Incline Lodge*. A luxury boutique hotel, it has the laid-back vibe the area is known for, with a hint of sophistication. Top-floor High Sierra rooms have a shared veranda and vaulted ceilings, while Alpine View rooms have private balconies with a forest view. But even the standard rooms come with custom-designed furnishings and curated art, and all have electric kettles and steamers in addition to the usual amenities. After a hard day on the slopes or the lake, relax in the heated indoor pool or grab a drink at the lobby bar. Rooms start at $139; 1-bedroom suites also are available. The Incline Lodge is at 1003 Tahoe Blvd. in Incline Village. Visit theinclinelodge.com or call (775) 260-5750.

Since you've come this far, you may prefer lodging on the lake. The lakeside cottages at the *Hyatt Regency Lake Tahoe* are worth the splurge, especially if you are splitting the cost with friends or family members. You'll have an amazing sense of serenity as you contemplate the views of the opal-colored lake waters and Canada geese descending on the sand. Nightly rates start at $376 in the winter, $581 in the summer, and go up to $1,851. Regular hotel rooms also are available. The Hyatt Regency Lake Tahoe Resort & Casino is at 111 Country Club Dr. in Incline Village; visit hyatt.com or (775) 832-1234.

Likewise, *Lake Tahoe Balloons* delivers hours of panoramic vistas beyond your wildest imagination. The classic package includes what they say is the world's only balloon-aircraft recovery vessel, since the balloons launch and land on a boat on the lake. Then, there's the 1-hour flight over the breath-takingly scenic areas on and around the lake. It's $399 per person, and private tours are available. Visit laketahoeballoons.com or call (530) 544-1221.

You'll recognize hints of the arts-and-crafts architecture the area is known for at *Cedar Glen Lodge* in Tahoe Vista. The newly renovated resort is in the woods across the street from the lake, where there's a sandy beach. Right on the property there's a seasonal heated pool, year-round hot tub, firepit, put-ting green, and lawn area for relaxing. There's also an indoor wine bar with fireplace and great views. You can stay in one of the cozy cottages spaced around the property or in a room in the lodge. Rates start at $179. The lodge is at 6589 N. Lake Blvd.; visit tahoecedarglen.com or call (530) 546-4281.

Spend 1 or 2 days experiencing Lake Tahoe itself. The best way to get the lay of the land, and in this case water, lies in driving the 72-mile rim of the lake. It's one of a number of road trips detailed on the website of the Reno-Sparks Convention and Visitors Authority at visitrenotahoe.com.

Lake Tahoe ranks as the highest alpine lake of its size in the country, with a surface elevation of 6,225 feet. It earns its name honestly, Tahoe is Washoe for "big water," with a length of 22 miles and a width of 12 miles. Its crystal-clear waters have enthralled visitors for more than a century. In some places, objects can be seen to depths of up to 75 feet. Lake Tahoe's depth of 1,645 feet makes it the 3rd-deepest lake in North America and the 10th-deepest in the world. Its 40 trillion gallons would cover a flat area the size of California to a depth of 14 inches but would take 700-plus years to refill. Freel Peak rises to 10,881 feet, while Mount Tallac on the shoreline rises to 9,735 feet.

One of the more interesting landmarks is Cave Rock on the east side of Lake Tahoe in the US 50 stretch. Washoe Native Americans considered it a

A Bit of Scandinavia on the Shores of Lake Tahoe

We'd seen the dire warnings: "It is to be stressed . . . that this is a steep trail," the California Department of Parks and Recreation cautions of the mile-long path. And how. The good news is that, getting there, you'll walk a mile downhill. The bad news is that you have to walk that mile back up—and rides are not available. Is it worth it? Definitely. For one thing, Vikingsholm tours run in the summer and early fall, when Lake Tahoe's weather is at its most glorious. For another, that mile-long walk in both directions offers almost continual views of Emerald Bay and the rest of the breathtaking lake. And then there's the magnificent house that Lora Knight commissioned at the head of the bay in the late 1920s, which is now part of Emerald Bay State Park.

Knight—who also purchased the lake's only island—was intrigued by the area's resemblance to Scandinavia and commissioned her niece's husband, a Swedish architect, to design her home. Knight, her niece, and the architect undertook a grand tour of Scandinavia to do research. The result is a home with numerous design features that faithfully evoke ancient Scandinavian buildings and is considered one of the finest examples of Scandinavian architecture in the country. Knight also commissioned a teahouse on the island—which is also the site of the only waterfall that flows directly into the lake—and would take friends by boat to her parties there.

Tours run daily from Memorial Day weekend to Sept 30. Besides the trail, parking is the only obstacle; the Vikingsholm lot on SR 89 tends to fill up, so arrive early or expect to circle—and circle. For more information, visit vikingsholm.com or call (530) 525-3384.

sacred spot, lying their deceased to rest in the cold waters below the out-cropping. Today the highway passes through 25 yards of solid stone at Cave Rock—clearly an improvement on the original Lincoln Highway route, since only a thin ledge exists today where that road passed around it.

Thunderbird Lodge, a magnificent estate on the shore of Lake Tahoe, was built in 1936 by wealthy San Franciscan George Whittell Jr. and is listed in the National Register of Historic Places. At one time Whittell controlled 27 miles of Lake Tahoe shoreline, from Crystal Bay to Zephyr Cove, and 5,300 acres became Lake Tahoe State Park. The current site of 6.6 acres—of the original 140—include the main house and is owned and operated by the Thunderbird Lodge and Yacht—Lake Tahoe preservation society. Tours are available by reservation, although the property's also available for weddings and other events. Visit thunderbirdtahoe.org or call (775) 832-8750.

Continue around the lake and discover more special places. More energetic visitors can leave their vehicles and traffic behind and travel by foot or horseback on the **Tahoe Rim Trail,** where trailheads offer a variety of hiking and riding experiences. A guide, complete with interactive maps, is available at the website of the Tahoe Rim Trail Association, tahoerimtrail.org. Or call (775) 298-0012 for more information.

Myriad excursions offer new perspectives from which to view Lake Tahoe, and few can equal the view from the water. The **MS Dixie II** paddle wheeler cruises the surface while the captain points out historic sites along the shoreline. Depending on the season, you might take a sunny late-morning or afternoon trip or relax on an evening dinner cruise. Rates run from $99 to $140 for adults and from $55 to $75 for children 3 to 11. The boat leaves from Zephyr Cove, 4 miles north of Stateline on US 50. Visit zephyrcove.com or call (800) 238-2463.

For an even more awe-inspiring view of the lake and its environs, take off on a **parasail** from Zephyr Cove. You'll be launched from a boat connected by a 1,000-foot rope and can sail single or tandem. You can even take your camera along to get some amazing shots! It's $95; visit zephyrcove.com or call (800) 238-2463.

Or stay grounded and test your casting skills with **Alpine Fly Fishing** in South Lake Tahoe. Alpine's guides, with a combined 60 years of experience, can teach fishers of any skill level the intricacies of making just the right cast. You'll fish one of many rivers in the area that are known for brown and rainbow trout and other fish. The gear's included, or you can bring your own. Half-day trips are $395 for 1 or 2 anglers, $550 for 3, or make it a full day for $550 or $695. Visit alpineflyfishing.com or call (530) 318-6717.

A premier event, the *Lake Tahoe Shakespeare Festival,* combines open-air performances on beautiful Lake Tahoe with quality productions of Shakespeare's best-loved works. Dynamic sets, fabulous costumes, and professional theater would make even the Bard envious. The Shakespeare season runs during July and August; the schedule also includes the Young Shakespeare program for children and a few non-Shakespeare events. Shows are presented at Sand Harbor State Park in Incline Village, where you can dig your feet into the sand and enjoy a picnic while you are entertained. Performances Thurs through Sat start at $22 for youths 25 and younger and go up to $469 for table seating for 4 with wait service. Tues, Wed, and Sun performances start at $17 for youths and go to $440 for a table for 4. For tickets and more information, visit laketahoe shakespeare.com or call (800) 74-SHOWS (747-4697).

trivia

Wayne Newton has performed in the Silver State more than any other entertainer, signing his first contract in 1959 at the age of 16.

Other Lake Tahoe annual events include Lake Tahoe Snowfest in early Mar, Classical Tahoe in late Jul to early Aug, the Battle Born BeerFest & Chili Cookoff in Oct, and Northern Lights Festival in Nov and Dec. Visit tahoe.com.

The *Chart House* chain that once spread across the country and overseas is mostly gone now, but one still lives on in Stateline—and, perched high atop Kingsbury Grade, it has a stunning view of the lake. Entrées include herb-crusted prime rib and a broad selection of seafood; prices are moderate to expensive. Dinner is served from 4 to 9 p.m. Sun through Thurs and 4 to 9:30 p.m. Fri and Sat. It's at 392 Kingsbury Grade. Visit chart-house.com/location/chart-house-lake-tahoe-nv/ or call (775) 588-6176.

For a bit of classic French cooking with pan-Asian flair while you're in the Lake Tahoe area, consider the cozy, intimate *Le Bistro Restaurant & Bar,* where menu items may include foie gras, duck, filet mignon, or fresh fish; breads and desserts are freshly baked. Dinner is served from 6 to 9 p.m. Tues through Thurs and 6 to 9:30 p.m. Fri and Sat. Visit lebistrotahoe.com or call (775) 831-0800 for reservations. The restaurant and bar are at 120 Country Club Dr. in Incline Village.

Azzara's Italian Restaurant has been pleasing customers since 1978. Start with the stuffed artichoke or bruschetta and move on to a main course of saltimbocca alla romana, ravioli di aragosta, or lasagne al forno. Finish with coffee and tiramisu. Azzara's, which begins serving at 5 p.m. Tues through Sun, is at 930 Tahoe Blvd. in Incline Village. Visit azzaras.com or call (775) 831-0346.

The *Mount Rose Wilderness* encompasses 30,000 acres of rugged terrain within minutes of Lake Tahoe and the urban communities of Reno and Sparks. Elevations range from 6,400 feet along canyon bottoms to 10,778 feet at the summit of Mount Rose. Trails totaling up to 25 miles, including 7 miles of the Tahoe Rim Trail, lead from several trailheads. Wilderness permits are not required. Access the area from the Mount Rose Highway, which is SR 431, via SR 28 on the north shore. Maps are available at fs.usda.gov/ltbmu. Call (530) 543-2600 for more information.

If you lack equipment or would like a guide, *Tahoe Trips and Trails* offers getaways into the spectacular country around Lake Tahoe. It offers an array of hiking and multisport tours in the Lake Tahoe area and throughout the West for individuals, families, and groups of all athletic abilities. Call (800) 581-4453.

Located in *Spooner Lake & Backcountry State Park* in the Lake Tahoe Basin, Wild Cat Cabin is a beautiful, hand-hewn, Scandinavian-style log cabin 3 miles from the Spooner trailhead that sleeps 2 and has wood stoves for heat and cooking. The nearby Spooner Lake Cabin is similarly outfitted and sleeps 4. Both are available May 1 through Oct 1. The Spooner Lake Visitor Center and Amphitheater serve as the heart of the park's natural and cultural history programs and provide access to more than 60 miles of paths and trails. Visit parks.nv.gov/parks/spooner-lake or call (775) 831-0494.

Driving north on SR 431 brings you to I-580 North into Reno, the BIGGEST LITTLE CITY IN THE WORLD—the slogan on the famous Reno Arch, completed in October 1926, which was derived from a contest. G. A. Burns came up with the winning slogan and donated the $100 prize to charity. During the Great Depression in 1932, the city fathers voted to turn off the lights on the arch in order to save money. The business community responded with an outcry and raised enough money to turn them back on again within three months, and they still light up Virginia Street.

On the campus of the University of Nevada, Reno, the *Fleischmann Planetarium* presents a series of programs to educate and delight adults and children alike. Full-dome theater shows, provided on Fri and Sat, rotate periodically and include such presentations as *Constellations and Planet Earth* and *Exploring Space and Time.*

An adjacent exhibit hall contains more than 100 space-themed objects such as a meteorite collection that includes the largest one known to have fallen in Nevada, one of only four Rand-McNally Oceanic Earth Globes in the world, a companion moon globe and interactive exhibits such as a gravity well and NASA modules in which visitors can drive on the moon or mars.

Nine Stops along the Scenic Drive around Lake Tahoe (from South Lake Tahoe)

1. Off of Highway 89 near South Lake Tahoe, **Fallen Leaf Lake** is a large alpine lake where scenes from *The Bodyguard* were filmed with Kevin Costner and Whitney Houston.

2. **Emerald Bay** is Tahoe's most photographed site, a glacier-carved bay surrounded by magnificent granite peaks. The bay is 3 miles long by 1 mile wide, and you can find impressive vantage points along Highway 89, or by taking a lake cruise through the bay.

3. **Eagle Falls** is a series of three waterfalls that pour into Emerald Bay. You can hike to the foot of the lower falls or hike up to Eagle Lake and Desolation Wilderness. Parking is scarce.

4. **Ed Z'Berg Sugar Pine Point State Park.** Hellman-Ehrman Mansion, a three-story rock-and-wood estate, was designed by well-known architect Walter Danford Bliss. Tours provide views of the spacious living and dining rooms with their oak floors and polished wood ceilings. It's open for tours during the summer; visit sierrastate parks.org/our-parks#sugar-pine or call (530) 525-3384.

5. Side trip to **Palisades Tahoe** (formerly known as Squaw Valley). The site of the 1960 Winter Olympics and one of the great ski destinations in the world. In addition to skiing, you can ice-skate, mountain bike, bungee jump, and hear live music in the Plaza Bar (palisadestahoe.com or 800-403-0206).

6. Side trip to **Donner Memorial State Park,** 12593 Donner Pass Rd., Truckee, California (parks.ca.gov). A 1918 monument to the tragedy of the Donner Party stands 22 feet high (the depth of the snow they were trapped in). The visitor center displays exhibits on the Donner Party, local Native Americans, and builders of the transcontinental railroad; expect to spend about an hour.

7. **Sand Harbor State Park.** Over a mile of white, sandy beaches on the North Shore of Lake Tahoe, Sand Harbor is arguably the most popular beach on the lake. In summer it is the site of the Shakespeare Festival. Because of its popularity, arrive early for parking.

8. **Vikingsholm.** An elaborately detailed Scandinavian lodge may seem out of place on the Nevada/California border, but Vikingsholm is just the sort of place, and it's worth the effort that it takes to get there. Tours are offered from Memorial Day to Sept 30, and the views of the lake—both from the parking lot at the top of the trail to the home and from the home itself—are hard to beat. Off Highway 89 at the head of Emerald Bay.

9. **Heavenly ski resort gondola.** Take a 2.4-mile trip up to 9,123 feet—near the top of Monument Peak—where you can really appreciate the grandeur of Lake Tahoe. On your way up (or down,) stop at the observation deck to relax and have a latte. Adults $69, teens 13 to 18 and seniors $54, and kids 5 through 12 $34. 3860 Saddle Rd., South Lake Tahoe; visit skiheavenly.com or call (775) 586-7000.

There are science-fiction exhibits as well, such as replicas of the *Star Wars Millennium Falcon*, *Star Trek* communicator, *Dr. Who* TARDIS, and the tesseract from *The Avengers*. Future artifact themes include "Dreams and Dystopias" and "Cyberspace Time and Technology."

Hours are 2:30 to 8 p.m. Fri and 10 a.m. to 1 p.m. and 2:30 to 8 p.m. Sat. Tickets for full-dome theater shows are $15 for most adults and $10 for students (age 3 through college), seniors, and service members and include the exhibits. Or view just the exhibits for $3. The planetarium is at 1664 N. Virginia St. Visit unr.edu/planetarium or call (775) 784-4812.

Moving from the universe to planet Earth, stop in at the **Wilbur D. May Arboretum & Botanical Garden** in Rancho San Rafael Regional Park at 1595 N. Sierra St. A map of the gardens and accompanying guide will lead you through the seven-circle labyrinth, Songbird Garden, Rose Garden, and Rock Garden—all of which are self-explanatory—and such spaces as Kristen's Garden, a secluded space with water feature and gazebo planted with a shade garden and grape and honeysuckle vines, and Rowley Grove, with a mix of native conifers including Ponderosa pine, lodgepole, and white fir.

The arboretum and botanical garden is a great escape from the city. It's open daily from 8 a.m. to 9 p.m. in spring and summer, 8 a.m. to 7 p.m. in the fall, and 8 a.m. to 5 p.m. in the winter. Admission is free. Visit washoecounty.gov/parks/maycenterhome/arboretum/ or call (775) 785-4153.

Trace the history of the automobile at the **National Automobile Museum,** 1 Museum Dr., which is Reno's premier museum and, arguably, the finest automobile collection in the country. See such classics as a 1936 Mercedes-Benz Type 500K Special Roadster, Duesenbergs that are real doozies, and celebrity cars such as James Dean's 1949 Mercury, Al Jolson's 1933 V-16 Cadillac, Lana Turner's 1941 Chrysler Newport (one of only six made), and the 1912 Rambler 73-CC Cross Country used in the movie *Titanic*. There also are rarities such as a sleek 1938 Phantom Corsair and the 1907 Thomas Flyer that won "the Great Race" from New York to Paris. Admission is $15 for most adults, $13 for seniors, and $10 for children ages 6 through 15, first responders, veterans, and active-duty military members. Hours are 9 a.m. to 5 p.m. Mon through Sat and 10 a.m. to 5 p.m. Sun. Visit automuseum.org or call (775) 333-9300.

The **Nevada Historical Society,** founded in 1904, is Nevada's oldest museum and serves as the repository of much of the state's interesting history. Within its walls you will find priceless works by famous Washoe basket-maker Datsolalee and artifacts representing explorer, buckaroo, settler, and casino history, telling five interlinked stories about life in early Nevada. Among them are the Gridley Flour Sack (see page 156), the repeated auction of which throughout the country raised about $250,000 for the Civil War–era US Sanitary

Commission, which aided wounded Union soldiers. Temporary exhibits display such collections as watercolors of the state, and the museum's archives contain more than 500,000 historical photographs and numerous book and manuscript collections. Admission is $6 for adults and free for those 18 and younger. The museum is at 1650 N. Virginia St. and is open from 10 a.m. to 4 p.m. Wed through Sat. Visit nvhistoricalsociety.org or call (775) 688-1190.

Reno hosts the **National Championship Air Races,** the nation's longest consecutive running air race, in the fall of each year. Watch top aviators thrill the audience with death-defying aerobatic feats and maneuvers at Reno Stead Airport, north of Reno. Flying formations, solo performers, and flybys with antique biplanes are on the schedule. A variety of ticket packages are available. For information, visit the website of the Reno Air Racing Association at airrace .org or call (775) 972-6663.

The **Reno Rodeo** in June, which calls itself "the Wildest, Richest Rodeo in the West," has bull riding, extreme bull riding, roping, steer wrestling, and more; visit renorodeo.com or call (775) 329-3877. The **Nevada State Fair,** also in June, has exhibits, vendors, and midway carnival rides; nevadastatefair.org or (775) 400-1102. For more information on these and other Reno activities, visit the Reno Sparks Convention and Visitors Authority website at visitrenotahoe .com or call (775) 682-3800.

Louis' Basque Corner, at 301 E. 4th St., serves authentic Basque foods, family style, and is a Reno tradition. Lunch served Tues through Sat; dinner daily; louisbasquecorner.com or (775) 323-7203. Locals also favor **The Stone House Café,** in a historic house at 1907 Arlington Ave., where "gourmet all day" includes breakfast, lunch, and dinner; visit stonehousecafereno.com or call (775) 284-3895.

International appetites journey to **Soochow Chinese Restaurant,** 656 E. Prater Way in Sparks, for an extensive menu of Chinese classics; soochow restaurant.com or (775) 359-5207. For classic Italian fare, try the landmark **Johnny's Ristorante Italiano** at 4245 W. 4th St., in business since 1966 and known for dishes such as Parmesan-crusted Petrale sole; johnnysristorante .com or (775) 747-4511. For northern Italian, the nod goes to **La Strada** in the Eldorado hotel-casino, 345 N. Virginia St., for its signature mushroom ravioli in porcini cream sauce; visit caesars.com/eldorado-reno or call (775) 348-3401.

Sparks grew up as a railroad town and division point of the Southern Pacific Railroad, beginning in 1903, and had one of the world's largest roundhouses during the steam era. So it's only fitting that you start your tour of "The Rail City" at the **Sparks Heritage Museum & Cultural Center,** 814 Victorian Ave., which is partially housed in a replica of the original Sparks Southern

Pacific Depot. You'll also see an outdoor train exhibit with steam locomotive, cupola caboose, and Pullman executive car.

Inside the museum, which tells the story of Sparks from the earliest settlers to today with vintage artifacts and interactive iPad kiosks, you'll find a turn-of-the-20th-century barbershop, a display on Prohibition, and, of course, details of railroad history. As you step into the railroad exhibit room, a train whistle blows. Visit sparksmuseum.org or call (775) 355-1144.

The museum is in Victorian Square, home to events including the Best in the West Nugget Rib Cook-Off in September, and Sparks Hometown Christmas Parade & Tree Lighting in early December. For information on these and other events, visit cityofsparks.us or call (775) 353-7856.

Pyramid Lake holds just as much intrigue and mystery today as it did when explorer John C. Frémont first set eyes on it. As described in Frémont's 1843 journal,

It broke upon our eyes like the ocean. The waves were curling in the breeze, and their dark-green color showed it to be a body of deep water, . . . [and it] was set like a gem in the mountains.

We encamped on the shore, opposite a very remarkable rock in the lake, which had attracted our attention for many miles. It rose, according to our estimate, 600 feet above the water, and from the point we viewed it, presented a pretty exact outline of the great pyramid of Cheops. . . . I called it Pyramid Lake.

To reach Pyramid Lake, take SR 445 north out of Sparks for 28 miles. Along the way you'll pass the Palomino Valley Wild Horse and Burro Center. When you approach the shore of the lake (the first view of which will doubtless be as memorable as Frémont's), bear left on SR 445 to reach the *Pyramid Lake Paiute Tribe and Visitor Center.* There, you can learn about the Native inhabitants of the area, plus indigenous animals and plant life. Exhibits delve into the people's history and culture and offer insight on why the tribe holds the lake and surrounding landscape sacred. The Pyramid Lake Reservation was set aside in 1859. As noted in the Pony Express Territory chapter, the

trivia

Anaho Island, a rocky island in Pyramid Lake, is home to one of only eight nesting colonies of American white pelicans in the Western United States and Canada. Public access is closed because the birds need solitude for nesting; frightened adult birds leave unhatched eggs or their young, which, if abandoned, die in the hot summer sun or are attacked and eaten by gulls.

Pyramid Lake Legend

Pyramid Lake Road, north of Reno via SR 445, is the only byway in the nation entirely within a tribal reservation. Stop by the museum for information about the lake and its native Paiute tribe. The formation of this huge lake was once a riddle. Now we know the deep azure waters as the remnants of an ancient inland sea extending south to Walker Lake. Native American legend attributes the lake's appearance to another cause, and the famous rock formation at the lake's southeast shore serves as a clue. The rock represents the Great Stone Mother waiting for her lost children to return to her. Since the basket at her feet remained empty, her tears over time filled Pyramid Lake.

1860 Pyramid Lake War led to one of the bloodiest slaughters of Native Americans in Nevada history.

Visit the tribe's website for information on permits and rules and note that some areas are off-limits to the public. Camping permits are $32 for 1 night, $82 for 3.

Plan to spend the better part of a day or more at the lake. There's usually a good breeze here, so bring along your kite. Lahontan trout season runs from Oct 1 to Jun 30; Sacramento perch season is year-round.

Pyramid Lake is a high desert lake with water about one-sixth as salty as seawater. The lake is flanked on the east and west by rugged mountain ranges, and large tufa (calcium carbonate deposits) formations spot the beach areas. Across from the marina is the large rock formation for which the lake was named. To get to the pyramid, follow Route 445 southeast until it becomes Route 446. Swing north on Route 447 at the junction near Nixon. Continue up Route 447 until you see the sign for the pyramid, which is about 5 miles past Marble Bluff Dam. Turn left and prepare yourself for 8 miles of bone-jarring washboard roads. Stay on the main hard-packed road and be sure to stay out of roads leading into soft sand, unless you want to spend the rest of the day digging yourself out. The main road will swing and circle around to the beach area, where you can get close to Pyramid Rock.

Before you arrive at Pyramid Rock, however, you will pass Anaho Island National Wildlife Refuge, safe nesting habitat for white pelicans, which is closed to the public. But look up and see the sun reflecting off circling pelicans as if a giant mobile filled the sky.

To the left of Pyramid Rock, with a little sleuthing, you will find Great Stone Mother, a tufa rock formation that resembles a woman with an open basket next to her. Legend has it that the woman shed tears for her children, filling the lake.

A Hidden World within Casinos

Check out these amusement centers for kids—no matter how you define them.

Circus Circus, Reno
caesars.com/circus-circus-reno
(800) 648-5010
Circus Circus lives up to its name by providing a carnival experience with acrobatic performances, an arcade, and games including *Pac-Man* and *Space Invaders*. You'll play with an ATM-style card and can redeem points for prizes.

Grand Sierra Fun Quest
Grand Sierra Resort, Reno
grandsierraresort.com
(775) 789-1127
The 40,000-square-foot center has a laser-tag arena, bumper cars, arcade games including balloon pop and bean-bag toss, and more than 125 video, arcade, and ride games.

Harrah's Lake Tahoe Arcade
Harrah's Lake Tahoe, Stateline
caesars.com/harrahs-tahoe
(800) 427-7247
Get away from the madding casino crowds in this smoke-free, alcohol-free space with video games like *Jurassic Park* and classic arcade games such as air hockey and Skee-Ball. Spend $20 and get 4 hours of free parking.

Nugget Skywalk Arcade
Nugget Casino Resort, Sparks
cnty.com/nugget/
(888) 868-4438
In the Skywalk Arcade, kids can prove their pinball wizardry, shoot some air hockey, or work on becoming the next LeBron with basketball hoops. Games are available for little kids and teenagers, and points can be redeemed for prizes.

North of Nixon 56 miles on SR 447, you'll arrive at *Gerlach* (population 21), the gateway to the Black Rock Desert. *Bruno's Country Club* is a café and sports bar plus motel with rooms, some with kitchenettes, and apartments. According to TripAdvisor, it's no. 1 of the one hotel in Gerlach. Call (775) 557-2220.

Out-of-the-way Nevada places seem to seem to attract potters, and Gerlach is no exception. Stop at John and Rachel Bogard's *Planet X Pottery,* a solar-powered pottery studio that was established in 1974. John Bogard has a reputation for crafting innovative and strikingly beautiful pots, dishes, and vases. Planet X has a working studio and four show galleries, which also display paintings of the area. To get there, drive north out of Gerlach, take the left fork (SR 447), and continue for 8 miles. Visit planetxpottery.net or call (775) 442-1919.

We'll leave you at the *Black Rock Desert,* which has seen its share of history over the eons. The Black Rock Desert was at the bottom of ancient Lake Lahontan; in places the silt is estimated to be 10,000 feet deep, and in 1992, with the help of excavators, a large mammoth fossil emerged from its depths.

One of the main wagon routes to the West crossed the desert, and at High Rock Canyon pioneers chiseled their names in the canyon rock walls between 1841 and 1849. In the 1940s and 1950s, the desert was used as a bombing range;

unexploded shells still appear from time to time—if you see any, leave them where they lie and give them a wide berth.

Today, it's most well known as the site of the annual **Burning Man,** a week-long event devoted to "community, art, self-expression and self-reliance" that draws upward of 80,000 people to the desert playa in Aug. Visit burningman.org.

To learn more about the area, stop at the **BLM Black Rock Station Visitor Contact Center,** which is open Thur through Mon from Apr through Oct. It's just west of Gerlach at the entrance to the Black Rock Desert-High Rock Canyon Emigrant Trails National Conservation Area. At the center, visitors can learn about the recreational, cultural, and national resources of the area through interpretive panels and maps and obtain important safety information.

Caution: The playa is unpassable when wet, and there are several bog areas to avoid. Inquire locally about road conditions before you head out. Tell someone where you are going and when you expect to return. Visit blm.gov/office/black-rock-station or call (775) 623-1500.

A New Emphasis in Reno

With the rise of Native American casinos in California, Reno gradually has identified less as a gambling mecca and more eagerly embraced the activities so popular in the Sierra Nevada and the Lake Tahoe area.

The river runs through it, and the City of Reno has capitalized on that proximity with its *Truckee River Whitewater Park* at Wingfield Park, 2 S. Arlington Ave. Grab a kayak, canoe, inner tube, or raft and launch yourself through the 11 drop-pools that cover 0.5 mile. The water temperature's a moderate 50 to 70 degrees, and there are 7,000 tons of smooth boulders and flat-top rocks along the edges for easy access, spectating, and kayak maneuvers. There's also a grassy park with amphi-theater. Helmets and flotation jackets are required.

You don't need to be an expert; reps stress that kayakers of all levels, especially, can enjoy the park and can start their adventure anywhere upstream. Kayak rentals, rafting trips, and instruction are available from Sierra Adventures at wildsierra.com or (775) 323-8928. For more information, go to reno.gov or call (775) 334-4636.

If you want to go rock climbing but can't quite get to a nearby mountain, try your skills at *Base Camp Big Wall* at the Whitney Peak Hotel just down the block. Con-structed on the exterior wall of the hotel at 255 N. Virginia St., it received a Guinness World Record as the world's largest climbing wall and offers a variety of climbing options. The $35 fee includes gear rental. Visit whitneypeakhotel.com or call (775) 398-5443.

For something a little tamer that the whole family can enjoy, there's the *Wild Island Family Adventure Park* in Sparks. It has a waterpark with about 12 slides and other attractions (including the Little Lagoon Kiddie Pool), bowling (with private two-lane rooms), black light go-karts, and laser tag. Visit wildisland.com or call (775) 359-2927.

Places to Stay in Reno–Tahoe Territory

CARSON CITY/ CARSON VALLEY

Deer Run Ranch Bed & Breakfast
5440 Eastlake Blvd.
bbonline.com/united
-states/nevada/carson-city/
deerrun.html
(775) 882-3643

The Federal Hotel
900 S. Carson St.
thefederalhotelnv.com
(775) 883-0900

Gold Dust West Carson City
2171 E. William St.
gdwcasino.com
(775) 885-9000

Hardman House Hotel
917 N. Carson St.
hardmanhousehotel.com
(775) 882-7744

GARDNERVILLE

Best Western Topaz Lake Inn
3210 Sandy Bowers Ave.
bestwestern.com
(775) 266-4661

GENOA

Holiday Inn Club Vacations David Walley's Resort
2001 Foothill Rd.
holidayinnclub.com
(775) 782-8155

White House Inn
195 Genoa Ln.
whitehouseinngenoanv
.com
(775) 870-7203

LAKE TAHOE—NORTH

Hyatt Regency Resort & Casino & Lakeside Cottages
111 Country Club Dr.,
Incline Village
hyatt.com
(775) 832-1234

The Incline Lodge
1003 Tahoe Blvd.,
Incline Village
theinclinelodge.com
(775) 260-5750

LAKE TAHOE—SOUTH

Camp Richardson Resort
1900 Jameson Beach Rd.,
South Lake Tahoe
camprichardsonresort.com
(530) 494-2228

Fireside Lodge Bed & Breakfast
515 Emerald Bay Rd.,
South Lake Tahoe
tahoefiresidelodge.com
(530) 544-5515

Harrah's Lake Tahoe
15 US 50, Stateline
caesars.com
(800) 427-7247

Margaritaville Resort Lake Tahoe
4130 Lake Tahoe Blvd.,
South Lake Tahoe
margaritavilleresorts.com
(530) 444-5400

RENO/SPARKS

Circus Circus Hotel Casino
500 N. Sierra St.
caesars.com
(800) 648-5010

Eldorado Hotel/Casino
345 N. Virginia St.
caesars.com
(800) 879-8879

Grand Sierra Resort
2500 E. 2nd St.
grandsierraresort.com
(775) 789-2000

Nugget Casino Resort
1100 Nugget Ave., Sparks
cnty.com/nugget
(888) 868-4438

Whitney Peak Hotel
255 N. Virginia St.
whitneypeakhotel.com
(775) 398-5400

VIRGINIA CITY

Cobb Mansion Bed & Breakfast
18 S. A St.
cobbmansion.com
(775) 847-9006

Gold Hill Hotel
1540 Main St., Gold Hill
goldhillhotel.net
(775) 847-0111

Silver Queen Hotel
28 N. C St.
silverqueenhotel.net
(775) 847-0440

Places to Eat in Reno-Tahoe Territory

CARSON CITY

Eve's Eatery
(Modern American)
402 N. Carson St.
eveseaterynv.com
(775) 461-0352

Glen Eagles (Continental)
3700 N. Carson St.
gleneaglesrestaurant.com
(775) 884-4414

Great Basin Brewery
(American)
302 N. Carson St.
greatbasinbrewingco.com
(775) 885-7307

Heidi's Family Restaurant
1020 N. Carson St.
(775) 882-0486.

Mom & Pop's Diner
224 S. Carson St.
(775) 884-4411

Nashville Social Club
(Southern)
1105 S. Carson St.
thenashvilleclub.com
(775) 515-0020

GARDNERVILLE

J. T. Basque Bar & Dining Room (Basque)
1426 US 395 N.
jtbasquenv.com
(775) 782-2074

GENOA

The Pink House
(Modern American)
193 Genoa Lane
thepinkhousegenoa.com
(775) 392-4279

GERLACH

Bruno's Country Club
(American)
445 Main St.
(775) 557-2220

LAKE TAHOE—NORTH

Azzara's Restaurant
(Italian)
930 Tahoe Blvd.,
ncline Village
azzaras.com
(775) 831-0346

Big Water Grill
(American/Californian)
341 Ski Way, Incline Village
bigwatergrille.com
(775) 833-0606

Gar Woods Grill & Pier
5000 N. Lake Blvd.,
Carnelian Bay
garwoods.com
(530) 546-3366

La Fondue (French)
120 Country Club Dr.,
Incline Village
laketahoefondue.com
(775) 831-6104

Le Bistro (French)
120 Country Club Dr.,
Incline Village
lebistrotahoe.com
(775) 831-0800

Lone Eagle Grille, Hyatt Regency Lake Tahoe
(American)
111 Country Club Dr.,
Incline Village
loneeaglegrille.com
(775) 886-6899

T's Mesquite Rotisserie
(American Grill)
901 Tahoe Blvd.,
Incline Village
tsrotisserie.com
(775) 831-2832

LAKE TAHOE—SOUTH

Chart House (American)
392 Kingsbury Grade,
Stateline
chart-house.com
(775) 588-6276

Tahoe Tavern & Grill
(American)
219 Kingsbury Grade,
Stateline
tahoetavernandgrill.com
(775) 580-6226

RENO

The Kitchen Table
(American)
530 W. Plumb Ln.
thekitchentablereno.com
(775) 384-3959

La Strada, Eldorado hotel-casino (Italian)
345 N. Virginia St.
caesars.com
(775) 348-3401

Louis' Basque Corner
301 E. 4th St.
louisbasquecorner.com
775) 323-7203

Oyster Bar, Nugget Casino Resort
1100 Nugget Ave., Sparks
cnty.com/nugget
(775) 356-3300

Step Korean Bistro
2855 N. McCarran Blvd.,
Sparks
stepkoreanbistro.com
(775) 622-8925

FOR MORE INFORMATION IN RENO–TAHOE TERRITORY

Lake Tahoe Visitors Authority
4114 Lake Tahoe Blvd.,
South Lake Tahoe
visitlaketahoe.com
(530) 542-4637

North Lake Tahoe Community Alliance
100 N. Lake Blvd., Tahoe City
gotahoenorth.com
(530) 581-6900

**Reno-Sparks Convention
and Visitors Authority**
4065 S. Virginia St.
visitrenotahoe.com
(775) 827-7600

Virginia City Tourism Commission
86 S. C St.
visitvirginiacitynv.com
(775) 847-7500

Visit Carson City
716 N. Carson St.
visitcarsoncity.com
(775) 687-7410

Visit Carson Valley
1477 UA 395 N., Gardnerville
visitcarsonvalley.org
(775) 782-8145

Cowboy Country

Elko County

You want to really find Nevada off the beaten path? Journey into ***Jarbidge.*** In fact, this part of Nevada is impassable from within the state for more than six months of the year; snow blocks the mountain passes and roads. To arrive at Jarbidge, enter through Idaho to the north. Take US 93 about 76 miles out of Twin Falls to Beaver Lane in Owyhee County, Idaho. After crossing into Elko County, Nevada, take SR 746/North Fork of Charleston Road about 15 miles to head into Jarbidge Canyon. You can't miss the border; it's doubly marked, with a boulder on the left slope that has ID/NV painted on it and a used road-grader blade containing similar markings on the left shoulder. And note that while the first 76 miles will take you about 1 hour and 45 minutes, the last 15 on a dirt/gravel road will take just over an hour. Get used to it; there are no paved roads within 20 miles of Jarbidge. And the Jarbidge Community Association points out that instead of trusting your GPS, it's best to get advice from a local. Luckily, members maintain an active Facebook page to answer questions.

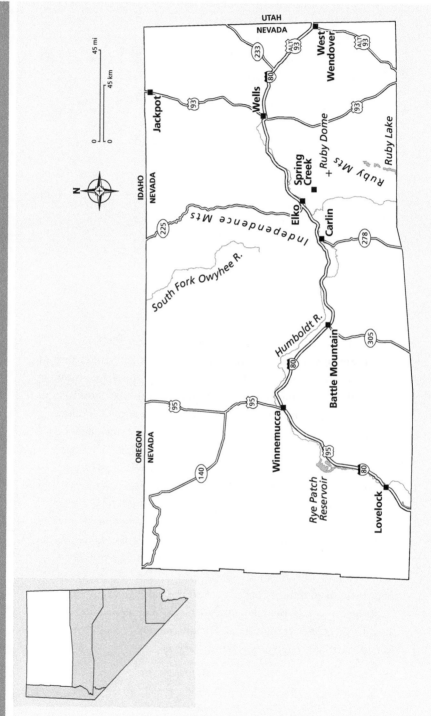

COWBOY COUNTRY

As in nearly every Nevada drive, be alert for open-range cattle. You may round a bend to find a cattle drive in progress on the roadbed. When you aren't dodging cattle, look out across the fields for a lone coyote.

The winding gravel road leads you by towering rock spires rising along the banks of the gorge. Twisted evergreens cling to the rocky banks. Keep the window rolled down to experience the roar of the tumbling Jarbidge River.

Past the state border 8 miles, after you enter the beautiful Humboldt-Toiyabe National Forest, you come upon the ***Jarbidge Historical Marker,*** designating Jarbidge Canyon as the site of the West's last stagecoach robbery and murder. The foul deed took place on windswept, snow-covered December 5, 1916. The stage, bound from Three Creek, Idaho, to Jarbidge, carried pay for the men at the mines and mills, as well as $3,200 in small bills for Crumley & Walker, owners of the Success Saloon and Restaurant, and a $1,000 cashier's check for the proprietor of the candy store.

A search party, formed after the stagecoach failed to arrive on time, found the dead body of driver Fred Searcy sprawled on the seat. Mr. J. T. McCormick, owner of the general store and an excellent hunter, made casts of dog prints found at the site. After a bit of sleuthing, the search party found the stray dog that had made the prints. The dog in turn led them to a slashed mail sack with a bloody palm print later linked to gambler Ben Kuhl.

Kuhl and several associates were charged with the robbery and murder. The trial was noteworthy because it was the first time prints were introduced as evidence. On October 16, 1917, the jury delivered a guilty verdict of murder in the first degree, carrying the penalty of death by shooting or hanging, at the option of the defendant. Kuhl's sentence was commuted to life imprisonment on December 13, 1918. He served 35 years before being released on parole and died of pneumonia five years later.

Accomplice Edward "Cut-Lip Swede" Beck was found guilty of conspiracy and received a life sentence, serving six years in the state prison. William McGraw, who lent the murder

it's jarbidge (not jarbridge)

How did they come up with that name? Jarbidge, a onetime mining town in the scenic far north, is one of Nevada's most mispronounced places. Jarbidge is the anglicized version of *Tsaw-haw-bitts*, a word from Shoshone folklore. The giant Tsawhawbitts lived in Jarbidge Canyon and preyed on natives, tossing them into a basket slung across his back. Reaching home, he tossed them into a kettle to cook up for dinner. The Shoshone avoided the canyon until it filled up with people during the mining boom. They pronounced the canyon "Ja-ha-bich," eventually spelling it Jarbidge.

weapon to Beck, was never put on trial due to lack of evidence. The loot was never recovered.

Continue another 0.5 mile to enter Jarbidge and go back in time to a century or so ago. Jarbidge (pronounced like garbage with a J) derives from the Native American word *Tsawhawbitts*, meaning "bad or evil spirit" and relating to a legendary cannibalistic giant who roamed the nearby mountains and valleys, capturing people, putting them into a basket, and then returning to Jarbidge Canyon to devour them. Evidence of Native American hunting parties in the area trace back more than 10,000 years.

The cry of "Gold!" by prospector David Bourne in 1909 forced Congress to carve Jarbidge out of the boundaries of the Humboldt National Forest, which had been created in 1908. More than 1,500 miners flooded into the region, helping the Jarbidge district replace Goldfield as Nevada's premier gold-producing region. The Elkoro Mining Company ranked as Nevada's number one gold producer in 1918 and 1919. Overall, Jarbidge mines produced more than $9 million in gold before they played out in the late 1920s, with the last mine (Elkoro) giving up the ghost in the 1930s. In the early years, rooming was so scarce that hostelers rented out their bunks on a three-shift basis.

As early as the 1880s, a Basque sheepherder claimed he discovered a rich vein of gold quartz in the canyon; however, he died before he could return to the property. Some versions of the story claim that a fight broke out with a partner, who was killed. In any event, the famed Lost Sheepherder's Ledge has never been relocated and awaits your discovery.

Today around a dozen residents keep Jarbidge alive year-round, with the population exploding to more than 100 during the summer. Residents know how to enjoy themselves with an annual Memorial Day Weekend parade and barbecue and Labor Day Weekend parade, plus Jarbidge Days in August, the Jarbidge Arts Council Wine Walk in September, and a Halloween Pig Roast

AUTHOR'S TOP PICKS

Cowboy Poetry Gathering, Elko

Basque Festivals,
Elko and Winnemucca
Jarbidge

Elko and Winnemucca

Angel Lake, Wells

Cottonwood Guest Ranch and Hunting Service, Wells

Ruby 360 Ranch and Ruby Mountain Helicopter Skiing

Wild Horse State Recreation Area

Northeastern Nevada Museum

J. K. Capriola Co.

and Costume Party. In addition, Jarbidgeites are always open to spontaneous reasons to celebrate. Weather permitting, opening of mountain passes and an influx of visitors take place around mid- to late June.

Jarbidge is truly off the beaten path. Mail arrives on Mon, Wed, and Fri; not until the 1980s, after nearly 40 years of being "out of service," did the telephone return to the town. But that doesn't mean there's not plenty to see and do in the area. A walk down the center of town on the dirt street offers both history and entertainment.

But first settle into the *Tsawhawbitts Ranch Bed & Breakfast* at 1052 W. Side Dr., which is on the right as you come into the north end of town. Look for the stone walls and log arch entrance to the property. The log structure nestled in the pines was built in 1974 as a hunting retreat and purchased in 1989 by present owners Krinn and Chuck McCoy. Buildings include the main house, carriage house (originally a dairy barn in the mining days and later a machine shop), and party house. The carriage house sleeps 8 and contains a full kitchen and laundry facilities. The party house sleeps 4.

The spacious main house has 3 bedrooms on the ground floor and 3 upstairs, with a large common area for reading, watching television, playing games, or pursuing other forms of relaxation. Be sure to look at the historic photos on the wall in the common area, the topographic map near the river entrance, and unique area antiques. If you study the old photos of the tent-town days, you'll see the names JAHABITTS and JAHABICH painted on a board

TOP ANNUAL EVENTS

Cowboy Poetry Gathering
Elko, Jan
westernfolklife.org
(775) 738-7508

Lamoille Country Fair
Lamoille, Jun
gfwclamoillewomensclubnv.org
(775) 777-1400.

Annual Winnemucca Basque Festival
Winnemucca, Jun
euskalkazeta.com

National Basque Festival
Elko, Jul
elkobasqueclub.com
(775) 934-3217

Silver State Stampede
Elko, Jul
silverstatestampede.com

Bonneville Salt Flats Speed Week
West Wendover, Aug
saltflats.com
(801) 977-4300

Elko County Fair
Elko, Labor Day Weekend
elkocountyfair.com
(775) 738-3616

Elko Gold Rush Challenge
Elko, Sept
elkogoldrushchallenge.com

above the tent flaps. That gives you a clue as to how tongues got twisted from Tsawhawbitts to Jarbidge. Call (775) 488-2338.

Take a stroll through town, crossing the wooden bridge on the north end. Your first stop should be the **Trading Post,** a true one-stop shop for snacks, groceries, candles, beer and wine, and hunting and fishing gear. On a chilly morning, the old woodstove will provide comfort, as will the conversation and advice from owner Cindy Wilmarth and other local residents. The building was constructed in 1912 and moved to Jarbidge in 1923, after the mines around nearby Pavlak played out. It's at 889 W. Side Ave.; call (775) 488-2315.

The 1911 **Historic Jarbidge Jail,** right next door at 899 W. Side Ave., is managed and protected by the town of Jarbidge. Inside its stone walls, visitors, who are on the honor system, can see the old iron cell that confined the likes of Ben Kuhl, as well as an original prisoner cot, and look through original old mining claims and records such as 1920s purchase orders for the Elkoro Mine Company, headquartered at 120 Broadway in New York City. Don't miss the old mining implements hanging on the outside of the jail. For more information, ask at the Trading Post.

Just beyond the jail on the right is the old red-light district, whose log structures with caved-in roofs provide a new definition of air-conditioning. There are plenty of interesting structures left over from the mining days, such as a house with dozens of antlers on the porch roof.

The late local writer Helen Wilson, author of *Gold Fever*, was a native of Jarbidge and spent part of each year there, well into her 90s. *Gold Fever* is a Nevadan tale about Jarbidgeites. It relates stories about Helen's mother and father, hardships endured, and letters tied in a bundle with a blue ribbon. Helen's 1910 cabin is noted by a sign.

For food and entertainment, there are the **Outdoor Inn** and the **Red Dog Saloon.** The wood-clad Outdoor Inn features an ornate solid-mahogany bar and backbar crafted in Europe. After its trip around the Horn in 1890, it survived the 1906 San Francisco earthquake and later resided in the Golden Nugget Saloon in Las Vegas before making the journey to Jarbidge. Tall, carved-wood statues of Greek mythological figures Pan and Aphrodite highlight the backbar. The Outdoor Inn is owned by Jason Stegall, who purchased the historic structure in 2018 and also owns the Outdoor Inn Motel and The Barn Hotel & RV Park. For more information, call (775) 488-2311.

While the Outdoor Inn is open seasonally, its sister establishment the Red Dog Saloon serves all year. It tempts visitors with its sign promising "ice-cold beer and pop" and serves breakfast, lunch, and dinner. As you'd imagine, the interior is filled with historical artifacts. The Red Dog is at 599 Main St.; call (775) 488-2311.

Continuing up the street, you pass over a creek race with mining equipment alongside. Stop and read the historical marker near the school. The tiny school, which eventually served as few as six students, has closed.

The **Humboldt-Toiyabe National Forest** surrounding Jarbidge provides a host of recreational opportunities. The forest is broken into several distinct pieces, and we visit other parts of it in this and other sections of this book. Combined, the segments encompass 6.3 million acres, making it the largest national forest in the lower 48 states. Terrain and scenery range from sage-covered lowlands to canyons with sheer rock walls to towering mountain peaks. Southeast of Jarbidge, Mount Matterhorn (no, the other one) rises to a height of 10,843 feet. For maps, publications, weather, road and avalanche information, and permits including one that will enable you to cut your own Christmas tree, visit fs.usda.gov/htnf or call (775) 738-5171 or (775) 331-6444.

The **Jarbidge Wilderness** remains one of the nation's least-visited wilderness areas. Its varied terrain ranges from desert at about 5,000 feet to mountains of more than 10,000. There are about 170 miles of trail extending from several trailheads, some of them improved dirt roads, others accessible only by four-wheel-drive vehicles. The Jarbidge Wilderness provides some of the best mountain biking and brook-trout fishing in the country. This truly is wilderness; you can travel for days without seeing another person. Many of the wilderness's most breathtaking sights, such as pristine Emerald Lake, at an elevation of 9,200 feet, are best reached on horseback. Information is available from the Mountain City–Ruby Mountains–Jarbidge Ranger District offices in Elko or Wells at (775) 738-5171 or (775) 752-1799.

The services of a professional guide are recommended. They provide everything from pack and transport animals, gear, food, and expertise. The Prunty family's **Jarbidge Wilderness Guide and Packing** has a long tradition of guide trips in the Jarbidge Wilderness dating back to the 1940s and involving four generations of the family. The Prunty family homesteaded in Charleston, Nevada, only 3 miles from the wilderness, and became well known in rodeo circles for their bucking stock.

Groups are limited to 6, although larger group tours may be arranged; families with children older than 6 also are welcome. The fee for a 6-day pack trip including food, tents, sleeping pads, and related equipment (you'll bring your sleeping bag and personal gear) is $2,700 per person, with a $1,000 non-refundable deposit. Base-camp adventures for 3 days are $1,500 per person with a $500 deposit. For reservations and more information, visit jarbidge adventures.com or call (208) 857-2270.

Backtrack to Rogerson, Idaho, turn right onto US 93 South and drive about 85 miles to **Wells** (population 1,267). Wells started out as an important resting spot and watering hole along the California Trail. From 1845 through 1870, thousands of emigrants traveling by covered wagon each year rested from their grueling trip and prepared themselves for the rest of the journey across the Humboldt Valley to California. Humboldt Wells was formally established upon completion of the Central Pacific Railroad in 1869; its name was shortened to Wells in 1873.

Wells is the gateway to **Angel Lake,** which is reached via the 12-mile **Angel Lake Scenic Byway,** also known as Angel Lake Road. The lake itself is at an elevation of 8,500 feet in the beautiful Ruby Mountains, and as you make your way to the recreation area, you'll wind through pine, quaking aspen, mountain mahogany, piñon pine, and sagebrush. Keep your eyes open for wildlife, which include pronghorn antelope, mule deer, bighorn sheep, and mountain goats, some of which you may see on the drive up.

Angel Lake, which is surrounded by glacial cirques—bowl-shaped depressions—is a good place to catch rainbow, tiger, and brook trout. Motorized boats are prohibited, but fishing from canoes or float tubes is fine. Ambitious hikers may be inspired by Hole-in-the-Mountain Peak, the highest point in the East Humboldts. The numerous hiking trails include the Smith Lake Trail, which begins at the Angel Lake Campground (26 sites available by reservation, plus day-use picnic areas) to the northern edge of the East Humboldt Wilderness. For more information, call (775) 752-3357. For campground reservations and information, visit fs.usda.gov.

The Krenka Ranch in Ruby Valley is home to **Hidden Lake Outfitters,** where owner and head guide Henry Krenka offers hunting services as well as fishing, camping, photography trips, and trail rides from his family's 125-year-old ranch. Visit hiddenlakeoutfitters.com or call (775) 779-2268.

Annual events in Wells include the 4th of July Parade, Independence Day Golf Scramble, and fireworks in July, junior rodeo in August, and Christmas Parade of Lights in December. Visit cityofwellsnv.com or call (775) 752-3355.

Wells is also the center of an important agricultural region, and Nevada's only agricultural ghost town, **Metropolis,** lies 14 miles northwest of the city. To reach Metropolis from downtown Wells, cross the railroad track at 7th Street, turn left on 8th Street and follow the road as it winds out of town, heading west and bypassing the railroad overpass. The road turns to gravel 11 miles later, and 1 mile down the road you'll cross a cattle guard. Make an immediate left and continue another 1.5 miles; you'll spot the ruins on your right. Faded wooden signs mark the way.

Born out of an investment dream for an innovative agricultural community, Metropolis was virtually carved out of the sagebrush with grand aspirations. East Coast financier Harry L. Pierce organized investors to form the Metropolis

Land Improvement Company and related Pacific Reclamation Company (PRC) in 1910. In 1911 the PRC completed the 100-foot-high Bishop Creek Dam, partly with brick rubble left over from the 1906 San Francisco earthquake. Plans were in place to irrigate, with water diverted from the dam, 40,000 acres of land purchased by the PRC.

The PRC recruited industrious Mormon farmers with track records of improving the land under the most adverse conditions. The PRC sold land to the farmers for $75 and up per acre for irrigated land and $10 to $15 per acre for dry-farming plots. Town lots sold for $100 to $300. More than 700 farmers, approximately two-thirds Mormons, settled into the Metropolis area. Investors envisioned a thriving town of 7,500 residents.

Streets, lots, and parks were plotted in 1911. By the fall of 1911, the Southern Pacific Railroad built an 8-mile railroad spur that carried impressed visitors into the fast-growing town. The Amusement Hall was the first Metropolis building, quickly followed by Hotel Metropolis in January 1912. The $75,000 hotel was proclaimed the largest between Denver and San Francisco. Its three stories of red pressed brick boasted steam heat, electric lights, running water, a marble-tiled lobby, a billiard room, a barbershop, a newsstand, and a bank. Out of its 50 rooms, 30 had baths. A lavish grand opening on December 29, 1911, formally opened Hotel Metropolis. The four-block commercial district had graded streets, concrete sidewalks, fire hydrants, and electric streetlights.

All of this was reported in the town's newspaper, the *Metropolis Chronicle*, which began publication in September 1911. All started out well; the land proved productive, with turkey red wheat growing to shoulder height, yielding 30 bushels per unirrigated acre.

Legal battles, however, initiated by local ranchers and farmers over water rights, proved disastrous for the PRC and Metropolis. The courts found in favor of the locals, limiting the amount of water the PRC could draw to one-tenth the amount needed to irrigate 40,000 acres. The company went into receivership in April 1913 and finally went bankrupt in 1920.

Other problems befell Metropolis. Several years of drought, followed by an invasion of crop-eating jackrabbits, put the final nail in its coffin.

Hotel Metropolis closed in 1913 (and burned in 1936); the newspaper stopped its presses in late 1913; the last train departed Metropolis in 1925; the Lincoln School (opened in September 1914 at a cost of $25,000 with a student capacity of 180) discontinued high school classes in 1940 and grammar classes in 1949; and the Metropolis US Post Office canceled its last stamp in 1942.

The farmers and ranchers who did remain proved successful, as the exodus of others left adequate water supplies. Likewise, the Metropolis area social life flourished, with dances, parties, hot springs outings, quiltings, and other social gatherings. Today, no one lives in town, and all that remains are foundations for Hotel Metropolis and the lone entrance arch of the two-story Lincoln School.

Stop at the Metropolis memorial plaque across the road from the schoolhouse arch. It gives a brief history of the town and includes historic photographs. The arch represents a fantastic and memorable photo opportunity. For safety's sake, don't climb over the ruins. If you continue down the dirt road between the sagebrush that brought you to Metropolis, you will arrive at the newer cemetery (the old one contains only a few remaining graves and headstones, and you'll need a guide to get you there).

After a day among the ruins, head back to Wells. On the east side of the Jarbidge wilderness you'll find the **Cottonwood Guest Ranch,** a working horse and cattle ranch owned by six generations of the Smith family. Activities include ATV riding and mountain biking, snowmobiling in winter, and bird- and wildlife-watching.

Lodge rooms sleep 2 to 3 people and have private baths. An optional meal package covers continental breakfast, sack lunch, dinner, or any combination of the three. There's also an RV park, dry camping, and periodic retreats for postwar service members. Visit cottonwoodguestranch.com or call (755) 472-0222.

If you're interested in rifle, archery, or muzzle-loader hunting, the affiliated **Cottonwood Ranch Hunting Service** is the place to arrange and experience high-country hunts on horseback. The service has a sole-use permit for half of the wilderness and ability to access about 75 percent of it. Drop-camp service is available for independent hunters who'd rather go it alone.

Jason Molsbee has been guiding for the service for more than 20 years and makes his home at the ranch. Colleague Blain Jackson has been guiding for more than 28 years in the wilderness and surrounding areas. They can lead you on hunts for elk, mule deer, pronghorn antelope, bighorn sheep, mountain lions, and "varmints" such as coyotes and squirrels. Trips range from $8,900 for a 6-day fully guided bull elk hunt to $4,000 for a 3-day guided antelope hunt. Predator and varmint hunts are $575 a day. For more information or reservations, visit cottonwoodranchhs.com or call Jackson at (435) 770-8092 or Molsbee at (208) 852-6199.

Head west from Wells about 30 miles on I-80, and you'll come to the Halleck Interchange. A Nevada Historic Marker at the site tells the story of Camp Halleck (1867), later renamed Fort Halleck (1879). It was originally built to provide protection for travelers along the California Trail and construction workers laying the tracks for the Central Pacific Railroad. Ironically, Fort Halleck troops never engaged local tribes in battle but did participate in skirmishes with the Modoc tribe of California (1873), the Nez Percé in Idaho (1877), the Bannock tribe in Oregon (1878), and the Apaches in Arizona (1883). The government disbanded the fort on December 1, 1886.

Continuing west an additional 20 miles brings you to **Elko** (population 21,048), once voted "Best Small Town in America." A midsize-to-large town by Nevada standards, Elko keeps going due to a boom in gold mining in the immediate area that more than doubled the city's population from 1985 to 1995. A number of gold-mining companies maintain offices in Elko and operate mines in the vicinity. Nevada is the gold capital of North America, producing more than 75 percent of gold mined in the United States, which is fourth in production in the world.

Fur trappers visited the area in the 1820s, as did famed explorers John C. Frémont and Kit Carson. The forty-niners trod the California Trail near Elko as they followed the Humboldt River westward.

Elko rose out of the Nevada landscape as a rough-and-tumble tent city alongside the track of the Central Pacific Railroad in December 1868. Legend has it that the railroad's Charles Crocker liked to name railhead towns after animals and added an "o" to make the pronunciation easier. When the Golden Spike linked the Central Pacific and Union Pacific at Promontory Point, Utah, many of the Central Pacific's Chinese track crew were simply abandoned. A number of them made their way to Elko, where they raised vegetables. They are credited with building the city's first water system, consisting of a reservoir and a nearly 10-mile ditch to carry water through what is now City Park.

In 1869 the state legislature created Elko County out of Lander County and made Elko the county seat, complete with a new courthouse. A year later, Josiah and Elizabeth Potts climbed the gallows and were hanged. The Pottses had been convicted of murdering a wealthy old horse trader, Miles Faucett. Upon hearing the reading of the death warrant, Elizabeth Potts proclaimed, "I am innocent, so help me God!" She attempted to cheat the gallows the morning before the scheduled hanging by slitting her wrists with a razor, but her efforts were thwarted by the death watch of J. Stanley Taber. Elizabeth was the only woman ever legally hanged in Nevada. The gallows was constructed in Placerville, California, tested with weights, and then knocked down for shipment to Elko, where it was rebuilt in a corner of the jail yard adjacent to the courthouse.

Covering the hanging, the San Francisco *Daily Report* commented, "It is to the credit of Elko, that it hangs a woman guilty of murder. It is a dreadful thing to hang a woman, but not so dreadful as for a woman to be a murderer. . . . In San Francisco Mrs. Potts would certainly have either been acquitted or pronounced insane, and would have walked out of court a free woman."

Other Elko firsts include the first high school in Nevada and the first site for the University of Nevada, from 1874 to 1885. Continuing its firsts in education,

Elko became home to Nevada's first community college, in 1967. *Nellie Brown*, one of the first novels written by a Black American, was published in 1871 by Thomas Detter, proprietor of Elko's Silver Brick shaving saloon and bathing establishment. He was instrumental in forcing change in the Nevada law that prohibited Black children from attending public schools. In 1875 Detter delivered a major speech in San Francisco at the anniversary celebration of the Emancipation Proclamation. Elko became the first town to relocate the railroad tracks that formed a barrier through the middle of town.

Near the Elko Airport is the site of the nation's first successful oil shale distillation facility. Robert M. Catlin Sr. drove the main shaft beginning in 1916. The plant operated for a few years in the 1920s, producing an average of 36 gallons of crude oil per ton of shale but not enough to compete with cheaper fossil fuels. The airport hosted another first. On April 6, 1926, Varney Air Lines pilot Leon Cuddeback landed his biplane at Elko, completing the first scheduled airmail run in the United States. A historical marker at the Elko Airport terminal commemorates the 460-mile flight from Pasco, Washington, to Elko with an intermediate stop at Boise, Idaho, for fuel and mail.

Your first stop in Elko should be the ***Northeastern Nevada Museum,*** which contains a wealth of Elko County and Nevada history and art, starting with the 1860 Ruby Valley Pony Express Cabin outside of the museum. Originally located 60 miles south of Elko, it was moved in 1960 in celebration of the 100th anniversary of the Pony Express. Although the Pony Express lasted only 18 months, it left its mark on Western history forever.

trivia

The *Northeastern Nevada Museum* in Elko displays the "hoof-shoes" worn by 1930s cattle rustler Crazy Tex, who fooled experienced trackers by perfecting the stride of a cow.

Inside the museum, you'll will find more than 40 custom cases displaying historic artifacts covering explorations, railroads, mining, and ranching. Other displays evoke the early lives of the Native American, cowboy, Basque, and Chinese people in the area.

The museum's R. C. & Mary Ellis Gallery exhibits a collection of works by Will James, who was a legendary Western artist, author, and cowboy. The Halleck Bar Gallery displays the legendary bar as well as rotating art and cultural exhibits, and the Barrick Gallery shows rotating exhibits.

The museum is at 1515 Idaho St. and is open Tues through Sat from 9 a.m. to 5 p.m. and Sun from 1 to 5 p.m. Admission is $8 for most adults, $4 for seniors, students, and children 13 to 18, and $2 for children younger than 13. Visit museumelko.org or call (775) 738-3418.

The historic Pioneer Building, which began life as a saloon and then a hotel, houses the **Western Folklife Center** at 501 Railroad St. Its mission is to give voice to old and new cultures of the West, which it does through permanent and changing exhibitions. They might include collections such as *Right Where We Belong: Thirty Years of Contemporary Cowboy Gear*, with exhibits of utilitarian craftsmanship such as saddles, bits, and spurs. A recent temporary exhibit, *The Pioneer Hotel: A Place Where We Belong*, traced its history from the first bar in Elko to its current status as a cultural center complete with theaters, saloon, and gift shop as well as the exhibit gallery.

But the center is perhaps best known for the annual National Cowboy Poetry Gathering in late January, which since 1985 has celebrated the bards of the West as well as Western artists and musicians. Celebrated cowboy poets such as Waddie Mitchell enlighten and entertain audiences with their tales. Workshops on such topics as rawhide braiding, leather stamping, Basque cooking, journaling, music marketing, and daily ranch life also are presented during the weeklong event.

The gift shop and gallery are open from 10 a.m. to 5:30 p.m. weekdays and 10 a.m. to 5 p.m. Sat. For more information, visit westernfolklife.org or call (775) 738-7508.

Make time for a historic walking tour of Court Street. Start at the intersection of 4th Street, where you'll see the Map House, built in 1849 and the oldest house in Elko. Just down the block is Pythian Castle Hall, built for the fraternal order in 1927 at 421 Ct. You'll notice the Palladian-style windows, the red brick adorned with terra-cotta medallions, and the Roman numerals CDXXI, for 421. Now move along to the intersection of 6th Street to view the first county high school in Nevada, opened in 1895; Elko County offices now occupy the building. The Bradley House, at 643 Court St., was built in 1904 for John Rueben Bradley, the son of Nevada's second governor (an Elko cattleman), and is highlighted by a rounded turret and white trim. At 705 Court St., the 1910 McBride Home is surrounded by massive pines and other lush greenery. Wind up your tour at the Dewar Home at 745 Court St., built in 1869, soon after the town was established. Its red brick and white porch are now surrounded by large pines.

As you wander around town, watch for the **Centennial Boots** public-art installations, dozens of 6-foot-tall hand-painted cowboy boots at local businesses and parks that add a dash of color to the drabbest winter landscape.

You'll see real western horsemanship—and lots of normal-sized cowboy boots—at the **Spring Creek Horse Palace.** The 1,500-seat arena with a 150-by-300-foot show floor (there's also a lighted outdoor arena) welcomes spectators watching such events as the Spring Creek Kick-Off Rodeo in April.

Because the center is open daily, you also might catch cowboys—or novices or experienced equine aficionados—perfecting their art.

The center, which includes a bar and coffee shop, is in Spring Creek just southwest of Elko via SR 227. Visit springcreeknv.org or call (775) 753-6295.

The area is rich in Basque heritage, traced to the sheepherders who came from the Pyrenees Mountains in Spain and France. So it's only fitting that it's home to the annual *National Basque Festival,* a 2-day event over the 4th of July weekend. For more than 60 years, the festival has drawn a wide pool of ethnic Basques and those interested in the culture. Events include a parade in native clothing, traditional Basque music, jota (Basque folk) dancing, and strength competitions. Basque or not, you can be sure you'll be greeted whole-heartedly with *ongi etorri* (welcome).

The Elko Euzkaldunak, the organization that sponsors the festival, also presents the Sheepherder's Ball in March. Open to the public, the event includes a full Basque dinner and silent auction. For more information on the ball or festival, visit elkobasqueclub.com or call (775) 934-3217.

trivia

The *Cowboy Poetry Gathering* was voted the best special event in rural Nevada in a *Nevada Magazine* reader's poll.

A variety of Elko-area events in addition to the National Cowboy Poetry Gathering and National Basque Festival await your participation: Fire in the Hole Cornhole Tournament in May; the Silver State Stampede, a rodeo more than 100 years old, in Jul; Elko Art in the Park in Jul; Elko Gold Rush Challenge bucking bulls competition in Sept; and Ruby Mountain Balloon Festival in Spring Creek in Sept.

Pick up a souvenir of the West or stock up on supplies at world-renowned *J. M. Capriola & Co.* at 500 Commercial St., which has been family owned and operated for nearly 100 years. This is where the real cowboys shop for handmade saddles, bits, and spurs, crafted right there in the upstairs shop. Choose some new duds from a large selection of ranch wear, cowboy boots, and hats for the whole family, plus stirrups, ropes, silver collectibles, and everything needed for the ranch house. Capriola's made the saddle that won the gold medal at the 1904 St. Louis World's Fair, and then another at the Lewis and Clark Exposition in Portland, Oregon, making it the only saddle in history to win two gold medals. A legion of famous people is on its client list. Hours are 9 a.m. to 5 p.m. Mon through Sat. Visit capriolas.com or call (775) 738-5816.

By now you should have worked up an appetite and can enjoy some good dining, Elko style. To be sure, you must partake of at least one Basque meal

Waddie Mitchell Recites His Poetry

When **Waddie Mitchell,** America's favorite cowboy poet, threw a leg over his horse, a few of us inside the chuck wagon heard a seam rip. "Think I've worn out my britches," he grinned behind his waxed mustache, and followed the tiny chuck wagon down a dirt road. Crossing an old stagecoach road, the wagon pulled up to a clearing where, under a lone juniper tree, Sam the camp cook was setting out lunch meat, rolls, and potato salad. With sandwiches on our laps, Waddie began talking. He likes to do recitations, he told us, outdoors under the Nevada sky. The cowboys and Nevada: It's a natural fit. Ranchers attracted by the unfenced land brought long-horns up from Texas after the Civil War. Ranch life since then has been simple, basic, yet has spawned a lot of creativity. Cowboys find time to paint, compose songs, and to write poetry and practice reciting it around campfires. Mitchell's words spoke volumes of the loneliness of cowboy life on cattle drives. We were moved by a poem about his daughter, a true story, measured out in rhyme and meter, of how she had grown up before he knew it.

He has been busy for the past couple of decades. He was out on a cattle drive when the call came from Johnny Carson to appear on the *Tonight Show*. Invitations blew in from everywhere. He has recited poetry at the Rainbow Room in Manhattan, for black-tie events, and at Stanford University. Now he's the headliner at the Poetry Gathering. When Waddie Mitchell and Hal Cannon conceived an event in Nevada centered on cowboy poetry, Waddie was against the idea of calling it a festival. "This is what it's like out there on a cattle drive; cowboys gathering wherever the chuck wagon bell clangs, just as we are now." A beetle the size of the cowboy's famous handlebar mustache whirled by as he spoke. His horse neighed; Sam the camp cook clanked the kettle; and Waddie's boyhood friend, Don Farmer, just smiled. Full sun broke across the plain and sped east up the flanks of the Ruby Mountains.

before leaving town. ***The Star Hotel,*** which dates to 1910, is at 246 Silver St. and offers family-style dining in an old-world atmosphere. Dinner includes cabbage soup, tossed salad, French bread, Basque beans, pasta, green beans, french fries, and coffee or tea—and that's just getting started. Entrée choices include baked lamb, fried chicken, lamb chops, and pork chops, plus a number of steaks and variety of seafood. Lunch is only slightly lighter—and be sure to try a Picon punch. Visit elkostarhotel.com or call (775) 738-9925.

Toki Ona, 1550 Idaho St., also puts on the Basque feedbag, though in a lighter, updated way. Visit eattokiona.com or call (775) 778-3606.

And ***Ogi Basque Deli, Bar & Pintxos*** at 460 Commercial St. is even more updated, serving a grilled Basque breakfast wrap, Basque-style sandwiches, salads, and desserts. Visit ogideli.com or call (775) 753-9290.

Take SR 227 East out of Elko for about 25 miles, and you'll come to the town of ***Lamoille*** (population 55), at the base of the glacier-carved Ruby Mountains. Thomas Waterman, one of the first settlers in the valley, named it after an area in his beautiful native Vermont. The name stems from the French

LaMoutte, meaning "gull-inhabited," which was given to the Lamoille River in Vermont. The Lamoille Valley served as an important stopping point. Waterman's store, hotel, and blacksmith shop provided rest, supplies, and wagon repairs to emigrants continuing to point west.

The picturesque Lamoille Valley rivals any Swiss valley setting. Continue through the town to reach the Lamoille Community Presbyterian Church—"the Little Church of the Crossroads"—for a photo opportunity that sets the tone for a relaxing and rejuvenating stay. The church's steeple is framed by the majestic backdrop of the Ruby Mountains.

The long-standing **Pine Lodge Dinner House** sits south of the main road into Lamoille, among the pines, and is a favorite of locals and visitors alike. Drawing your attention around the interior of the restaurant are numerous taxidermied wildlife such as bear, deer, sheep, and rattlesnakes, captured in striking poses. On the menu are crispy artichoke hearts, marinated venison, shrimp scampi, and pesto gnocchi with chicken—and you can finish it off with cinnamon-vanilla bread pudding. It's open Wed through Sat; call (775) 753-6363.

The modern **Ruby 360 Lodge** at 301 Mountain View Dr. is quite a contrast to the historic buildings you've been seeing. It has the advertised 360-degree view of the glorious Ruby Mountains and 10 rooms, plus a ski room for changing or equipment storage. There are also 2 fully furnished yurts, one of which is at 9,700 feet. There are firepits around the property, a hot tub, and a full-service bar Thurs through Sat. Rooms include morning coffee and biscotti, although a heavier breakfast can be arranged. Dinners also can be arranged Thurs through Sat, summer through Oct. Visit rubylodge360 .com or call (775) 753-6867.

Joe and Francy Royer built the lodge to complement their **Ruby Mountain Helicopter Skiing,** which has been in business since 1977. This is a sure way to get a bird's-eye view of Lamoille Valley and the Ruby Mountains. When the weather's right, skiers and boarders can land and take off from 11,387-foot Ruby Dome and 14 other peaks above 11,000 feet.

Guided single-day heli-skiing is $1,882, which includes equipment, breakfast and lunch, and lodging on the first night. A guided 3-day trip with all meals and lodging is $5,950, and heli-assist group tours are available. Visit helicopter skiing.com or call (775) 753-6867.

No visit to the Elko/Lamoille area is complete without a trip up **Lamoille Canyon.** A two-lane, 12-mile paved scenic byway winds its way to a trailhead at an elevation of 8,600 feet. Along the way you'll see cascading waterfalls tumbling over glacier-carved rock formations as the river draws you deeper into the Ruby Mountain Area. Stop at one of the numerous trailheads or picnicking spots for viewing wildlife that include massive elk, bighorn sheep, cougars, grouse, hawks, and golden eagles; especially keep your eyes open for beaver ponds.

Rugged glaciated peaks that frequently draw comparisons to the Swiss Alps rise to more than 11,000 feet. On the return trip, you'll see rock formations and other sights from new perspectives and in a different light at various times of the day. Outbursts of bright wildflowers such as bluebells, iris, lupine, and larkspur mingle among the rocks. Pines and oak dot the mountainsides.

One of the most spectacular trails is the 43-mile **Ruby Crest National Recreation Trail,** which follows the crest of the Rubies to Harrison Pass to the south. Thru-hiking takes several days. A recommended thru-hiking itinerary is at travelnevada.com, which also lists a number of day hikes with varying degrees of difficulty.

For those with less time, a mile-long easy round trip on the Nature Trail takes off 0.5 mile north of Terraces Campground. For a moderately difficult 4- to 6-hour round-trip journey, take the Thomas Canyon Trail from Thomas Canyon Campground.

Campsites in Lamoille Canyon are typically in demand, so call for a reservation at (877) 444-6777 or recreation.gov. Rates, in season, run about $19; they're lower in the offseason.

For more information on the Ruby Mountains area, visit fs.usda.gov or call (775) 331-6444.

There are miles of roads and trails in this part of Nevada that are suitable for biking, from paved roads to trails of varying difficulties. Those with mountain biking on their minds can get information—and equipment and tune-ups—at **T-Rix Mountain Bikes,** 1490 Idaho St. in Elko; call (775) 777-8804.

Elko County contains 121 of the state's 535 streams and more than 33 percent of Nevada's reservoirs. Most of them contain trout, but a number are managed to provide game fishing of both largemouth and smallmouth bass, crappie, and catfish. Frozen reservoirs in the winter also allow fishers to experience ice fishing.

One of Nevada's newer state parks, **South Fork State Recreation Area,** is about 22 miles southwest of Lamoille. The park's 1,659-foot dam creates a reservoir for a diversity of water sports, such as boating, waterskiing, and fishing. Overnight camping is available at 25 campsites within 2,200 acres of scenic meadowland and rolling hills. The campground comes complete with restrooms, running water, and showers, and some hookups are available.

To get to South Fork State Recreation Area from Lamoille, take SR 227 about 13 miles to SR 228, and then travel about 14 miles to the park. Entrance fees are $5 per vehicle ($10 for non-Nevada vehicles); camping is $15 to $20,

and more for hookups. For more information, visit parks.nv.gov/parks/south
-fork or call (775) 744-4346.

Now prepare yourself for a ride (depending on weather conditions and
time of year) across the Rubies through Harrison Pass to the **Ruby Lake
National Wildlife Refuge.** From South Fork, return to SR 228 and head south
about 32 miles to Ruby Valley Road, then turn right on Ruby Valley. Along the
way you'll pass through **Jiggs** (population about 2).

You may think Jiggs is an unusual name, but the town and area post office
have sported a number of monikers, starting as Mound Valley and proceeding
through Cottonwood, Dry Creek, Hilton, and Skelton before a US postmaster
with a sense of humor rechristened the town Jiggs in 1918 after the *Bringing
Up Father* comic strip. Through the years, Jiggs has been a social center for area
ranchers who first set up shop here in the 1860s, although all that remains is
the Jiggs Bar (775-744-4311).

The road to the wildlife refuge is steep, winding, and rough and is closed
during certain times of the year due to weather. Note that Harrison Pass is not
maintained during the winter. Before starting out, check road conditions with
the US Forest Service at fws.gov/refuge/ruby-lake or (775) 779-2237.

The alternate route begins on I-80 about 20 miles east of Elko, at the Halleck interchange. Follow SR 229 southeast about 35 miles until you reach the
refuge headquarters, an additional 30-plus miles.

Either way, you will enjoy a spectacular drive around or through the
Rubies. Limited amounts of gasoline can be obtained on a seasonal basis at
Shantytown, so begin your trip with a full tank.

Established in 1938 by President Franklin D. Roosevelt, the refuge encompasses 39,928 acres of marshes, meadows, grasslands, and brush-covered upland
habitats. As many as 200-plus species of birds can be sighted. Be sure to take
along your binoculars to zero in on the graceful sandhill crane, great blue heron,
or red-tailed hawk. Birds such as the trumpeter swan and bald and golden eagles
may also be sighted. In a good year the refuge can produce 5,000 canvasback
and 4,000 redhead ducks.

Other wildlife also make the refuge their home. Keep a watchful eye out for
antelopes, badgers, beavers, bobcats, coyotes, mountain lions, mule deer, porcu-
pines, weasels, and other critters. A guide to birds, mammals, fish, amphibians,
reptiles, and their habitats in the refuge can be obtained at the refuge headquarters or at fws.gov/refuge/ruby-lake.

Note: You'll need to obtain licenses and duck stamps before arriving at the
refuge. Visit fws.gov/refuge/ruby-lake or call (775) 779-2237.

Here's a chance to see wildlife in a completely different form, on the other
side of the Humboldt River: 67 miles north of Elko, off SR 225, is the 120-acre

Wild Horse State Recreation Area on the northeast shore of Wild Horse Reservoir. The park is open year-round and offers a host of boating, camping, picnicking, and fishing activities—though no hunting.

The reservoir was formed by the construction of the original dam in 1937, with a 1970 enlargement bringing it to 3,000 acres. It's a great place to catch German and rainbow brown trout, small-mouth bass, yellow perch, and catfish. There's a boat ramp next to the beach. The 34 campsites include some pull-through sites for large RVs—a rarity in this part of the country—and restrooms and showers. The park also has 3 cabins for rent.

Admission is $5 per vehicle, or $10 for non-Nevada vehicles. There's a $10 fee for the boat ramp, and camping rates range from $15 to $20. For details, go to parks.nv.gov/parks/wild-horse or call (775) 385-5939.

While you may well see elk, pronghorn antelope, mule deer, and a variety of game birds in the park, ranching in the area has made the sighting of wild horses there less likely. But the animals who roamed so freely in the area that they led to the names of the park and reservoir can be spotted on the Owyhee Desert to the west.

westward bound

The world's greatest peacetime migration started in 1840. For nearly 30 years, more than 200,000 emigrants passed through Nevada on their way west in search of a better life. They walked beside oxen-drawn wagons over dusty ruts, across dry desert basins, muddy hills, rocks, mountains, and rivers. The ***Emigrant Trail,*** or California National Historic Trail, designated in 1992, has been marked across the state. To learn more about it, visit the California Trail Interpretive Center at 1 Interpretive Center Way in Elko. Visit californiatrailcenter.org or call (775) 738-4949.

Wild horses and burros roam much of the Nevada countryside. In fact, Nevada ranks first in the nation in the number of wild horses and burros, with an estimated 44,786 wild horses and 4,482 burros. The federal Bureau of Land Management manages 26.9 million acres of land across 10 Western states to help control the wild horse and burro populations, which can double every four years. The 1971 Wild-Free Roaming Horses and Burros Act declares them "living symbols of the historic and pioneer spirit of the West" and authorizes the BLM and US Forest Service to manage and protect the herds. To that end, they use some anti-fertility measures and also remove wild animals for placement in private care.

Thus, the BLM adoption and sales program, which has put nearly 290,000 wild horses and burros in private care since 1971. Those interested in owning a wild horse or burro must meet a detailed set of qualifications. There are permanent year-round adoption centers in Reno and Carson City, and online adoptions are now possible. When an animal has been adopted for a year, and the owner provides the proper paperwork, ownership is transferred to them. Animals that are more than 10 years old or have been offered for adoption three times can be purchased immediately by those meeting the qualifications.

For more information on the BLM Wild Horse and Burro Program, go to blm.gov/whb or call (866) 4MUSTANGS, or (866) 468-7826.

Backtracking a few miles south on SR 225, take a right (west) turn at the Lone Mountain Station Corner onto SR 226 to travel a mere 24 miles (branching left onto SR 789 for the last 6 miles), but back in history more than a century and a half to the ghost of the mining town of *Tuscarora* (population 89). During its peak mining days in 1878, Tuscarora's population rose to 5,000, exceeding that of the county seat Elko. At one time, more Chinese lived in Tuscarora than in any other place in America except San Francisco. Many of them arrived here after they were abandoned by the railroad.

Tuscarora sprang out of the earth with the discovery of gold by John and Steve Beard in 1867. Four years later, W. O. Weed discovered the rich Mount Blitzen silver lodes. The only Tuscarora gold mine, The Dexter, operated continuously until 1898. Major silver mines, such as the Argenta, Belle Isle, Commonwealth, Grand Prize, and Navajo, produced more than $7 million between 1871 and 1910. Overall, production estimates range from $10 million to $40 million. Due to the lack of wood in the area, almost all of the available sagebrush was collected to fire the mills. Six mills with a combined 80 stamps processed ore from the district's most productive mines. By 1915 only a handful of people resided in town—as is true today, despite a brief flurry of gold-mining activity that threatened to devour the town in the 1990s before the mining company collapsed in a flood of lawsuits.

A single-mill stack towers over the town like a lone sentinel waiting for the return of prosperity. Other remaining structures include a number of houses and the *Tuscarora Pottery School,* founded in 1966 by the late Dennis and Julie Parks. Art students have come here from all over the world. The facility includes galleries with the works of both Parks and his son, Ben, who now works as an ICU/medical-surgical nurse at Northeastern Nevada Regional Hospital in Elko when he's not creating art or directing the operation of Patho Phizz, which specializes in scrub tops adorned with patterns inspired by pathogens.

A dedicated staff, headed by president Cody Breese, a sculptural ceramicist and instructor, helps keep things humming. Workshops, with classes of no more than eight students, include community firings and topics such as soda firing.

The school has two showrooms and student residences in the old Zweifel Rooming House at 138 Main St., which dates to the mid-1800s and was moved to Tuscarora from the declining mining town of Cornucopia. The building also held the post office, as evidenced by the row of mailboxes in the hallway.

A geodesic dome dedicated to wheel throwing is Tuscarora's first new building since the time of the mines.

Public collections that include Parks's works cover the globe, from the Nevada Museum of Art to the Musée Ariana in Switzerland and from the Museum of Ceramics in Italy to Mimar Sinan Üniversitesi in Turkey. Often the school is open with not a soul in sight, but someone will arrive soon to visit with you and take you on a tour. For more information, visit tuscarorapottery.com.

The only other business surviving in town is the post office, which serves ranches throughout the valley, so you can stop in and mail a letter if you wish.

After visiting with the Tuscarora living, stop at the well-kept cemetery at the end of town to browse among the dead and read the tombstones. Tuscarora regained a brief bit of the limelight in 1992 when director David Schickele introduced his film *Tuscarora Lives* (detailing Tuscarora citizens' battle with an open-pit mining company) at the San Francisco Film Arts Festival.

Another nearly forgotten mining-town treat awaits you as you maneuver your vehicle over 42 miles of graveled, sometimes rutted, SR 789 west to **Midas.** Riding the ruts gives you a slight taste of what the emigrants and pioneers had to endure as they traveled by wagons across these old trails and roads. Pack your fishing rod, because along the way you'll pass Willow Creek Reservoir (ndow.org/waters/willow-creek-reservoir), with excellent angling. Be careful as you round the curves—many hundreds of sheep may be blocking the roadway. At the only fork in the road, turn right for the last 2 miles into Midas.

Gold was discovered here in 1907. The camp was originally called Gold Circle, because many gold mines encircled it. The name was changed to Midas in November 1907 with the establishment of the post office because postal officials worried that too many Nevada towns already had the word *gold* affixed to their names. By 1908 more than 2,000 people with hopes of striking it rich filled the tent city. The first murder occurred in a duel that year. Less than a year later, fewer than 250 miners remained, as low-grade ore and high transportation costs hampered operations.

Midas rebounded in 1915 with the construction of a 50-ton cyanide mill. Seven years later, fire destroyed the mill and mining ceased. In 1926 Gold Circle Consolidated Mines built a 75-ton mill and operated it until late 1929. Other mine and mill production continued until the beginning of World War II before shutting down. Overall, Midas-area mines produced more than $4 million in gold. After 1942 the town rapidly declined. The post office closed that year, followed by the school one year later. Today, the population of Midas is lower than the pounds of air in your tires.

Yet the future is a bit brighter. Mining is once again stirring in the area. Some newer houses and mobile homes are scattered among period mining shacks and abandoned machinery. Towering cottonwoods embrace the town as they stretch over the main street from both sides, creating a tunnel effect.

The organization *Friends of Midas*—which likes to say, "Midas is home to a few full-time residents and the hearts of many more"—has also brought new life to the old mining town. Its volunteers maintain the 1908 cemetery, which has only three granite markers, as others have been lost to weather and theft. Sales of the book *A Century of Enthusiasm: Midas, Nevada, 1907–2007* benefit the organization and are available on its website, friendsofmidas.com. Friends of Midas also maintains archives that it opens to those researching family history in the area.

If you're feeling thirsty—and it's open—stop at the seasonal *Midas Bighorn Saloon,* in a historic building in the center of town. The saloon doesn't serve much in the way of food but does have beer, wine, whiskey, and snacks. Call (775) 529-0203.

At this time, you can continue on to Golconda in Humboldt County, but we recommend a loop back to I-80 at Elko, to head west, virtually following the route of the Donner Party in 1846. Note the red rock structures as you proceed west from Elko.

Eureka County

A little beyond Carlin you enter Eureka County. At this point emigrants had to make an important decision: They could push on along the Humboldt River with fresh water and grasses for the oxen or take a more direct route and climb over Emigrant Pass, an elevation of 6,114 feet, as I-80 does today. On the Humboldt River Route through *Palisade,* travelers encountered steep, 800-foot basalt cliffs, leaving little room alongside the river for wagons. Most emigrants opted for the Emigrant Pass route, except when the river was low in dry years, and they could use the riverbed as the road.

Take a diversion to cover the 10-mile drive to Palisade and see where the Donner Party traveled. Follow SR 278 south to the Palisade cutoff on the right (west). It's easy to see how Palisade (originally called Palisades) derived its name from the red cliffs. As you maneuver the narrow dirt road hugging the mountain, peer over the left shoulder (it's very close) and see where the train enters a tunnel below you. You drop off the mountain ledge into what remains of Palisade. The wooden shack, built of railroad ties, at the fork is unique and a great photo opportunity. Turn right and go over the railroad track to get a better view of the Humboldt River and canyon route. It's also a handy place to get a wonderful shot of the railroad trestle and tunnel through the mountainside.

The town was laid out by the Central Pacific Railroad in February 1870. It rivaled Elko and Carlin as a departure point for wagon, freight, and stage lines to Eureka and points south. At its peak the railroad community of Palisade reached a population of 300 people. After the Eureka mines played out and closed in 1885, Palisade went into a decline. The Western Pacific began running through the town in 1908, but a flood in 1910 damaged the rail lines and swept away Palisade's hopes for revival. The post office finally shut down in 1962.

A gravel road from Palisade joins I-80 just east of Emigrant Pass but may require a four-wheel-drive vehicle and good weather. Check locally for road conditions before venturing out. To be on the safe side, it's only a little more than 10 miles back to the interstate at Carlin. On the other side of the pass, the trail once again struck the Humboldt River at Gravelly Ford, east of Beowawe (where there's a mining operation and geothermal power plant). This was the sight of several deaths, and three fenced graves remain here on private land.

Lander County

The **Battle Mountain** (population 4,187) area first drew attention around the 1830s, due to plentiful beavers in nearby rivers. By 1841 the first organized party of emigrants made its way through what is now the town. An estimated 60,000 wagons traveled along this route in 1852 alone. In 1866 prospectors discovered gold and silver in the hills southwest of town. Two years later, the Central Pacific Railroad reached here, and the town was born.

Ranching and mining have long been the main industries, with 19 major mines currently active in Lander County, including Nevada Gold Mine's Phoenix Project and Cortez mine, Hecla Mining Company, and various barite mines (barite being the principal ore for the element barium).

The origin of the name Battle Mountain remains a mystery. Various versions report a skirmish between Native Americans and a wagon train (1850), a survey crew (1857), and another emigrant party (1865). Take your pick.

For a trip through a historic mining area, take SR 305 south. Just after the overpass over I-80, turn left and follow the road to the foot of Lewis Canyon, where you veer left. As you enter the canyon, look for old mill sites, wooden water pipes, and other mining relics.

Some area history provides a little color. The town of Argenta stood 13 miles to the east. The first stage from Argenta to Austin carried 16 passengers.

The first passenger train arrived there on November 12, 1868, and the population shortly thereafter boomed to 500. On November 25, 1868, a drunken stage driver rolled over the Austin-bound stage (twice). The first fatal shooting took place on December 12, 1868: A desperado was shot dead, with "everyone taking credit." In February 1869, two men murdered another man in Winnemucca and fled to Argenta, where they terrorized the town before riding away. Argenta had to pack a lot of living into its short history. In March 1870 the rail began running from Battle Mountain instead of Argenta, sealing that community's fate. Argenta migrated lock, stock, and barrel to Battle Mountain.

Battle Mountain figured prominently in the women's suffrage movement as the location for the first recorded Woman Suffrage Convention, in 1870. Nevada, like a number of other western states, approved the vote for women prior to passage of the 1920 US constitutional amendment. Nevada women first went to the polls in 1915.

Humboldt County

The road out of Battle Mountain follows the Humboldt River northwest, crossing into Humboldt County. East of Golconda the Donner Party suffered a tragedy that foretold the panic and fear setting in and foreshadowed the even greater tragedies awaiting them in the future. On October 5, 1846, one of the Donner Party's leaders, James Reed, stabbed John Snyder to death during a dispute about driving the party's wagons over a steep, sandy hill approximately 10 miles east of *Golconda* (population 51). Reed pleaded self-defense but was contradicted by witness accounts reported to the council formed to investigate the matter. Some members wanted to hang Reed, but instead the council banished him from the party and, as a result, deprived the Donner Party of much-needed leadership.

trivia

It took the **Donner Party** two long months to cross present-day Nevada. Virginia Reed, whose entire family survived, gave this advice: "Never take no cut-offs and walk as fast as you can."

Pull off the interstate for a brief tour through Golconda. The town originated as an ore-shipping station along the Central Pacific Railroad in 1868 but was a long-awaited stopping-off spot on the California Trail, due to the presence of soothing hot springs. Around the turn of the 20th century, Golconda's fashionable Hot Springs Hotel attracted travelers.

The town grew to a population of 500 by 1899, due to the discovery of gold and silver in the area and the construction of the Golconda and Adelaide Railroad to the Adelaide Mine, making Golconda the center of the Edna Mountains Mining District. Two Golconda mills (90-ton and 100-ton) processed ore from nearby mines. Foundations of the mills remain. In addition to gold and silver, area mines have produced manganese and tungsten from time to time. Today mining activity has renewed in the area, but Golconda's glory days are gone. Take a picture of the Golconda Community Hall (the former schoolhouse) with the bright red roof and browse around the streets for other historic structures and foundations.

East of Winnemucca 80 miles you'll see a sign designating **Button Point.** Don't try to distinguish the shape of a button on the surrounding hills, because the name came from Frank and his uncle I. V. Button, of the famous Double Square brand. The Buttons raised thousands of horses on 4,000 square miles of ranchland.

Enter **Winnemucca** (population 8,064), the only Nevada town named after a Native American. The town began as French Ford, but Central Pacific Railroad officials renamed it in honor of the famous Chief Winnemucca of the Northern Paiute (called Winamuck by his people).

For years Winnemucca laid false claim to a big event in Western history that involved other important figures. The story went that on Wednesday morning, September 19, 1900, George Leroy Parker (Butch Cassidy), Harry Longabaugh (the Sundance Kid), and Will Carver pulled their last US bank job, robbing the First National Bank of Winnemucca and riding off with sacks filled with $32,640 in gold coins. Refreshed with a change of horses near Button Point, they allegedly escaped to Tuscarora, Nevada, and later Wyoming and Fort Worth, Texas, where they took the famous portrait that they mailed back to the bank president with their sincere appreciation for his generosity. Although this makes for a wonderful story, it never actually happened. Butch Cassidy reportedly was in Wyoming planning a train robbery on that day. But residents told the story for decades before it was proven false and even used to hold a Butch Cassidy festival. The bank building has been restored and now houses another business; it can be viewed at the northwest corner of Bridge and 4th Streets.

Charley Hymer, at 22 years old, owns the dubious distinction of being on the wrong end of Winnemucca's first hanging, for killing a man over a seating-arrangement dispute at a dance hall in 1880. According to legend, Hymer's dying wish was to have his "sad fate serve at least as an example for all wayward and non-law-abiding youth."

The Humboldt (or Old French) Canal originated near Golconda and ran through Winnemucca at Bridge and West 5th Streets. Several portions of the canal are still visible near Golconda, in Winnemucca, and at Rose Creek, south of Winnemucca. A grand scheme conceived in 1862 to supply water to more

Sarah Winnemucca

Chief Winnemucca's daughter, Sarah, was notable in her own right. She traveled to Washington, DC, with her father to plead for improved conditions for their people. Their meeting with Secretary of the Interior Carl Schurz and President Rutherford B. Hayes produced promises but little action on the part of the US government. She is credited with the first English book written by a Native American, *Life Among the Paiutes* (1882), and frequently gave lectures on the conditions of Native Americans. She served as an interpreter in the 1860s at Fort McDermitt and founded a Native American school in 1884 near Lovelock. A statue of her has been placed in the National Statuary Hall Collection in Washington, DC.

Sarah was a Paiute, from one of the tribes that inhabited the Great Basin Desert region comprising most of Nevada and parts of Utah, Idaho, Wyoming, Oregon, and California. At the time of the wagon trains, the Paiutes thrived in a land that tested the hardiest emigrants. She began by telling of her grandfather, who greeted the wagon trains as a sign that the two sides (the dark skinned and white skinned) of a great family would at last be reunited. According to Paiute tradition, the Great Spirit, tired of their constant bickering, had separated the members of the family. She also talked about the men who came for her sister Mary, only 10 years old but fair skinned and pretty, when their father was away with the white ranchers. The men dragged her out of the barn and returned her in the morning. Mary, never the same, sat with the life gone out of her.

Sarah married twice, both times to soldiers she met when translating for the army. Learn more about Sarah Winnemucca's life in her autobiography, *Life Among the Paiutes*.

than 40 stamp mills as well as to help transport barge traffic, the canal was designed to run 66 miles and cost $160,000. French investors sunk $100,000 into the canal before severe seepage and other engineering problems halted construction.

The canal investors may have suffered, but about 50 years later, an enterprising French couple would launch a business that survives today. The Roman Tavern and Restaurant, which had opened in 1898 at 94 W. Railroad St., was renamed ***The Martin Hotel*** after it was purchased by French expats Augustine A. and Elisee Martin in 1913. A 1920 fire prompted an expansion to 25 rooms and a restaurant, and the upstairs was a popular speakeasy during Prohibition—at least until government agents confiscated the booze and poured it down Melarkey Street, prompting local residents to come out with their cups.

After Augustine Martin's health declined, the business was owned by a succession of Basque families. While it's no longer a hotel, it thrives today as a Basque restaurant serving lunch weekdays and dinner 6 nights a week. By now you may have noted that the Basques have a tradition of hearty eating; meals at the Martin include wine, soup, salad, Basque beans, mashed potatoes, a Basque side dish, a vegetable, freshly baked bread, hand-cut fries, and bread pudding, with entrée choices including local lamb chops or shank, sweetbreads, chicken, pork, and various cuts of beef. Visit themartinhotel.com or call (775) 623-3197.

Take a walking tour of 72 historic Winnemucca points of interest with the help of the guide at historicwinnemucca.stqry.app, sponsored by the North Central Historical Society and Humboldt Museum and best viewed on mobile devices. There's also a 40-page online visitor guide at the website of the Winnemucca Convention & Visitors Authority, winnemucca.com.

In 1919 noted Nevada architect Frederic J. DeLongchamps designed the **Humboldt County Courthouse** at 40 5th St. DeLongchamps employed a neoclassical design finished with buff-colored brick and cream terra-cotta and highlighted by Corinthian columns supporting the pediment. That same year, Winnemucca missed becoming the state capital by one vote. The courthouse opened on January 1, 1921, and in 1983 joined the ranks of buildings on the National Register of Historic Places. For additional information on DeLong-champs, turn to the Lovelock discussion later in this section.

With its Spanish Mission–style architecture, the 1924 **St. Paul's Catholic Church,** at the corner of 4th and Melarkey Streets, is worth a look, as is the 1927 **Winnemucca Grammar School,** at 5th and Lay Streets. The 1901 **Shone House,** at Bridge and 6th Streets, is an example of a splendid restoration. Unfortunately, all that remains of the town's pride and joy, the **Nixon Opera House,** is a plaque in the lot west of the chamber of commerce's office. The 1908 opera house burned down in 1992. The city of Winnemucca and the Friends of the Nixon Opera House posted a $21,500 reward for information leading to the conviction of the person or persons responsible for the fire. In its prime the opera house was the largest theater between Salt Lake City and San Francisco.

On the corner of the spot vacated by the opera house stands a most unlikely sight in the middle of sagebrush country. The more-than-6-feet-tall slab of redwood represents the remains of what has to be one of the largest pieces of driftwood in history. The 1,477-year-old tree yielded in excess of 45,000 board feet of lumber. It drifted onto a Crescent, California, beach during the 1964 flood. The slab proclaims Winnemucca as the GATEWAY TO THE PACIFIC NORTHWEST and marks the Winnemucca to the Sea Highway, via SR 140, north of the city. The **Humboldt County Library,** at 85 E. 5th St., maintains a Nevada Room, offering many interesting resources on Nevada and Humboldt County history.

Enter the **Buckaroo Hall of Fame and Western Heritage Museum** through the Visitor's Center at 50 W. Winnemucca Blvd. A number of fine collections will keep you enthralled there for some time. Our favorite is the

name that outlaw

Western legend **Butch Cassidy** was born George Leroy Parker in Beaver, Utah, on April 13, 1866. He took the name Cassidy after Mike Cassidy, a fellow cattle rustler in Utah and Colorado, and earned the nickname Butch while working as a butcher in Rock Springs, Wyoming.

buckaroo clothing and gear used on the "96" Ranch in Paradise Valley. Learn about *tapederos* (stirrup covers used to keep snow and brush off the rider's boots and legs) and see fine-tooled leather cuffs to protect wrists from thorns and rope burns. Don't miss the collection of branding irons, saddles, western bronzes, and artwork. Wrap up your visit with a look at the photo of Will Rogers at the 1930 Winnemucca Rodeo.

Hall of fame nominees must have been born before 1900, worked within a 200-mile radius of Winnemucca, made a living on horseback, and mastered the skills of a buckaroo. Admission is free. For more information, call (775) 623-2225.

Winnemucca annual events include the Ranch Hand Rodeo in late Feb, Winnemucca Basque Festival in Jul, and the Tri-County Fair & Stampede and Buckaroo Heritage Western Art Roundup, both Labor Day weekend. Visit the website of the Winnemucca Convention & Visitors Authority at winnemucca .com or call (775) 623-5071.

Drive to the intersection of Maple Avenue and Jungo Road for a peek at regional history at the ***Humboldt Museum*** in the former 1907 St. Mary's Episcopal Church and a more recently constructed brick building. Exhibits include 13,000-year-old mammoth bones; a collection of playbills, posters and other ephemera from the Nixon Opera House; the piano that survived the opera house fire in 1992; an 1857 Wilcox and Gibbs sewing machine; and artifacts from Basque and Native American culture. The museum, at 175 Museum Way, is open from 9 a.m. to 4 p.m. Wed through Fri and 10 a.m. to 4 p.m. Sat. Visit humboldtmuseum.org or call (775) 623-2912.

The Smithsonian Institution in Washington, DC, reportedly owns one of Ken Tipton's hand-tooled saddles, but you don't have to go east to see his handiwork. Stop at ***Tips Western*** to peruse fancy horse bits, show spurs, chinks and chaps, wallets and checkbook covers, luggage, boots, and saddle pads. You can order any item with your own brand or initials tooled into the leather and even purchase a custom saddle, made by the same three master saddlemakers for nearly 50 years and requiring two to three weeks for design and eight to nine years for delivery. Tips Western is at 1150 E. National Ave. Visit tipswestern.com or call (775) 623-3300.

On the food front, Winnemucca also comes in strong. If you haven't had your fill of Basque food, consider **Ormacheas Basque House** at 180 Melarkey St.; (775) 623-3455. For Mexican food, there's the family-owned **Chihuahua's Cantina and Grill** at 71 Giroux St.; chihuahuasgrill.com or (775) 625-4613. For Korean, try **Koreana Korean Cuisine** at 329 E. Winnemucca Blvd.; koreana .live or (775) 625-7032. And for good ol' all-American, there's **The Pig BBQ & Pub** at 1139 W. Winnemucca Blvd.; (775) 623-4104 or **The Griddle** at 460 W. Winnemucca Blvd.; (775) 623-2977.

Vesco City Park, at Mizpah and Haskell Streets, has softball, volleyball, tennis, swimming, and skate-park facilities, restrooms, a playground and picnic tables, so it's a great place to take a break and let the kids run around.

As you head north out of town on US 95/I-11, sand dunes will start to encroach upon the roadbed. About 22 miles north of Winnemucca, you turn off US 95/I-11 onto SR 290 for a trip to **Paradise Valley** (population 71), 18 miles away. Hudson Bay Company's Peter Skene Ogden passed through Paradise Valley in 1828. First settled in 1863, the fertile valley evolved into the granary and fruit-raising center for the central and eastern Nevada mining camps and fast-growing towns. The community of Scottsdale emerged in 1866 and took its name from nearby Camp Scott, established to ward off Native American attacks on valley ranchers. The name changed to Paradise City in 1869 and today the town is called Paradise Valley. By 1871 the Paradise Valley Post Office opened, and 100 people lived in town. Today, fewer than that remain, along with some interesting historic buildings worthy of photographing.

trivia

Northeastern Nevada is prime grazing land for cattle such as Texas longhorns and sheep.

William F. Stock, founder of the famous "96" Ranch, first saw Paradise Valley in 1863 and homesteaded in 1864. The ranch is currently owned by the fifth generation of his direct descendants. Paradise Valley has a somewhat unique— in Nevada, at least—mix of old stone buildings created by Italian masons and the adobe structures that predate them.

In town you pass an old stone church on the right before you reach one of the town's major social gathering spots, the post office, on the left. You cannot help but see the massive, gnarled cottonwood tree stump reaching to the sky.

A little farther along, you arrive at one of the other social hangouts, the **Paradise Valley Saloon & Bar G** at 95 Main St., constructed out of granite block in 1910. Inside you find overstuffed sofas, an antler chandelier, and a mounted wild boar "sipping suds." Excellent photographs of the town's early days cover the walls. The dollar bills that used to paper the ceiling were removed—by the order, depending on who you talk to, of either the health department or the fire marshal—but plenty of them adorn the walls.

One of the other things that just got to be a thing around the saloon is the report of ghosts. Once a picture flew off the wall, and on frequent occasions the doors connecting the saloon to the back of the building sound like someone is opening and closing them without the benefit of anyone entering the saloon. Then there are the sounds of bartenders working late into the night, even though the bar is closed.

Adjacent to the saloon is a mercantile store with ice cream, food, and collectibles. It's worth a browse to see what treasure you might turn up. In any event, an ice cream cone will do your disposition wonders. The saloon is reachable at (775) 578-3090.

At the end of the main drag, turn right, but not before you get a look at the Flying A gas sign, a relic of earlier days. Get ready for some more photo opportunities. Historic buildings such as the Micca Hotel, which dates to 1902, are lined up like a Hollywood movie set; the only thing missing is Gary Cooper strolling to his fate. When we pulled through town, a horse was tied up to the hitching post with a feed sack over its head at the last house before you veer left and leave Paradise. Across the road you can just barely make out the faded letters on the old blacksmith shed and stable.

That's all the exploring for today. It's time to return 5 miles south of town and turn left at the sign for the **Stonehouse Country Inn.** At the end of the drive, you pass under a welcoming arch and are greeted by a three-story ranch house with spacious rooms. Built in 1941, the ranch is surrounded by the beautiful Santa Rosa Mountains, which deliver wonderful sunset and sunrise vistas. All rooms have private baths for your convenience—and all of them have views. Plenty of reading material makes for a relaxing evening. We recommend *Buckaroos in Paradise*, depicting life at the historic "96" Ranch. The book came about as a by-product of the Smithsonian Institution's 1981 exhibit *Views of a Western Way of Life*, on ranch life in Paradise Valley. Western art and historic photographs bring to life the real West. Ask to see the photographs of the ranch's original stone house structure and notice how small the cottonwoods are in the picture compared with their current height.

Steve Lucas, the proprietor, and innkeeper Claudia specialize in tantalizing home-cooked meals, featuring prime rib, barbecued steak, lamb, pork, or seafood. If you still have room, a tempting dessert awaits you.

After a few of these meals, you will probably need to get some exercise. The Stonehouse Country Inn offers a variety of activities to get you active. Those in good shape or desiring to achieve that goal can enjoy hiking or biking along the Paradise Valley Trail or the Santa Rosa Mountain Trail. If you choose to relax near the ranch, an afternoon of pitching horseshoes can fill the day. For the more sedate, sit back in the solarium (the ranch hands call it the porch) and watch the birds and animals crisscross the meadow. No matter how you spend it, you will enjoy your stay in Paradise.

Room rates run from $70 to $105 on weekdays and from $75 to $120 on weekends and holidays. Seasonal RV sites with hookups are available for $20 per night. Those wishing to fly in can land at a 0.5-mile airstrip adjoining the Stonehouse property. Accommodations for horses also are available. For information and reservations, visit stonehouse.freeservers.com or call (775) 578-3530.

Take the scenic route out of Paradise Valley through the Humboldt National Forest on your way to McDermitt on the Nevada-Oregon border. It's a well-maintained gravel road, although steep and winding. The road was constructed by the Paradise Civilian Conservation Corps in 1938. You will traverse Hinkley Summit, at 8,520 feet in elevation. The drive transports you through striated lava, interesting volcanic formations, rhyolite towers, and car-stopping views.

Creekside picnicking and camping can be had in the mountains at *Lye Creek Campground.* Turn left at road sign 087 and travel about 1.5 miles past the US Forest Service Station. Granite Peak, at 9,732 feet in elevation, towers over the remaining countryside. Hiking trails abound in the area, but the forest-service roads are suitable only for high-clearance vehicles, which precludes RVs and trailers. The campground in a grove of aspen trees along Lye Creek is typically open from Jun through mid-Oct and has 14 sites. Overnight fees are $8 to $10, or $25 for groups. For more information, visit fs.usda.gov or call (775) 331-6444.

The drive back to US 95/I-11 is just as enjoyable. You go over Windy Gap Summit, at 7,380 feet in elevation, and reach the blacktop 13 miles south of McDermitt. *Fort McDermitt* started out as Quinn River Camp, an outpost established in 1865 to protect travelers and area ranchers. That summer Lieutenant Colonel Charles F. McDermitt was killed in a Native American ambush, and later the fort was renamed in his honor. Twenty-four years of continuous operation made it the US Army's longest active fort in Nevada. It also ranked as the last Nevada army post in service when it was converted into a Native American reservation school and incorporated into Fort McDermitt Reservation in 1889. One original building remains on the reservation 3 miles from town.

In March 1891 the post office moved off the reservation to McDermitt, Nevada, then to McDermitt, Oregon, and finally back to McDermitt, Nevada. Today, this is one of few towns in the country that are in two states. The state line runs right through one historic building, the White Horse Inn, with the gambling saloon on the Nevada side and the rest in Oregon.

The **McDermitt Ranch Hand Rodeo** runs every year during the 4th of July weekend. The rodeo spun off from the 1920s street horse races held in McDermitt. Visit whatinthemucc.com or call (775) 623-8631 or (775) 532-8240.

Pershing County

Miles of traveling through the desert and sagebrush take you to your next oasis, in the form of the living ghost town of **Unionville.** Retrace your tracks 71 miles on US 95/I-11 to Winnemucca, where you will pick up I-80 going west. Exit at Mill City and turn south on SR 400. Along the 21-mile route to the Unionville cutoff, you will pass the **Star City Historic Marker.** Star City bloomed with the discovery of a silver lode and the opening of the Sheba Mine. The town received its name because it rested in the shadow of Star Peak, with an elevation of 9,835 feet. The town rapidly grew to a population of 1,400 and in 1864 supported a Wells Fargo office and more than a dozen saloons. Just four years later, the boom collapsed and all but a few people deserted the town.

When the Sheba Mine company stock was listed on the volatile and speculative San Francisco Stock and Exchange, it immediately shot up to $400 per share. The price peaked at $600 per share, creating a market value of $60 million. During its years of operation, the Sheba Mine produced more than $5 million in silver.

At the Unionville cutoff, take the dirt road to the right and head toward the mountains for 2 miles. Ironically, Southern sympathizers settling into the Buena Vista Canyon area prospecting for silver first named the town Dixie in 1861. Later that same year, the more numerous Northern partisans forced the town to change its name to Unionville. Growth from mining activity helped the town garner the county seat, a distinction it held until 1873, when Winnemucca wrestled it away.

What Rolling Mountain Thunder Built

Thunder Mountain Monument, dedicated to Native Americans, is found at Imlay, on the north side of Interstate 80, 42 miles north of Lovelock. This outdoor art installation, constructed mainly of found objects, was built in the 1970s by the late World War II veteran and Creek Indian Frank Van Zant, known as Chief Rolling Mountain Thunder. He attracted volunteers who helped with the construction, using concrete and desert flotsam to erect this fascinating work of art. Visitors are welcome on self-guided tours. The experience has been described as "powerful, intriguing, as visionary as the Watts Towers." Visit thundermountainmonument.com.

During its boom years, Unionville boasted fine houses and business establishments. Samuel Clemens (prior to arriving at Virginia City and taking on the name Mark Twain) arrived in Unionville in 1861; it was where he realized he was "allergic to shovels." By April 1863 approximately 20 stagecoaches arrived daily in the town. The Arizona Mine proved to be the most productive mine by far. In the early 1870s three ten-stamp mills treated its ore, producing wealth for the mine's owners. Underground, more than 17 miles of tunnels ferreted out veins of silver.

The 1870 census listed many Chinese laborers as part of the town population. Numerous interesting occupations showed up on the census records, such as blacksmith, hurdy dancer, tanner, candy store owner, and prostitute. A teamster's freight rig was valued at $300. A fire in 1872 and a lessening in ore quality contributed to the decline of Unionville. By the late 1870s most mining ceased and Unionville grew into a sleepy mining ghost town, with a few stalwart, self-sufficient residents remaining to keep the town alive.

Today some twenty-seven people inhabit Unionville and keep it a charming place to live and visit. A true delight after a day on the backroads of Nevada or a hike in the canyons of the Humboldt Mountains is an evening or more at the *Old Pioneer Garden Country Inn.* The mother-and-son hosting duo are your guides back to a simpler time. For entertainment, you can gather eggs for breakfast, milk the goats, or just listen to the geese honk up a storm. A gazebo is a spot for a quiet getaway. A stream passes by the old homestead and murmurs you to sleep at night as you huddle under a down quilt.

You have your choice of accommodations, with private baths and either one queen bed or a queen and a twin. Everywhere you look, there's something to make you smile: a grouping of pictures, overstuffed easy chairs, a collection of antiques, lots of books, or the chairs by the creek. Meals aren't provided but you can access the kitchen and cook your own. Rates are $110 a night. Call (775) 538-7585.

Returning to I-80, you'll find *Rye Patch State Recreation Area* at exit 129, 20 miles southwest of Mill City. The Rye Patch area is full of history. There are ancient petroglyphs to be found, a 12-mile stretch of trail taken by the Donner Party, and mill foundations from early mining efforts. Inquire about programs with park officials. Rye Patch includes an 11,000-surface-acre reservoir perfect for boating, fishing, swimming, and waterskiing. Picnic during the day or stay overnight at one of the two campgrounds, which have a combined 47 sites, flush toilets, and showers. For more information, visit parks.nv.gov/parks/rye-patch or call (775) 442-0135.

Moving on 22 miles down the interstate brings you to *Lovelock* (population 2,400). Make it a point to stop at the Pershing County Courthouse, opened on June 21, 1921. It was designed by noted Nevada architect Frederic J. DeLongchamps and contains one of only two round court chambers in use in the United States. Located adjacent to the courthouse are Bicentennial Park and a large swimming pool in which to cool off from all your sightseeing. The courthouse is at the corner of Main Street and Central Avenue.

During DeLongchamps's 60-year career, he designed more than 500 buildings, including seven Nevada county courthouses. He apprenticed in San Francisco following the 1906 earthquake and returned to his native Nevada ready to put to use the design concepts he learned in San Francisco's reconstruction. Many of his creations serve as the cornerstones of Nevada's towns and cities. He also won awards for the Nevada buildings he designed for the 1915 Panama-Pacific International Expositions in San Francisco and San Diego, and he added the wings on the Nevada State Capitol in 1913.

On the south end of town, find Marzen Lane just off the Cornell Avenue main drag and stop for a visit at the **Marzen House Museum.** Outside you will find a collection of agricultural and mining equipment. Inside view the Paiute artifacts, such as baskets, beads, and arrowheads; typical period western rooms and clothes, saddles, and brands; and an old dentist's office. You will learn that a dust storm forced Amelia Earhart to land in Lovelock on June 8, 1931, and that Edna Purviance, costar and love interest of Charlie Chaplin, was born in Paradise Valley and raised in Lovelock. Admission is free. Museum hours are noon to 4 p.m. Wed through Sat and at other times by prior arrangement. For more information, visit pershingcounty.net or call (775) 273-2115.

Lovelock also is noted for archaeological treasure. In 1911, thousands of artifacts dating to between 2000 BC and AD 1000 were found in Lovelock Cave. They included eleven tule duck decoys, determined to be the oldest found anywhere on earth and destined to be Nevada's state artifact. They're now in the Smithsonian's National Museum of the American Indian in Washington, DC. Replicas are in the Marzen House Museum.

The Lady Loves a Tramp

Charlie Chaplin's first leading lady, *Edna Purviance,* starred in 40 films with the good-hearted tramp. Edna helped out at her mother's boardinghouse in Lovelock, then moved to San Francisco. While living the life of a bohemian (she walked a duck on a leash), she was discovered by Chaplin, who described her as "quiet and reserved with large, beautiful eyes, beautiful teeth and a sensitive mouth." Edna became his lover and leading lady for 10 years. He supported her until her death in 1958 from cancer.

While in Lovelock, consider a different kind of prospecting—for pizza. *Gold Diggers Saloon* is a lively place, hosting pool tournaments, St. Patrick's Day and pretty much any other reason for a party, music festivals and more. It's at 2210 Rye Patch Reservoir Rd.; call (775) 538-7000.

For a good time, schedule your visit to coincide with the Lovelock Ranch Rodeo in May, Junior Rodeo in June, or Frontier Days in August. For information, visit pershingchamber.com, or call (775) 273-2400.

Leaving Lovelock, follow the Humboldt River southwest until it disappears into the Humboldt Sink, never to reappear.

Places to Stay in Cowboy Country

ELKO

Ruby Crest Ranch
197 Western Hills,
Spring Creek
elkoguideservice.com
(775) 744-2277

Ramada Hotel & Stockmen's Casino
340 Commercial St.
stockmenscasino.com
(775) 738-5141

Shutters Hotel Elko
3650 E. Idaho St.
shuttershotelelko.com
(775) 777-1200

JARBIDGE

Outdoor Inn
Main Street
(775) 488-2311

Tsawhawbitts Ranch Bed & Breakfast
1052 W. Side Dr.
(775) 488-2338

LAMOILLE

Ruby 360 Lodge
301 N. Mountain View Dr.
ruby360lodge.com
(775) 553-0096

LOVELOCK

Cadillac Inn
1395 Cornell Ave.
(775) 273-2798

PARADISE VALLEY

Stonehouse Country Inn
SR 290
stonehouse.freeservers
.com
(775) 578-3530

UNIONVILLE

Old Pioneer Garden Country Inn
2805 Unionville Rd.
(775) 538-7585

WELLS

Cottonwood Guest Ranch
O'Neil Route
cottonwoodguestranch
.com
(775) 472-0222

Sharon Motel
635 6th St.
sharonmotelwells.com
(775) 752-3232

WEST WENDOVER

Wendover Nugget Hotel & Casino
101 Wendover Blvd.
maverickgaming.com/
wendover-nugget
(775) 664-2221

WINNEMUCCA

Best Western Plus Gold Country Inn
921 W. Winnemucca Blvd.
bestwestern.com
(775) 623-6999r

Regency Inn & Suites
705 W. Winnemucca Blvd.
regencyinn.net
(775) 623-4898

Scott Shady Court Motel
400 W. 1st St.
scottshadycourtmotel.com
(775) 623-3646

The Winnemucca Inn
741 W. Winnemucca Blvd.
winnemuccainn.com
(775) 623-2565

Places to Eat in Cowboy Country

BATTLE MOUNTAIN

El Aguila Real Mexican Restaurant
254 E. Front St.
(775) 635-8390

ELKO

Cook's Steakhouse & Saloon
245 3rd St.
cookssteakhouseand saloon.com
(775) 738-0882

La Fiesta (Mexican)
780 Commercial St.
(775) 738-1622.

Luciano's
(Modern American)
351 Silver St.
lucianosnv.com
(775) 777-1808

Star Hotel (Basque)
246 Silver St.
elkostarhotel.com
(775) 738-9925

LAMOILLE

Pine Lodge Dinner House
(American)
915 Lamoille Hwy.
(775) 753-6363

LOVELOCK

Mendoza's Authentic Mexican Food
410 Cornell Ave.
(775) 273-7773

MIDAS

Midas Bighorn Saloon
(American)
348 N. Main St.
(775) 529-0203

WELLS

Betaso's Restaurant & Bar (Mexican)
765 Humboldt Ave.
(775) 752-3670

Iron Skillet
1440 6th St.
(775) 752-2000

Sher-E Punjab Dhaba Indian Restaurant
143 US 93
(775) 752-1350

WEST WENDOVER

Steak House
Rainbow Hotel-Casino
1045 Wendover Blvd.
wendoverfun.com
(800) 217-0049

WINNEMUCCA

Garden Café (American)
Winnemucca Inn & Casino
741 W. Winnemucca Blvd.
winnemuccainn.com
(775) 623-2565

Martin Hotel (Basque)
94 W. Railroad St.
themartinhotel.com
(775) 623-3197

The Pig Bar-B-Q and Pub
1139 W. Winnemucca Blvd.
(775) 623-4104

Silver Peak Bar & Grill
(Modern American)
485 W. Winnemucca Blvd.
silverpeakwinnemucca.com
(775) 625-1582

FOR MORE INFORMATION

**City of West Wendover Tourism
& Convention Bureau**
735 Wendover Blvd.
westwendovercity.com
(775) 664-3138

Elko Area Chamber of Commerce
1405 Idaho St.
elkonevada.com
(775) 738-7135

Elko Convention & Visitors Authority
700 Moren Way
exploreelko.com
(775) 738-4091

**Lander County Convention
& Tourism Authority**
470 S. Broad St., Battle Mountain
landercountytourism.com
(775) 635-1112

**Pershing County
Chamber of Commerce**
1005 W. Broadway, Lovelock
pershingchamber.com
(775) 273-2400

Town of Jackpot
1594 Pond Dr.
townofjackpot.com
(775) 755-2448

Wells Chamber of Commerce
395 6th St.
(775) 752-3540

**Winnemucca Convention
& Visitors Authority**
50 W. Winnemucca Blvd.
winnemucca.com
(775) 623-5071

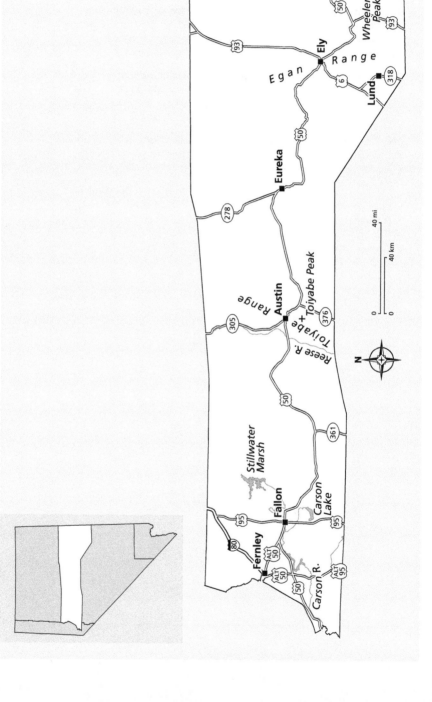

Pony Express Territory

Churchill County

To reach Pony Express Territory from Lovelock, continue on I-80 west, then turn south on US 95/I-11 to **Fallon** (population 9,655). The intersection marks the beginning of I-80 and SR 95 marks the beginning of the 40-mile desert, the most dreaded section of the California Trail. If possible, emigrants traveled the route at night to avoid the intense heat, although traveling at night had its own perils, as clearly pointed out in the diary of one 40-mile-desert emigrant, Sarah Royce:

> Then the conviction, which had been gaining ground in my mind, took possession of the whole party. We had passed the forks of the road before daylight, that morning, and were now miles out on the desert without a mouthful of food for the cattle and only two or three quarts of water in a little cask.
>
> What could be done? Halt we must, for the oxen were nearly worn out and night was coming on. The animals must at least rest, if they could not be fed: and, that they might rest, they were chained securely

to the wagon, for, hungry and thirsty as they were, they would, if loose, start off frantically in search of water and food, and soon drop down exhausted. . . .

So there was nothing to be done but to turn back and try to find the meadows. Turn back! What a chill the words sent through one. Turn back, on a journey like that, in which every mile had been gained by most earnest labor, growing more and more intense, until, of late, it had seemed that the certainty of advance with every step, was all that made the next step possible.

Although the Royces made it to California safely, the 40-mile desert was not so merciful at other times. The barren, waterless alkali wasteland claimed many an oxen team and its owners. According to an 1850 survey, more than 1,000 mules, 5,000 horses, nearly 4,000 cattle, and 953 graves marked the treacherous 40-mile stretch. An estimated $1 million in personal property was discarded along the route to lighten the load and save the animals. More than 3,000 wagons were abandoned in the desert, the heaviest use of which occurred from 1849 to 1869.

Lyon County

Before exploring Fallon, track west on US 50 to Lyon County and the towns of **Dayton** (population 14,258), **Stagecoach** (population 2,022), and **Silver Springs** (population 5,629)—all of which have grown precipitously in the past decade or so, thanks to their proximity to the Reno metropolitan area. This region has been at the crossroads of the American West for more than a century. Explorer John C. Frémont camped near here in 1844 and later, prospectors

AUTHOR'S TOP PICKS

Lehman Caves,
Great Basin National Park

Northern Nevada Railway Museum,
Ely

Walking tour of Old Town Dayton

Renaissance Village, Ely

Wheeler Peak Scenic Drive,
Great Basin National Park

Fort Churchill State Historic Park

Historic Eureka

Cold Springs Pony Express Station

Lahontan State Recreation Area

Historic Austin

on their way to California goldfields made their way through. They in turn were followed by emigrants along the California Trail or other trails that traversed the valley. Finally, with the Lincoln Highway and now US 50, motorized traffic continued the journey.

In Dayton, be sure to stop in the historic district. The **Union Hotel,** built in the early 1870s, still stands (and is undergoing renovation), as do other historic buildings, making the town a charming place to visit. Next door is an original wall from the Pony Express station. For a historical walking tour of Old Town Dayton, visit daytonnvchamber.com or call (775) 246-6316.

Stop for a cold one at the 1863 **Odeon Hall & Saloon,** where part of *The Misfits* was filmed, at 65 Pike St. It's Dayton's oldest saloon but these days also a cultural/community gathering place, with music, dancing, lectures, and poetry. Visit odeonsaloon.com or call (775) 241-2316. Or mosey on down for a drink at the art deco bar at **Js' Old Town Bistro,** 30 Pike St.—or, if it's dinnertime and you're hungry, a plate of pasta, a pizza, or some bruschetta. The stone-and-timber mid-1800s building saw a number of uses over the years before it was restored in the early 2000s. Visit jsoldtownbistro.com or call (775) 246-4400.

The **Dayton Museum,** in the old grammar school at 135 Shady Ln. in Old Town Dayton, has photos, quilts, and other memorabilia from the town's history. It's open from 10 a.m. to 4 p.m. Sat, 1 to 4 p.m. Sun, and other days by appointment; visit daytonnvhistory.org or call (775) 246-6316.

Washoe Native Americans frequently used the Dayton area as a base camp for fishing along the Carson River, for pine-nut gathering, and as a winter village sheltered from the Sierra snows. It became Nevada's first settlement in a valley, in 1849. Among other firsts recorded at Dayton was the first dance at Hall's Station, on New Year's Eve in 1853. In attendance were 150 men and only 9 women.

When emigrants arrived on their way to California, the area took on the name Ponderers' Rest because wagon trains stopped here while the emigrants decided whether to continue westward or settle along the Carson River. It was at one time called Chinatown, after the Chinese brought to the area in 1856 to build the Reese Ditch from the Carson River to the entrance of Gold Canyon. In 1861 the town took the name of Dayton, after early settler John Day. Day also surveyed the town, becoming Nevada's surveyor general in 1870.

Gold was found in Gold Canyon as early as 1849, but the 1859 silver Comstock Lode discovery transformed Dayton into a bustling mining and mill town with 2,500 people in its peak year of 1865. Unlike other Nevada mining towns, Dayton was the site of large-scale dredging operations by the Carson River Placer Mining and Dredge Company. The firm spent $2 million to erect a dredge in 1865, but the effort proved futile.

Before leaving town, tour the **Dayton Cemetery,** at the top of the hill beyond the historic district. It dates to 1851 and is one of Nevada's oldest cemeteries in continuous use; it's a prime example of Nevada off the beaten path.

Plan a stop at **Dayton State Park,** about 1 mile northeast of Dayton off US 50. Stroll along the nature trail, picnic, or set up camp for the night. Within the park boundaries discover the remains of Rock Point Mill. It was constructed in 1861 and was one of the earliest large mills in Nevada to crush ore from the Comstock mines. Its 40 water-powered stamps were arranged in 8 batteries and could crush 50 tons of silver-bearing ore per day. An 1882 fire damaged the mill, but it was rebuilt in 1883. It continued operations until 1909, when another fire destroyed the mill.

The Nevada Mining Reduction and Power Company took over the original Rock Point Mill site in 1910, continuing ore crushing until the early 1920s, when the decline in Dayton-area silver mining forced its closure. The mill was then dismantled, moved to Silver City, and rebuilt at the Donovan Mill site. Foundations, retaining walls, and the reservoir head gate remain at the Rock Point Mill site.

The day-use fee is $5 per vehicle, or $10 for non-Nevada vehicles; camping is $15 to $20. Visit parks.nv.gov/parks/dayton or call (775) 687-5678.

Continue heading east on US 50 about 15 miles. Stop at the **Desert Well Station Historic Marker,** opposite the fire station at **Stagecoach.** One of the wells was used exclusively for camels brought to the Nevada desert to haul salt to the mines on the Comstock. The stage station gained a bit of fame when mentioned in Mark Twain's *Roughing It.* Twain related a story of how he narrowly escaped death in the 1860s while caught in a desert snowstorm with two companions. They had been traveling in a circle for hours, following their own tracks. They finally settled down for the night. One of the companions attempted to start a fire with sagebrush, using sparks from his pistol; he succeeded only in scaring off the horses. At the pits of despair, the men vowed reform, cast away their bottles of whiskey, and huddled together, awaiting death during the night. Morning found the eastern greenhorns camped not 15 steps away from a stage station reported to be the Desert Well Station.

From Stagecoach, drive east about 5 miles to Silver Springs and turn right onto Ramsey Cutoff/Ramsey Weeks Cutoff. In about 3.5 miles, turn right on US 50 Alt. Continue on California Emigrant Trail/Fort Churchill Road to **Fort Churchill State Historic Park.**

The US Army constructed Fort Churchill in 1860 to protect against Native American attacks in the wake of the Pyramid Lake Indian War. The fort guarded the Pony Express route and area settlers, and it served as the home post for hundreds of soldiers on excursions against the Native Americans. The military abandoned the garrison in 1869, and the remains of soldiers buried in the post cemetery were removed to Carson City in 1884. Over the years, the fort structures have served a variety of purposes. During the 1930s the National Park Service instituted some restoration plans that were carried out by the Civilian Conservation Corps. The Nevada Division of State Parks took over the site in 1957.

Start your tour at the visitor center, where you'll find an excellent pamphlet on Fort Churchill. It and the interpretive signs along the post pathway impart interesting knowledge about the fort and remaining structures. The 3-inch ordnance rifle on display represents the first rifled cannon mass-produced for the US Army. There are also a restored 130-year-old caisson (ammunition carrier) and a replica of a Pony Express Bible. Look over the fort schematic before embarking on the interpretive trail.

The fort was named after General Sylvester Churchill, then inspector general of the US Army, who served the area well for more than a decade controlling Native American uprisings. Post strength averaged around 200 soldiers, but it held as many as 600 men at one time. It ranked as one of Nevada's first, largest, and most strategic military posts, also serving as a Union recruiting station. The buildings stood on a square, facing a central parade ground. The eerie, partly restored adobe buildings on stone foundations stand in stark testimony to the harsh life of soldiers in the Nevada west. Fort Churchill was declared a National Historic Landmark in 1964.

A large tree-shaded area on the banks of the Carson River affords fine picnicking. Tables, cooking grills, and restrooms are available. A 20-site campground provides for overnight camping for tents, travel trailers, and motorhomes. The day-use fee is $5, or $10 for non-Nevada vehicles; camping is $15 to $20. For more information, visit parks.nv.gov/parks/fort-churchill or call (775) 577-2345.

Take a brief detour to **Buckland Station,** along the Carson River on US 50 Alt, a few miles south of Fort Churchill. Samuel S. Buckland settled here in 1859, began a ranching operation, and opened a station for the Overland Stage Company. He also constructed the first bridge across the Carson River downstream from Genoa. Buckland Station figured prominently in the Pyramid Lake Indian War, serving as the assembly point for the ill-fated volunteer units that rode off to

trivia

The renaissance of Nevada's mining has been called the *"Invisible Gold Era."* Commercial gold is no longer found in nuggets or veins. Instead, the exploration, assaying, extracting, and processing of precious metals relies heavily on technology. Nevada is the world's fifth-largest producer of gold and leads the nation in gold mining with 74 percent of the nation's gold production.

defeat and death. In 1864 Buckland opened a store and sold goods to travelers along the California Trail. When the US Army closed Fort Churchill, Buckland purchased the buildings at auction for $750 and used materials from the fort to build the large two-story hotel at present located at the Buckland Station site. Sam and his family are buried in the cemetery at Fort Churchill. Museum entrance is $1. For more information, visit parks.nv.gov/parks/buckland-station or call (775) 577-4880.

Retrace your steps to US 50 and drive about 26 miles east to return to Fallon.

Fallon sits in the high desert at 3,960 feet above sea level. The city was incorporated in 1908, six years after its founding. Its rich agricultural heritage stems from the Newlands Irrigation Project. The first land reclamation project in the country, this effort diverted water from the Carson and Truckee Rivers to reclaim the desert for the planting of food crops.

The irrigation project began in June 1903 under the authority of the Reclamation Act of 1902, signed by President Theodore Roosevelt. The first water from the Truckee River reached the Carson River in June 1905, when the Derby Diversion Dam was dedicated. The original scope of 400,000 acres of irrigated fields was never realized. The US Reclamation Service (later called the Bureau of Reclamation) underestimated the acre-feet of water required to properly irrigate the sandy soils, and a shortage of water almost sank the project in its first years. The construction of the Lahontan Dam between 1911 and 1915 finally corrected the problem, delivering enough water to irrigate more than 75,000 acres of farmland. Today, about 30,000 acres are irrigated by the reservoir, depending on the snowpack.

The **Lahontan State Recreation Area** around the 162-foot-high dam and 10,000-acre reservoir provides plenty of outdoor activities including boating, fishing, waterskiing, horseback riding, and camping. Developed campsites are available all year, and primitive camping is permitted on the beach. Admission is $5 per vehicle, or $10 per non-Nevada vehicle. Camping is $15 to $20, and the boat launch is $15 to $20. The recreation area is about 28 miles west of Fallon via US 50. Visit parks.nv.gov/parks/lahontan or call (775) 577-2226.

Buried under the waters of the reservoir lies **Williams Station** (also called Honey Lake Smith's), the scene of a tragic event that triggered the Pyramid Lake Indian War. In 1860 one of the Williams brothers and some hired hands kidnapped two Paiute women. Tribe members trailed them to the station and burned it down, killing five of the men trapped inside. When word of the attack reached Virginia City, a volunteer army of 105 men was organized and trailed the Native Americans to Pyramid Lake. During the ensuing battle, the volunteers suffered 69 casualties, including the death of the group's leader,

Lake Lahontan

Because Nevada sits squarely in the Great Basin Desert region of the western United States, its boundaries seem artificial. Parts of this vast, empty land shoot straight past borders into Idaho, Wyoming, Utah, Oregon, and California. Dry and arid now but formerly an immense inland sea fed by Ice Age–induced rains, Nevada provided sanctuary to birds, animals, and the first humans. Paiute Native Americans called this inland sea *Lake Lahontan.* By the time wagon trains arrived, the Paiutes had retreated to camps at Pyramid Lake and Walker Lake, remnants of Lake Lahontan. Its dried-up alkaline surface sapped the strength of pioneers and livestock. Although rainfall was too scarce to support trees and woody plants, trading posts sprang up along the trail, then mining camps at rich ore deposits, then railroad depots and small towns. Remnants of this activity abound throughout the state—proud outdoor museums, slowly decaying into the ancient lake bed of Lahontan.

experienced Native American fighter Major William Ormsby. Calls for reinforcements went out to California, and a second battle resulted in substantial Native American casualties. As a result of the Pyramid Lake Indian War, the government constructed Fort Churchill. "Honey Lake" Smith rebuilt the station.

In Fallon, a must-stop is the ***Churchill County Museum*** at 1050 S. Maine St. (on US 50, which is why the museum has been called the "best little museum on the loneliest road in America"). Its 10,000 square feet house a fine collection of Native artifacts, as well as historical Churchill County displays. Visitors enter though a virtual reality (VR) Hidden Cave (the real one's in the nearby Grimes Point/Hidden Cave Archaeological Site; more on that later) with interactive features and artifacts from the cave. A large diorama brings to life the Fallon area during the time of white settlement and includes a Stillwater Paiute home and information on difficulties pioneers faced crossing the desert.

More recent eras are evoked in exhibits such as the transportation collection that includes a steamroller used on the Lahontan Dam, a vintage school bus, and old fire trucks. The Woodliff Store on the museum grounds is one of the oldest commercial buildings in Fallon. There also are temporary exhibits on such topics as outlaws and lawmen.

Admission is $5. Summer hours Mar through Nov are 10 a.m. to 5 p.m. Tues through Sat and 10 a.m. to 3 p.m. Sun; they're slightly shorter in winter. Visit ccmuseum.org (which also has some virtual exhibits) or call (775) 423-3677.

As you travel around Fallon, don't be alarmed by the fighter planes streaking across the sky at low altitudes. Since 1996, Fallon has been home to the US Navy's Top Gun flight school. Naval Air Station Fallon also is home to the Naval Aviation Warfighting Development Center and is the only facility in the Navy where an entire carrier air wing can train together.

Fallon is the site of numerous annual events, such as Battle Born Broncs in Jun; 4th of July Parade, Maine Street Block Party and Fireworks in Jul; Fallon Cantaloupe Festival & Country Fair in Aug; and the Fallon Junior Rodeo and Lions Club Labor Day Parade on Labor Day weekend. For details, go to visitfallon nevada.com or call (775) 423-5104.

Pick up some wine and cheese for a picnic, or a charcuterie board, cheese plate, or peach crostini with goat cheese and prosciutto at ***Bottle & Brie,*** 65 S. Maine St.; bottleandbrie.com or (775) 423-2743. Have lunch at ***The Slanted Porch,*** 310 S. Taylor St., where the menu includes the likes of the Stillwater sandwich, with lemon-garlic chicken salad, lettuce, tomato, onion, and mayo; visit slantedporch.com or call (775) 423-4489. Or find something a little more substantial at ***Three Sisters Steakhouse*** at the Stockman's Casino, where they have the beef and a lot more; visit stocksmancasino.com or call (775) 423-2117.

Whether or not you opt for a Stillwater sandwich, you may want to visit the 81,322-acre ***Stillwater National Wildlife Refuge*** just east of Fallon, which was created in 1948 to provide habitat for migratory birds. In the mid-1980s record rain and snowfall swelled the Carson and Humboldt Rivers to unprecedented levels, flooding Stillwater Marsh. As a result, archaeologists discovered artifacts and bones dating back thousands of years. Today, the refuge's wetlands attract more than a quarter-million waterfowl, hundreds of thousands of shorebirds, and myriad other birds; more than 290 species have been spotted. Land-based wildlife includes coyotes, mule deer, and jackrabbits.

The website at fws.gov/refuge/stillwater has information on the refuge and outlines itineraries for visits of 15 minutes to a half day. To reach the refuge entrance, go about 4.5 miles east of Fallon on US 50, then head east on Stillwater Road. Call (775) 423-5128.

East of Fallon 8 miles on US 50, you can see the real cave you got a taste of at the Churchill County Museum. ***Grimes Point/Hidden Cave Archaeo-logical Site*** represents one of the largest and most accessible prehistoric petroglyph rock-carving sites in the country. A 0.75-mile, self-guided interpretive trail leads through a boulder-strewn area rife with rock carvings at every turn. Over a period of 8,000 years, the rock carvers left traces of their occupation of the area around the marshes of ancient Lake Lahontan.

Hidden Cave, which was formed about 20,000 years ago, was revealed in the mid-1920s by four local schoolboys who were the first 20th-century people to see it. It's been excavated three times—the last, in 1979 and 1980, by the American Museum of Natural History. Many of the artifacts were intact and in groups, indicating that this may have been a storage place. The free public tours on the second and fourth Saturdays of most months begin with a video showing at the Churchill County Museum, followed by guided tours of the cave.

For more information, visit blm.gov/visit/grimes-pointhidden-cave-archae ological-site or call (775) 885-6000.

Be on the lookout for an unusual memorial on Four Mile Flat about 17 miles along US 50, as you approach Sand Mountain. Look to the north about 150 yards from the road shoulder for wooden fencing bordered by rocks. It marks the **graves of the Le Beau children,** who died of diphtheria within three days of each other, around 1865. Over the years, various Good Samaritans have periodically spruced up the grave site, adding a picket fence and new crosses as time, weather, and souvenir-hunters have taken their toll. One grave tender added a plaque that read: DEDICATED TO THE MEMORY OF THE HUNDREDS OF MEN, WOMEN, AND CHILDREN, AND THOUSANDS OF ANIMALS THAT PERISHED ON THE OLD SIMPSON TRAIL TO CALIFORNIA 1846 TO THE 1880s.

A mile or so down the road, you'll find yet another natural wonder and recreational delight. **Sand Mountain,** 600 feet high, 3.5 miles long, and 1 mile wide, the largest single dune in the Great Basin, captures the imagination when you consider that each grain of sand had to be blown separately from the desert floor over millions of years. It's in the **Sand Mountain Recreation Area,** a designated off-highway-vehicle fee site managed by the Bureau of Land Management; blm.gov/visit/sand-mountain-recreation-area or call (775) 885-6000. Besides OHVs and dirt bikes, the area sometimes is used by sand sailors and sand boarders.

At the entrance to the recreation area are the ruins of the **Sand Springs Pony Express Station,** where self-guided interpretive trail signs provide the history of the site that, besides being a pony express station, was also an overland stage station, telegraph station, and home to two prospectors. The ruins had been buried in sand until 1976, when the site was excavated.

Past Middlegate proceeding east on US 50, be sure to stop for a look at the **Cold Springs Pony Express Station,** one of the best-preserved Pony Express stations in Nevada. Nearby you can view remnants of freight and telegraph relay stations. A moderate 1.5-mile hike takes you to the Cold Springs Pony Express Station. According to legend,

pony express riders

Strap on your chaps, cinch up your saddle, and put on your spurs. From April 1860 to October 1861, dozens of young men galloped the vast expanse of open range from St. Joseph, Missouri, to Sacramento, California. Despite sleet, rain, desperadoes, and fatigue, they delivered mail in an extraordinarily swift 10 days' time. With his mailbags slapping against the sides of his saddle, a rider would approach a pony express station, where another rider awaited him. The next in line quickly mounted a fresh horse and raced away with the mailbags.

an 1860 traveler noted that the station was "a wretched place, rudely built, and roofless and maintained by four rough-looking boys." Cold Springs is located 25 miles west of New Pass Summit.

Lander County

About 30 miles west along US 50, you pass into Lander County at New Pass Summit, at an elevation of 6,348 feet. The site also served as a stage station and freighter stop in the early 1860s. Completion of the first transcontinental railroad caused the eventual demise of the Overland Stage line.

Follow that lonely road another 28 miles, and you'll arrive in **Austin** (population 167). Early in 1862 an employee of the Overland Mail and Stage Company, William Talcott, discovered rich silver veins in Pony Canyon and started a rush of prospectors to Austin. By 1867 the town boasted 11 mills to process ore and had a population of more than 10,000, making the fledgling city Nevada's second-largest community. All in all, more than $50 million in silver was mined and processed at Austin.

Many of the brick buildings remain, giving the town a perfect setting for a period movie. It's one of the most photogenic of Nevada's small towns, with tall church spires, a large courthouse, and false-front buildings on Main Street. Through the years the Pony Express, Overland Stage, Transcontinental Telegraph lines, Lincoln Highway, and Highway 50 crossed right through the center of town, with very little change in scenery.

A few blocks into town stop at **Gridley Store,** the origin of a colorful bit of Austin history. The one-story stone structure was erected in late 1863 and operated as a general store by owner Reuel Colt Gridley. Mark Twain immortalized him in *Roughing It* after Gridley carried a 50-pound sack of flour down Austin's main street after losing an 1864 election bet.

The sack of flour became even more famous after Gridley auctioned it off, with the proceeds going to the US Sanitary Fund, a Civil War version of the Red Cross that aided wounded Union soldiers. He auctioned the sack of flour many times throughout Nevada and California. It even made it to the 1864 St. Louis World's Fair, where it was auctioned off yet again. It raised more than $275,000 for the relief fund. You can see the original flour sack on display at the Nevada Historical Society in Reno. Ironically, Gridley died six years later, almost penniless.

The presses of Nevada's oldest newspaper, *The Reese River Reveille,* stopped in 1993 after it had been published in the same location since 1863. Early dispatches were brought in by stage. Its files contained early news of the Civil War and the assassination of President Lincoln. *The Reveille* editor formed the

The Difficult Hanging of Rufus B. Anderson at the Lander County Courthouse

Rufus B. Anderson was baptized into the Roman Catholic faith a few hours before his scheduled hanging for murder. The material for the scaffold had been brought to the jail the night before and was assembled and erected in front of the Lander County Courthouse in Austin. Ten minutes before 1 p.m., Anderson was marched out and up the scaffold. He knelt in prayer with the priest, then rose and addressed the crowd, asking for forgiveness. Sheriff Sanborn read the death warrant; a deputy bound his arms, placed a black hood over his head, and slipped a noose around his neck. As the condemned man uttered the words, "I commend my soul to thee," the trap was sprung and he crashed to the ground. A cry went up from the crowd. Anderson was carried back up and once again the end of the noose slipped through the coil and he ended up on the ground. Men shouted, "For shame, for shame! It's butchery!" Unconscious, Anderson was tied in a chair, where he soon revived and asked for a drink of water. The rope was adjusted a third time, and he and the chair swung free when the trap was dropped. The body and chair dangled for 20 minutes. The body was cut down, removed from the chair, and placed on a bier and taken to the family home.

—Nevada Historical Society records, October 30, 1868

"Sazarac Lying Club," named after the Sazarac Saloon and fertile ground for newspaper articles.

The Reveille's printing press is in the collection of the *Austin Historical Museum,* 180 Main St., which also exhibits a historic kitchen, vintage clothing, and other local artifacts. Hours are 11 a.m. to 3 p.m. Fri through Sun. Visit austinmuseumnevada.com or call (775) 964-2200.

The Lander County Court House cornerstone was laid in September 1871. The courthouse gained notoriety in the early 1880s when a man who murdered a popular local rancher was taken from the jail on the lower floor of the building by vigilantes and lynched from the balcony over the front door.

Austin contains a number of historic churches. St. Augustine's Catholic Church, which opened on Christmas Eve 1866, is the only remaining of the first four Catholic churches in Nevada. Services are no longer offered there, and its artifacts have been moved to Reno as various restoration projects have been undertaken. Erected in 1866, the Old Methodist Church (now Austin's town hall) housed a famous pipe organ that made the trip around the Horn and arrived in Austin from San Francisco via freight wagon. Donations of mining-company stock helped finance the church's construction. Some of the companies behind the mining stock went bust, causing the church consternation, not to mention cash-flow problems.

On the western outskirts of town, **Stokes Castle** draws the curious. Modeled after a tower outside Rome, Stokes Castle is crafted from hand-hewn native granite stones raised into place by a hand-powered windlass in 1897. Anson Phelps Stokes, an eastern financier with substantial mineral interests in the Austin area, not only built the structure but also arranged financing for construction for the 92-mile Nevada Central Railroad from Battle Mountain to Austin.

The three-story castle with three fireplaces was used sparingly and eventually fell into disrepair. The remains are enclosed by a wire fence, but the site's view of up to 60 miles to the south and 35 miles to the north makes it a great place to picnic. To reach Stokes Castle, take Main Street west to Castle Road and turn left. Follow the winding dirt road and signs to the castle, about 1 mile from the highway.

trivia

Emma Wixom of Austin rose to fame as opera singer Emma Nevada. She sang at the coronation of George V and received a $100,000 diamond necklace from Queen Victoria.

Austin had another connection with eastern culture. Emma Wixom, daughter of a pioneer Austin doctor, graduated from the Austin Methodist Choir to become the famous opera singer Emma Nevada. She trained in Vienna beginning in 1877, sang at the coronation of George V, and was a favorite of Queen Victoria. During her triumphant tour of America in 1885, she ordered her managers to change her schedule so that she could travel to Austin and sing for her old friends.

Austin hosts Gridley Days Cowboy Contest every year in July. Fun-filled activities include fiddle competitions, Nevada Civil War Volunteer demonstrations, and flour-sack races. For information, go to visit austinnevada.com or call (775) 964-2200.

Mountain biking along the Pony Express Trail is another popular Austin-area activity. For more information, visit the website of the Greater Austin Chamber of Commerce, austinnevada.com. Or call (775) 964-2200.

For a place to stay near Austin, consider the **Paradise Ranch Castle** bed-and-breakfast in Reese Valley. Yes, it does look like a castle, and accommodations include the King & Queen's Quarters, the Blue Room, and the rock-lined Secret Room. Homemade hot breakfast is included, which you can partake of in the kitchen or at the King's Table. In the evening, there's a cash bar in the Dungeon downstairs, where there are a jukebox and poker and pool tables. Visit paradiseranchcastle.com or call (440) 781-8768.

If you're looking for a bite to eat, note that **Grandma's Restaurant & Bar** calls itself "Austin's Living Room," so you'll get a bit of local color. You'll also get the likes of pizzas, tacos, roast chicken, and more. Visit grandmas-austin-nv .com or call (775) 666-5255.

After you leave Austin, you'll go through a horseshoe bend and make a steep climb on a 6–7 percent grade along a twisting road, so make sure your brakes are in good condition. You'll cross **Austin Summit,** at 7,484 feet, and then **Bob Scott's Summit,** at 7,195 feet. At this spot you'll find **Bob Scott Campground** with picnic tables and restrooms (fs.usda.gov or 775-331-6444). A historic marker commemorates the surveyors who plotted the West, laying out railway routes, water transport, and wagon roads. The Honey-Lake-to-Fort-Kearny wagon road was completed in 1860 by Captain Lander, after whom Lander County is named.

Take a loop tour for a jaunt into Big Smoky Valley and some intriguing places including **Spencer's Hot Springs,** which have eased the weary bones of travelers for 100 years. To get there, take US 50 for about 6 miles east of Bob Scott's Summit and turn right on SR 376. Follow the road for 0.75 mile, then turn left onto a gravel road; you'll see the **Toquima Cave** historic marker. After 5.5 miles turn left onto a dirt road and follow it to the springs.

One of Nevada's best-kept secrets is its abundance of geothermal springs. The earth's molten core comes close to the surface in parts of the western United States, and water passing through the core can push its way close to the surface and, finding a weak spot such as a fault, burst out like a geyser, ooze out as a mud pot, or bubble up as a hot mineral spring. Spencer's Hot Springs is undeveloped, no more than a hot pool and a wooden bench; as is the case with all hot springs, test the temperature of the water (which can be scalding hot) before you commit. But you can enjoy the magnificent scenery of the Toiyabe Range.

Next, continue on the dirt road to the 7,900-foot Pete's Summit and Toquima Cave. The cave, which lies at the end of an easy 0.25-mile path from the picnic area, has paintings made by the ancient Shoshone tribe. There's also a campground, picnic area, and toilets. Visit fs.usda.gov or call (775) 331-6444. Retrace your steps to SR 376 and head north to return to US 50.

A few miles east of the SR 376 turnoff you come upon **Hickison Summit**, at 6,546 feet in elevation, and the **Hickison Petroglyph Recreation Area.** Turn north and follow the well-graded gravel road to the campground, where shaded picnic tables, restrooms, and 21 camping and trailer sites provide a refuge from the summer desert heat, which can easily rise above 90 degrees Fahrenheit. Make sure you bring your own water, since drinking water may not be available.

Petroglyphs (ancient rock art) are located on the cliff at the edge of the picnic area. Estimates place their origin between 1000 BC and AD 1500. A Bureau of Land Management brochure located in a box at the beginning of the trail provides an excellent tour guide, pointing out native plants as well as interesting petroglyphs on the cliff face. Archaeologists believe the horseshoe-shaped petroglyph symbolizes the female. Many of the glyphs may represent hunting or fertility magic. From the trail you can take a left fork to arrive at the US 50 overlook. The highway route roughly follows the routes taken by Frémont (1845) and Simpson (1859). Likewise, the Pony Express traveled through the area on the way to Austin and points west.

Continuing on the petroglyph trail, stop at site 11. The petroglyphs on this boulder are different from the others at the site, though they still resemble the curvilinear style. The petroglyph at the base of the boulder may be an animal, making it the only zoomorphic glyph at the site. For more information, visit blm.gov/visit/hickison-petroglyph-recreation-area or call (775) 635-4000.

Eureka County

About 10 miles east on US 50 you'll enter Eureka County (near the Geographic Center of the State of Nevada, which is to the south). The county seat of **Eureka** (population 414), is about 33 miles farther down the road. As you approach, you'll likely see references to it as THE FRIENDLIEST TOWN ON THE LONELIEST ROAD IN AMERICA—and for good reason.

Eureka lies in the Diamond Valley, first explored by Colonel John C. Frémont in 1845. Fourteen years later, Captain James A. Simpson mapped a route through the north end of the valley. Between 1860 and 1861 the Pony Express crossed the terrain. You can still see traces of the Pony Express route through the sagebrush as it crosses Highway 278 about 21 miles north of town. Early freight roads also crisscrossed the valley as mining camps boomed in the 1860s. The mining boom gave birth to an agricultural and dairy industry in Diamond Valley.

Historically, Eureka ranked as Nevada's second-largest mineral producer. But instead of gold or copper, Eureka produced lead and silver. The town exploded to a population of 9,000 in the 1870s and 1880s. The dark-red-brick 1879 **Eureka County Courthouse** is well worth a visit, as is the 1880 **Eureka Opera House,** both of which have been restored.

Notice the courthouse's original tin ceiling, its chandeliers, and the Silver Party flag in the court chambers. The Silver Party advocated minting silver dollars, which in 1873 were outlawed in the United States, a move that severely damaged Nevada's mining industry and economy. Also, peek into the treasurer's office on the second floor and look at the vault adorned with a mountain scene. The courthouse, at 10 South Main St., is on the National Register of Historic Places.

The Eureka Opera House at 31 S. Main St. is a center for culture and entertainment in the community, hosting events that may range from the VFW Veteran's Day Dinner to the Juvenile Probation Dance Recital.

Go to visiteurekanevada.net, call (775) 220-2232 or stop at any number of businesses around town for maps, a brochure, and other information on

Eureka, including a walking tour. The people of Eureka clearly are fond of their slogans; another is "Eureka! You've Found Us!"

The **Eureka Sentinel Museum** is, appropriately enough, in the building that housed the offices of the *Eureka Sentinel* newspaper. The building was erected in 1879 (and also is on the National Register of Historic Places), and the paper published from 1870 to 1960. The old pressroom and posters printed by the *Sentinel* are on the ground floor, as are reproductions of the historic front pages. The second floor is dedicated to exhibits depicting school life in early Eureka, as well as an old barbershop, parlor, and kitchen. There's also a mining-history room and displays of items from fire companies, fraternal organizations and the military.

The museum is at 10 N. Monroe St. and hours are 8 a.m. to 5 p.m. weekdays (closed for lunch from 12 to 1 p.m.) Visit visiteurekanevada.net or call (775) 237-5010.

The historic Jackson House, next to the opera house, dates to 1877. The building was gutted by fire in 1880 and rebuilt. In 1981, after many years of vacancy, it was restored as a historical building, and in 1994 the apartments were returned to guest rooms. A porch surrounds the second story for evening viewing of cars coming into town on Highway 50, and an upstairs parlor is a nice place to relax. Note the brass crib in the parlor.

The building now is the **Jackson House Hotel**, with 8 Victorian-themed rooms with modern conveniences. It's at 11 S. Main St.; call (775) 237-5347.

An interesting piece of Eureka history is the Charcoal War of 1879. It started when Italian charcoal suppliers to the smelters went on strike for higher prices, then 25 cents per pound. The armed workers virtually took over Eureka on August 11, 1879. The militia temporarily restored order. On August 18, a posse of miners (none Italian), headed by a deputy sheriff, engaged a number of charcoal burners at Fish Creek, and attempted to arrest them. The conflict climaxed with the shooting deaths of five charcoal burners and the wounding of six others. No one was convicted for the killings. With the strike broken, the owners reduced the price they would pay for charcoal by more than 20 percent.

By the early 1890s, the mines had mostly played out and the smelters closed. In 15 years, Eureka had produced more than $40 million in silver, $20 million in gold, and tons of lead. Brief mining operations spurted up over the years, but none lasted long. Today that picture is changing, with productive mines operating in northern Eureka County and the Ruby Hill gold and silver mine near the town of Eureka.

trivia

Famed for his music and knowledge of cowboy lore, **Don Edwards** appeared in Robert Redford's *The Horse Whisperer*. He sometimes sang and played guitar during the summer season. For more about him, visit donedwardsmusic.com.

The ***Owl Club Bar & Steakhouse*** serves more-than-ample good grub (look for the sign that says, COME IN, WE'RE AWESOME). Like almost everything else, the eatery is located on the main drag (US 50). The pine wainscoting and Western artwork on the walls give the place a comfortable feeling. Visit owlclubeureka.com or call (775) 237-5280. Farther east on US 50, ***DJ's Diner & Drive-In*** serves up burgers, pizza, and sandwiches. Call (775) 237-5389.

Before leaving Eureka, check out the ***Perdiz Sport Shooting Inc.*** range in Windfall Canyon, 2 miles south of town. It is open to the public and has a fully automatic sporting-clay course with 10 stations, each simulating a specific species of game. For a schedule of shoot dates and the focus of each shoot, visit eurekacountynv.gov or call (775) 237-7027.

White Pine County

Just a few miles east of Eureka you'll cross into White Pine County. The county seat of ***Ely*** (population 3,994) is about 78 miles east of Eureka.

From 1905 to 1906 the Nevada Consolidated Copper Company constructed a 150-mile rail line from the Copper Flats ore mines west of Ely to the smelter at McGill and then to Cobre on the Southern Pacific Line. During the first half of this century, the Ely area produced nearly $1 billion in copper, gold, and silver. Largest among the famed copper pits is the Liberty, which resumed operations temporarily in July 1995.

To experience one of Ely's top attractions, go to the north end of East 11th Street and pull up to the ***Nevada Northern Railway Museum*** to take a ride into Nevada's past. The rail station's unique architecture is worth a picture, but even more fascinating is the fact that it functions as a living-history, operating railroad facility. Steam and diesel locomotives chug down the tracks on varying schedules all year. In addition, there are special-event train rides—such as an evening ride with wine and hors d'oeuvres, a stargazing train, a fireworks train, a photographer's excursion, and Halloween and Santa's Reindeer trains. Steam Excursion Train rides 90 minutes long are $39 for most adults, $33 for seniors and $15 for children 4 to 12. For $150 extra you can ride with the engineer; for $200 extra you can ride in the caboose. Rides on diesel-powered trains are slightly less expensive. Don't forget to tour the general office, depot, dispatcher's office, roundhouse, and blacksmith shop.

For schedule information, rates and reservations, visit nnry.com or call (775) 289-2085.

Another of Ely's showpieces is ***Renaissance Village,*** a truly unique look at the cultures that shaped the area. The project, born in 1999, was launched with a number of murals and other public-art pieces all over the downtown area. The village itself is a parcel of land with 11 shotgun houses and a barn, furnished to reflect the multicultural population that settled the town, with artifacts provided by local families. Thus you'll encounter an Italian household, a Basque one, a Chinese one, and on and on. It's at 400 Ely St.

Another project of the Ely Renaissance Village organization is **Art Bank and Garnet Mercantile** at 399 Aultman St., which showcases works by local artists and changing exhibitions. Visit elyrenaissancevillage.com or call (775) 293-0550.

Although small, the **White Pine Public Museum** houses a fine collection of White Pine County memorabilia and photographs, including many from the Pony Express, and Great Basin Native American artifacts. Here you will learn that Thelma Catherine Patricia Ryan—later to become Pat Nixon—came from Ely.

There's also a cell from the old Ely City Jail and a one-room schoolhouse from nearby Baker. The museum is at 2000 Aultman St. Admission is $7 for those 13 and older, $4 for kids 5 to 12. Hours are 10 a.m. to 4 p.m. daily, opening an hour later in winter. Visit wpmuseum.org or call (775) 289-4710.

Head back downtown to seek a good night's sleep at the historic **Hotel Nevada**, built in 1929 and created to be Ely's best hotel. A casino was added with the legalization of gambling in 1931. Guests over the years reportedly have included Ingrid Bergman, Gary Cooper, Mickey Rooney, and Stephen King.

The 64 rooms and suites have all the modern amenities and include breakfast vouchers for the Denny's on-site, which also provides room service. There's a fitness center and guest laundry, and pets are permitted. And, like any self-respecting historic structure in the state, the Hotel Nevada is said to have its share of ghosts. It's at 501 E. Aultman St. Visit hotelnevada.com or call (775) 289-6665.

When it's time for dinner, consider **Rack's Bar & Grill** at 753 Aultman St. Dinner entrées include battered cod, steaks, and pork chops, and there are a host of burger and sandwich choices as well as salads and starters. Rack's also advertises that it has the only smoke-free bar in Ely. Visit racksbarnevada.com or call (775) 289-3131.

For something lighter and a throw back in time, stop at **Economy Drug** at 696 Aultman St. It's a working pharmacy—and has been since 1946—but in recent years the soda fountain has been made brand-spankin' new, while evoking something right out of *American Graffiti*. Therefore, you'll find USB ports over the tables so you can charge your devices while you're munching the Garnet, a sub with grilled chicken, bacon, provolone, cranberries, sunflower seeds, lettuce, and mayo. But of course you won't want to bypass an authentic malt. Visit economydrugely.com or call (775) 289-4929.

On your way out of town, check out the **Ely Cemetery** on your right along the Great Basin Highway/US 50/US 93. There you'll find, among the scores of

Nevada Wilderness

Desert Survivors is an organization that leads its members on more than 25 free trips a year through Great Basin National Park, Eastern Sierra sagebrush desert, the remote desert of western Nevada, and more. Many of these lands are designated Wilderness Study Areas where antelope, wild horses, and coyotes roam; where a moonrise and brilliant stars transform the night. Membership dues are $30 per individual adult per year, which includes the trips, a newsletter, and social events. Visit desert-survivors.org.

historic graves, many inscribed solely in Mandarin Chinese, a reminder that this was a major ethnic group during Ely's early history. You'll also note that the great majority of them are in a separate area from the main part of the cemetery—off to the side and down a little slope, testimony to the racism of the time.

In the Ely area, plan a number of day trips. **Cave Lake State Park,** approximately 15 miles southeast of town, delivers some of the best fishing for German brown trout and rainbow trout in Nevada. The 1,820-acre park includes a 32-acre reservoir and 2 developed campgrounds. Four developed hiking trails are maintained; the Steptoe Creek Trail is an easy, 3-mile round-trip journey that crosses a creek. The park is open all year. Fees are $15 to $20 per vehicle for overnight camping and $5 to $10 for day use. To get there from Ely, take US 50/US 93/Great Basin Boulevard about 7.5 miles south to SR 486. Turn left and proceed to park. Visit parks.nv.gov/parks/cave-lake or call (775) 728-8100.

The **Ely Elk Viewing Area** is a chance to spot these majestic animals feeding during the fall and spring, along the road or in the viewing-area pullout. The area is about 6 miles south of town along US 50/US 93/Great Basin Boulevard. Elk frequently can be sighted on either side of the road. Visit blm.gov/visit/ely-elk-viewing-area or call (775) 289-1800.

Finish your Ely-area sightseeing with a trip to **Ward Charcoal Ovens State Historic Park.** These six beehive-shaped brick ovens were built around 1876 and produced charcoal for the smelters serving area mines. The 30-foot-tall, 27-foot-diameter ovens were filled with as many as 35 cords of wood at a time. A 20-stamp leaching mill was built but never proved successful, due to the type of ore mined and the shortage of available water.

Many men were employed in the gathering and shipping of wood for the ovens. Piñon was used almost exclusively, and deadwood was preferred. The ovens contain a hole in the top and a window vent in the back. The entrances are large, but duck if you enter wearing a cowboy hat. The charcoal ovens were abandoned in the 1880s after the smelters shut down. For a time, they reportedly were used to house travelers (rumor has it they occasionally sheltered stagecoach bandits). And reportedly one was cleaned and whitewashed as a prospective home for a gambler and his bride-to-be—but never used, because the two lovebirds quarreled and never married.

The park has fishing, hiking, picnicking, and camping for any type of RV or camper. To reach it, head east out of Ely on US 50/US 93/Great Basin Boulevard for about 13 miles, then turn right on SR 16. After about 5 miles, you'll turn left onto Cave Valley Road/SR 45. Visit parks.nv.gov/parks/ward-charcoal -ovens or call (775) 289-1693.

Rockhounds will delight in spending a few hours at **Garnet Hill,** an internationally known site for gem collectors looking for garnets. They can be found by careful rock-breaking or scoping out surfaces and drainages. It's also a place to see the open-pit copper mines near Ruth. The site has picnic tables, barbecue grills, a group barbecue area, restroom, and undeveloped sites for tent camping, but no water.

From Ely, follow US 50/US 93/Great Basin Boulevard to a mile north of the Ruth turnoff, and turn right onto the access road. In about 3 miles you'll come to the parking area. For details: blm.gov/visit/garnet-hill or call (775) 289-1800.

Next, it's off to Nevada's only national park and one of the country's least-visited, **Great Basin National Park.** To get there, head east on US 50/US 93/ Great Basin Boulevard for about 56 miles to SR 487 and turn right, then right again on SR 488 (the park is well-marked with signs).

Great Basin is packed with more than 77,000 acres full of hiking, exploring, and camping activities. Venture into the wonder of **Lehman Caves,** visit a desert glacier, gaze up to view the six-story-high Lexington Arch, and see the world's oldest living organism, the ancient **bristlecone pine** *(Pinus longaeva).*

Living bristlecones are more than 4,000 years old; they predate the Egyptian pyramids by more than 1,000 years and the oldest giant sequoia by 1,500 years. Dead and fallen bristlecones trace back more than 9,000 years. Their gnarled shapes present wonderful photo opportunities, as does spectacular Lexington Arch in the southern part of the park. The Rhodes Log Cabin, near the visitor center, was used as a guesthouse in the 1920s and is on the National Register of Historic Places.

Within the park are five distinct ecological environments. The 12-mile Wheeler Peak Scenic Drive, which hugs the peaks of the South Snake Range, gains more than 4,000 feet to an elevation of more than 10,000 feet and crosses through numerous ecological zones, from desert to a sub-Alpine forest.

Wheeler Peak, the second highest in Nevada, boasts a permanent ice cap at 13,063 feet and intriguing glacial features. The 2-acre glacier remnant at the base of the peak is an Alpine glacier like those that carved the mountains of the Great Basin.

The park, home to some of the darkest skies in the lower 48 states, has been designated an International Dark Sky Park and obviously is a prime location for stargazing from virtually anywhere within its borders.

Things are dark, as well, in the depths of Lehman Caves, where visitors walk among giant limestone formations and through marble caverns. Access is only by a ranger-guided tour; depending on the season, 60- and 90-minute tours may be offered. Flickering candlelight talks bring home the mystery of the caves. On the 90-minute Grand Palace Tour, which accommodates a maximum of 20 people and no children younger than 5, you'll see the Rose Trellis Room, Music Room, Lodge Room, Inscription Room, and Cypress Swamp as well as the Grand Palace itself.

Absalom Lehman discovered the caves around 1885. They were designated a national monument in 1922 and became part of the national park in 1986. The temperature in the caves remains about 50 degrees all year, so wear warm clothing. Note that the tours are very popular and may sell out a week in advance; get reservations at recreation.gov. Walk-up spots are sometimes available but also sell out very quickly. Cave tours are $12 to $15 for adults, $6 to $8 for kids 5 through 15. Park admission is free, and those who have annual or senior passes can get a 50 percent discount on the tours.

Lower Lehman Creek Campground is open year-round, while four other developed campgrounds in the park operate on a seasonal basis. Primitive camping is available along Snake Road. Overnight camping is $20, $10 for senior pass holders or $30 for groups; reserve at recreation.gov.

Informational pamphlets and maps are available at the front desks of the visitor centers; the information also is available at nps.gov/grba or by calling (775) 234-7331.

From Great Basin, retrace your steps to Ely by heading west on US 50 for about 66 miles and turning north on US 93. At this junction you first encounter

Lehman Caves

Because rivers and streams in the Great Basin have no outlet to the sea, they flow inland, forming small lakes or soaking into the earth. This action produced the treasure of Great Basin National Park: *Lehman Caves.* Following a tour guide into the dark, damp chill, I walked through caverns with names like Gothic Palace, Cypress Swamp, and the Grand Palace. The ceilings and walls were an art gallery of stalactites and stalagmites. Seeping water full of calcite crystals has created amazing formations over hundreds of thousands of years. Open year-round. For information, call (775) 234-7331.

Good Story, but No Bones

The disaster at **Chinaman Mine** occurred in 1872. An unstable mass of rock gave way, sealing the mine's entrance, and trapping between 8 and 12 Chinese miners who had been working underground. The mine owners reportedly decided not to reopen the passage; since the mine had not been lucrative, they couldn't be bothered. Tragically, the Chinese men presumably died of suffocation. When the passage was mined years later, workers expected to find human bones. They found some ore carts, but no bones.

the original route of the *Lincoln Highway* in Nevada. This was the nation's first transcontinental highway, traversing the country from New York City to San Francisco.

The idea for the Lincoln Highway first took root in Indianapolis at a 1912 dinner meeting of automobile industry tycoons. At the time, the nation's 2 million miles of roads were largely unconnected; railroads represented the only practical means of coast-to-coast travel. Within three years, a patchwork made from existing roads wound its way across the country from Times Square in New York City via ferry to New Jersey and finally to Lincoln Park in San Francisco in time for the 1915 Panama-Pacific International Exposition, thereby creating the transcontinental highway.

Later improvements made the Lincoln Highway one of the premier roads of its day. The federal government took over the road system in the 1920s. To mark the event, the Boy Scouts of America installed more than 3,000 Lincoln Highway markers along every mile of the route in 1928. A number of these Nevada markers can still be found. One is located in front of the courthouse in Eureka and another near the Nevada State Museum (old Carson City Mint Building) in Carson City.

In Nevada, the Lincoln Highway traveled through Ely, Eureka, Austin, Fallon, Fernley, Carson City, Sparks, and Reno, taking one of two routes around Lake Tahoe into California. In Reno it went under the famed Reno Arch, which was erected in 1926 to celebrate the passing of the Lincoln Highway and the Victory Highway through Reno.

About 43 miles north of Ely, turn right onto SR 893 near the Schellbourne Rest Area and drive about 15 miles to the ghost town of *Schellbourne.* In 1859 an Overland Stage stop and mail station was built at Schellbourne, and the Pony Express used the spot as a stop on its route in 1860. In the 1870s it became a mining town with 500 residents. The post office closed in 1929, and what remains of the town is today on a private ranch.

Return to US 93 and drive about 6 miles north to SR 489, then head for the hills for about 8 miles to reach **Cherry Creek** ghost town. It may be hard to believe, but one of White Pine County's largest towns occupied this site beginning in 1872 with the discovery of gold and silver. The construction of one of the first five-stamp mills in eastern Nevada took place here. Mining continued through several booms and busts into the 1880s and then quieted down until brief boomlets in the 1905 to 1908 and 1935 to 1940 periods. Estimated gold and silver production through Cherry Creek's mills during its heyday ranged from $3 million to $20 million. Gold and silver mining gave way to tungsten in the 1950s, when the mills ran full force to handle production from ten operating properties. When the price of tungsten dropped from $63 to $12 a unit, the mines shut down once again.

Today Cherry Creek hangs on with about 55 residents, a far cry from the estimated 6,000 who once crowded its streets and gave the town a reputation for rip-snorting activity—along with fine properties such as restaurants and a luxury hotel. One of the town's two oldest structures is the oldest remaining one-room school in Nevada (1872), which was in service until 1941 and now

TOP ANNUAL EVENTS

Mardi Gras Parade
Baker, Feb or Mar
(775) 234-7323

Starry Starry Night
Fort Churchill, Silver Springs, Apr
parks.nv.gov/events
(775) 577-2345

Schellraiser Music Festival
McGill, May or Jun
schellraiser.com

Battle Born Broncs
Fallon, Jun
battlebornbroncs.com
(775) 741-9780

De Golyer Bucking Horse & Bull Bash
Fallon, Jun
(775) 427-0228

Ely Rock & Gem Swap
Ely, Jun
elynevada.net
(775) 289-3720

Gridley Days Cowboy Contest Rodeo
Austin, Jul
(775) 964-2200

**Fallon Cantaloupe Festival
& Country Fair**
Fallon, Aug
falloncantaloupefestival.com
(775) 866-8474

**Hot Austin Nights Lions Club
Poker Run**
Austin, Aug
(775) 964-2200

**White Pine County Fair
& Horse Races**
Ely, Aug
Elynevadal.net
(775) 289-3720

serves as the ***Cherry Creek Museum***. The museum's open by appointment only. One of its more delightful displays consists of early photos of Cherry Creek schoolchildren.

As you walk around town, pay particular attention to the stone structure with a sod roof. Originally, it was the root cellar for the mercantile store, which has long since vanished.

But you won't find the original Cherry Creek railroad depot in Cherry Creek. It and an adjoining private residence have been restored and moved to Ely, where they're on display at the White Pine Museum. Complete with period artifacts, it brings to mind a movie set. For more information on Cherry Creek, contact White Pine County Tourism & Recreation at elynevada.net, or call (775) 289-3720.

The Cherry Creek Post Office opened in 1873 and operated for more than 100 years. Today 12 or so mailboxes line a corner in town and serve the same function, as the local gathering spot.

Cherry Creek is another perfect example of Nevada off the beaten path.

Places to Stay in Pony Express Territory

AUSTIN

Magnolia Gallery & Inn
103 Main St.
magnoliagalleryandinn
(775) 530-2241

BAKER

Border Inn Casino
3777 E. US 50
bordertinncasino.com
(775) 234-7300

Hidden Canyon Retreat
500 Hidden Canyon Rd.
hiddencanyonretreat.com
(775) 293-3099

ELY

Bristlecone Motel
700 Ave. I
bristleconemotelnv.com
(800) 497-7404

Fireside Inn
955 N. McGill Hwy.
(702) 353-5204

Four Sevens Motel
500 High St.
hotelnevada.com
(775) 289-4747

**Hotel Nevada
& Gambling Hall**
501 Aultman St.
hotelnevada.com
(775) 289-6665

Jailhouse Motel & Casino
211 5th St.
jailhousecasino.com
(775) 289-3033

Prospector's Casino
1501 East Aultman St.
prospectorhotel.us
(800) 750-0557

EUREKA

Jackson House
11 S. Main St.
eurekagcinnandjackson
house.com
(775) 237-5247

Ruby Hill Motel
380 N. Main St.
(775) 237-5339

Sundown Lodge
60 N. Main St.
sundownlodgemotel.com
(775) 237-5334

Sure Stay Best Western
251 N. Main St.
bestwestern.com
(775) 237-5247

FALLON

Cold Springs Station Resort
52300 Austin Hwy.
cssresort.com
(775) 423-1233

Overland Hotel & Saloon
125 E. Center St.
(775) 423-2719

Places to Eat in Pony Express Territory

AUSTIN

Champ's Burgers
16 Main St.
champsburgers.com
(775) 964-2579

Grandma's Restaurant & Bar (American)
99 Main St.
grandmas-austin-nv.com
(775) 666-5255

BAKER

Sandra's Mexican Food
Pioche Street
(435) 294-7403

DAYTON

1st & 10 Bar & Grill
240 Dayton Valley Rd.
(775) 246-7900

Rose Creek Pizzeria
6998 US 50 E.
(775) 241-1001

ELY

Economy Drug
(soda fountain)
696 Aultman St.
economydrugely.com
(775) 289-4929

La Fiesta Fine Mexican Restaurant
700 Ave. H
lafiestamexrestely.com
(775) 289-4114

Mr. Gino's Italian Restaurant & Bar
484 Aultman St.
(775) 289-3540

Twin Wok Chinese Cuisine
700 Park Ave.
twinwok.com
(775) 289-3699

EUREKA

Clementine's Steakhouse
501 S. Main St.
(775) 237-5135

The Owl Bar & Steakhouse
61 N. Main St.
owlclubeureka.com
(775) 237-5280

Sacha's Pizza and Sugar Shack
21 S. Main St.
(775) 537-5158

The Urban Cowboy
(Mexican)
121 N. Main St.
(775) 237-5774

FALLON

Azteca Grill & Bakery
1740 W. Williams Ave.
(775) 423-4964

Courtyard Café & Bakery
55 E. Williams Ave.
(775) 423-5505

Maine Street Café
810 S. Maine St.
mainestreetcafe.com
(775) 423-1830

FOR MORE INFORMATION

Dayton Area Chamber of Commerce
daytonnvchamber.com
(775) 246-7909

Fallon Chamber of Commerce
fallonchamber.com
(775) 423-2544

Greater Austin Chamber of Commerce
austinnevada.com
(775) 964-2200

Greater Eureka Chamber of Commerce
eurekachamber.com
(775) 442-3738

White Pine Chamber of Commerce
whitepinechamber.org
(775) 289-8877

White Pine Tourism & Recreation
elynevada.net
(775) 289-3720

Index

Explore More

GLOBE PEQUOT IS YOUR GUIDE to special places, focusing on local pride close to home and helping you discover new destinations to explore from coast to coast. We publish books about iconic people and places, tapping into regional interest, history, cooking and food culture, folklore and the paranormal – all the things that make each region unique. With more than 75 years in publishing, we strive to give you the most up-to-date, regional information by local experts.

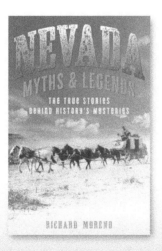

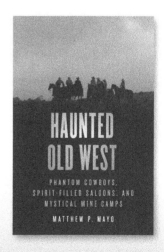